Decolonizing Anthropology

Decolonizing the Curriculum

Anna Bernard, *Decolonizing Literature*
Ali Meghji, *Decolonizing Sociology*
Sarah A. Radcliffe, *Decolonizing Geography*
Robbie Shilliam, *Decolonizing Politics*
Soumhya Venkatesan, *Decolonizing Anthropology*

Decolonizing Anthropology
An Introduction

Soumhya Venkatesan

polity

Copyright © Soumhya Venkatesan 2025

The right of Soumhya Venkatesan to be identified as Author of this Work has been asserted in accordance with the UK Copyright, Designs and Patents Act 1988.

First published in 2025 by Polity Press

Polity Press
65 Bridge Street
Cambridge CB2 1UR, UK

Polity Press
111 River Street
Hoboken, NJ 07030, USA

All rights reserved. Except for the quotation of short passages for the purpose of criticism and review, no part of this publication may be reproduced, stored in a retrieval system or transmitted, in any form or by any means, electronic, mechanical, photocopying, recording or otherwise, without the prior permission of the publisher.

ISBN-13: 978-1-5095-4059-4
ISBN-13: 978-1-5095-4060-0(pb)

A catalogue record for this book is available from the British Library.

Library of Congress Control Number: 2024935359

Typeset in 10.5 on 12.5pt Sabon
by Fakenham Prepress Solutions, Fakenham, Norfolk NR21 8NL
Printed and bound in Great Britain by CPI Group (UK) Ltd, Croydon

The publisher has used its best endeavours to ensure that the URLs for external websites referred to in this book are correct and active at the time of going to press. However, the publisher has no responsibility for the websites and can make no guarantee that a site will remain live or that the content is or will remain appropriate.

Every effort has been made to trace all copyright holders, but if any have been overlooked the publisher will be pleased to include any necessary credits in any subsequent reprint or edition.

For further information on Polity, visit our website:
politybooks.com

For
Appa: his caring detachment and love of Tamil
Amma: her courage and grace
Swathi: my sister and one of my best friends

Contents

Acknowledgements viii
Note on Racialized Terms xi

1 Introduction: Decolonizing Anthropology and a Decolonizing Anthropology 1
2 What is Decolonization? 28
3 Colonialism–Anthropology 62
4 Epistemological and Epistemic Justice 96
5 Ignorance and Ignoring 123
6 Understanding and Transforming Universities: The Potential of Ethnography and Anthropology 146
7 On Courses and in Classes 175
8 Conclusion 203

Notes 215
References 220
Index 243

Acknowledgements

This book has been a long time in the making, and I have many people to thank. When I began work on it in early 2020, COVID was just making its presence felt. My father's sudden death from COVID in India in October 2020 made the pandemic personal – something that was happening to us, his family and friends, and to the whole world in unfathomable and terrible ways that connected people yet revealed deep divisions in resources, approaches and access to health care and vaccines. Almost two years later, Queen Elizabeth II died, and this time the world came into view in a different way – for some people, even in far-flung places, it seemed to be a personal tragedy; for others, it was a chance to re-evaluate the past and future directions and to re-forge or seek to cut connections. As I finalized the revisions, the terrible Hamas attack and Israel's retaliation have renewed attention on what humans do to each other and how the past informs the present. Throughout these tumultuous and thought-provoking times, I read, thought about and discussed different aspects of colonization and decolonization with various people – students, friends and colleagues – and wrote draft chapter after draft chapter. Writing a synthetic book is a completely different project compared to one based on fieldwork, albeit no less immersive. I am grateful to all the people who suggested things to read, checked my understanding of work based on their own regional or topical expertise, and provided generous and rigorous critique.

Acknowledgements

As I describe in the Introduction, I wrote much of this book with the input of student volunteers, who discussed draft chapters with me extensively over the three years of the project. Some of them graduated and others took their place. Some, even after graduation, continued to participate, comment and inspire. The students are: Lucy Anderson, Charlotte Antilogus, Megan Bonfield, Florence Brown, Brendan Cox, Ruby Davis, Samuel Denny, Natalia Galindo Freire, Honor Gitsham, Regina Ho, Lauren Howie, Jack Keelan, Kasia De Kock Jewell, Clementine Lawrence, Michaela Lawrence, Patrick Jones-O'Brien, Ethan Butland O'Dwyer, Guendalina Magnoni Stella, Gabriele McGurk, Maria Obrebska, Megan Riley, Isabel Sturgess, Robin Tang, Xanthe Tsapparelli, Hannah Wheeler and Isabella Wimmer. My deepest thanks to all of them. My thanks also to the Social Anthropology department and the School of Social Sciences at Manchester for enabling financial compensation to the students for their intellectual labour. I also thank all my students and doctoral candidates at Manchester for critically engaging with my ideas and teaching me even as I taught them.

Tulasi Srinivas and Anthony Simpson read early drafts of the entire manuscript, and Stef Jansen read the final version in full. Their feedback has been invaluable. Elsayed Elsehamy Abdelhamid, Claire Alexander, Chloe Nahum-Claudel, Michelle Obeid and Chika Watanabe read and commented on different chapters. Sonja Dobroski and Peter Wade helped me grapple with complex questions and terminologies pertaining to race and indigeneity. I tried out some of the arguments at the Manchester Social Anthropology Research Away Day, the *Decolonising Anthropology?* studio sessions of the Association of Social Anthropology multi-part online conference, the Durham Anthropology Seminar, STAR2, comprising doctoral candidates at the Scottish universities, and with colleagues at the workshop held with Ngugi wa Thiong'o in Manchester. Molly Geidel, the translator of Silvia Rivera Cusicanqui, kindly checked over my understanding of Rivera Cusicanqui's ideas. I am very grateful to all of them.

Countless friends and colleagues have listened to, argued with and enriched my understandings of decolonization and related debates. I would particularly like to thank Kodili Chukwuma, Paolo Heywood, Leo Hopkinson, Stef Jansen, Sachiko Kubota, James Laidlaw, Nayanika Mookherjee, Michelle Obeid, Abeyami Ortega, Chimwemwe Phiri, Adam Reed, Angela De Souza Torresan and Peter Wade. Marilyn Strathern has been a constant inspiration.

At Polity Press, I am grateful to Ian Malcolm for his faith in the project, Pascal Porcheron, Ellen MacDonald-Kramer, Neil de Cort and other team members. I am grateful to the reviewers of this book for their critical and careful feedback. Thanks to Megan Caine of Monkeyproof and Gail Ferguson for copy-editing the manuscript.

My daughters, Aliya and Taylor, have put up with my obsession with decolonization for years, as has my good friend Imogen Stidworthy. Jon has lived with, read and critically engaged with almost every bit of (and also various other ideas that did not end up making it into) this book.

No piece of scholarship is ever the product of one person's thinking or work, and I cannot thank all these people and many, many others enough. No piece of scholarship is either fully finished or perfect – I take full responsibility for any shortcomings.

Note on Racialized Terms

It is hard to know what terminology to use when discussing people in terms of racial categories, especially when speaking across diverse national contexts and usages. Like any classification of people, racialized categories are relational and contextual. That is, one category is defined in relation to other categories in the series, and a person's identity is defined by interactions between what they think they are, what other people think they are and what they think other people think they are; and all categories can change depending on the specific context of who is speaking to whom, with what purposes and with what meanings each party attaches to the categories (meanings that are generated by historically changing social structures, such as hierarchies of power, wealth and value). When navigating this complex and shifting terrain, I will use terms such as 'Black', 'Native', 'European'/'non-European' and 'non-white' (this latter often specifically in relation to the 'whiteness' of anthropology) as shorthand devices to approximate familiar categories in world history, without making essentialist claims about any, or collapsing difference within each, category. When citing or engaging with the work of other authors, I follow their usage, including their capitalization.

–1–
Introduction: Decolonizing Anthropology and a Decolonizing Anthropology

Can we decolonize anthropology? Can anthropology enable decolonization? These questions have been asked before and doubtless will be again. They keep arising because, as a discipline, social-cultural anthropology promises much. Simultaneously focusing on human difference and human unity, the discipline seems to suggest the possibility of creating a shared world of common flourishing, without eradicating that which makes different forms of life and sociality viable and meaningful. And yet criticisms abound that the discipline has not lived up to that promise, neither in its own internal organization and practices, nor in its research practices or its modes of generating anthropological knowledge and applying this in the world. Thus Girish Daswani argues that 'anthropology is currently facing the dilemma of situating itself as a discipline that allows for the possibility of decolonial approaches while being unable to truly decolonize' (2021; see also Gupta and Stoolman 2022). Those who are both committed to, yet critical of, anthropology are concerned with two things: getting the anthropological house in order, and also enabling anthropology to make a positive difference in a world marked, and made profoundly unequal and unjust, by colonialism. These two aims often go under the term 'decolonization'. But the scope of the term remains vast, and

Jonathan Jansen, Professor of Education, who in 2009 became the first Black rector and vice-chancellor of the University of the Free State in South Africa, asks 'What does the word even mean? . . . Is decolonisation simply a byword for the proxy discontents in education and society?' (2019: 1–2).

In the simplest sense, decolonization refers to the formal end of colonial rule. Here, colonialism is understood as the domination of one people (the colonized) by another (the colonizer) through the claiming and implementation of political and other forms of control (Jansen and Osterhammel 2017). The colonized territory is not sovereign, neither able to make internal decisions nor enter into international agreements on its own behalf. Most territories formerly colonized by Europe are now independent sovereign states, even though only in theory because they remain subject to economic and military coercion by other more powerful states, often (but not always) former colonizers. Massive forced and other shifts of population into both colonized areas and the metropole, continuing Indigenous struggles in settler colonies, and patterns of wealth and other flows and impoverishment all mean that the term has a moral and political force beyond 'flag decolonization' (ibid.). Among other things, the term folds in anti-racism, self-examination, representational practices and demands for epistemological and epistemic justice. Its use is widespread, albeit not understood identically, in formerly colonized areas and in former colonial centres or the metropole, which further has what Harrison describes as its internal colonies (2010 [1991]: 2).

My own usage of the term 'decolonization' refers to the undoing of the logic of the colonizer (Gerber 2018; Mbembe 2021), i.e., the creation of and occupation of a centre and the definition of all others in relation to and for the benefit of this centre. European colonial powers followed this logic, of course, but it is not unique to them, although the scale of European colonization was unprecedented as were the effects. But there are many usages, and this is not the first publication to bear the title *Decolonizing Anthropology*. So let me explain my approach and contribution. My book has the subtitle 'An Introduction'. It thus begins with an exploration of the term 'decolonization' as adopted by different scholars and activists. I suggest that the term is wide in its scope and is used to pursue diverse and somewhat contradictory aims. In part, this is because of the different histories and practices of colonialism worldwide, and therefore the different aims and processes of decolonization in different contexts. For this reason, I suggest that the term itself merits critical anthropological scrutiny, and I advocate the adoption of more precise vocabularies for the hoped-for progressive changes in different places and by different kinds of people. I then turn to active attempts to decolonize anthropology, both in terms of reckoning with its colonial roots and as heralded by Faye Harrison's influential edited volume *Decolonizing Anthropology* (2010 [1991]). Harrison's volume is built around two key axes, the first of which is the promotion of deeper anthropological engagements with questions of race/racism by centring the work of African-American anthropologists and articulating new directions for anthropology based on this corpus, which begins from the Black experience as opposed to white problematizations. This includes re-examining anthropological framings. Second, Harrison outlines an 'anthropology for liberation', calling for anthropologists to actively shape a better world with, and for, their research participants. Harrison's work has set new research agendas and has been taken up widely. It has also encouraged more critical examinations of whiteness in anthropology and the reproduction of privilege, including along geographical lines that map onto colonizer/colonized distinctions. This is enormously significant work.

However, it remains important to maintain a distinction between anthropology (an academic discipline that seeks to understand and analyse) and activism (directed attempts to intervene in and shape the world). Different kinds of people – raced, gendered and Indigenous – have been trying to fight continuing inequities and oppression arising from, but not only from, colonization. Although it is important to work with and support them, it is equally important to understand what they do and why their attempts are/are not successful, and to communicate this understanding to research participants as well as more generally. Indeed, in some instances this might be more valuable than throwing one's efforts into activism, particularly when what is at stake for the anthropologist is different from what is at stake for those fighting for change on their own behalf and who may have disagreements among themselves about means and ends. We learn from them, but we can also inform in ways that enable future action and objections. For that reason, this book advocates the maintenance of a distinction between anthropological knowledge generation and activist theories of knowledge (knowing in oppositional ways and oriented towards transformation).

Key to this difference is anthropology's main tool – ethnography, which remains open-ended in its engagement with people and their life-worlds and committed to understanding diverse ways of being in the world. Part of anthropology's strength is the slowness and immersive nature of its research methodologies, based on intimate, long-term relations with people in order to try to holistically understand how they see, and live in, the world. Drawing on the growing focus in anthropology on right-wing actors, I suggest that expanding our focus to people (powerful or otherwise) who actively resist progressive or equitable change and fight to reproduce the status quo is perhaps as important as is supporting people in their struggles. Working only with anti-racists does not tell us about the quotidian and institutional ways in which racism is reproduced and defended by those not on the receiving end of it. Working with people who are identified as racist (even if they would not self-identify as such) can tell us why they understand and act in the world as they do, thus possibly enabling the building of common ground and a consensus towards change. This means stepping away from the assumption that the anthropologist must support research participants' aims and struggles. In other words, I suggest that a decolonizing anthropology is possible in other, albeit complementary, ways to what has come hitherto.

I extend this understanding of a decolonizing anthropology to the institution that most of us know best – the university. The university, in both its global and local instantiations, especially the metropolitan university, is increasingly the target of calls to decolonize – as are various diverse academic disciplines, including anthropology – yet this does not seem to be happening, and we need to do everything we can to build a better and more equitable university and anthropology. This includes asking how we, especially those of us in elite institutions, reproduce centres and margins that continue to look recognizably colonial. Equally, I suggest that we use anthropological methods and tools to understand the university, both as a global form and in its local instantiations. Such a focus includes asking why calls for radical transformation of universities or disciplines do not receive wider support, or are tamed, turned into box-ticking exercises at worst or restricted to the production of one or more radical courses for students. The revolutionary praxis of participant observation (Shah 2017) can be turned to the worlds we inhabit on a daily basis and in which we are deeply complicit.

On the whole then, I argue that decolonization is best understood as a set of demands and processes, some of them deeply contradictory and certainly not adding up to a clear-cut destination. These demands and processes can be engaged sympathetically and rigorously, thoughtfully supported, and studied and analysed – not with a view to debunking but with anthropological attention to nuance, contradiction, means and goals – and thus furthered or refined. We are trained as anthropologists and we teach as anthropologists. We can use this critical training to make a better world, not only by intervening in it but also by applying our discipline's methods, tools and approaches to better understand it. This book, then, is both about decolonizing anthropology and a decolonizing anthropology.

Colonial legacies

Colonial legacies are complicated. In his introduction to an edited journal issue on how we might think of these, Benoît de L'Estoile (2008) argues that one source of confusion with the phrase 'colonial legacies' is the implication that 'there is an essence of colonialism, overlooking the diversity of colonial practices and relations' and, further, that this places us in the position of passive recipients of a legacy from the past. De L'Estoile suggests that we might more usefully make a distinction between 'colonial relations' and 'colonization'. Colonial relations is a generic term that specifies a set of relations that have structured, albeit differently in different places and with respect to different kinds of person, the relations between Europeans and non-European inhabitants of the world from around the fifteenth century. These relations, although patterned, have played out on the ground in a multitude of ways that defy easy comprehension or disentanglement. De L'Estoile uses the more restricted term colonization to describe 'the political control of a territory by a foreign power with a view to incorporation and exploitation (but not necessarily including settlement); in that sense, colonisation is but one possible mode of colonial relations' (ibid.: 269).

Formerly colonized nations continue to work out their own escapes from, or modes of retaining or reshaping, colonial relations, for example, what to do with the colonial language and whether to maintain or dismantle colonial-era penal and civil laws, institutions, educational systems and their content, and infrastructural patterns. The crucial point is that in former colonies some colonial relations may continue to obtain after the end of colonization – some unconsciously – while others either fall by the wayside or are consciously dropped. Where active decisions are made, they can give rise to contestations and conflict. Several scholars argue that these kinds of working-out have not taken place in the metropole to the same extent, leading to imperfect decolonization, a lack of self-understanding and continued claims of exceptionalism. Thus, Priyamvada Gopal writes:

> 'Europe's' engagement with decolonisation must begin . . . [with] an unflinchingly truthful engagement with the pivotal role of empire and colonialism in its own making. This would encompass not just 'Europe's' own forays into and influence upon the world, a staple of

imperial history, but a sustained study of how those forays and the world itself – made 'Europe' and, certainly, the 'West'. (Gopal 2021: 879)

What form should such a sustained exploration take? In terms of a reckoning with the past, this must involve some form of epistemic and epistemological justice that not only retells the story of colonialism and colonization from the perspective of the colonized but reveals the ways in which colonialism materially benefited colonizing nations and shaped them in diverse ways that continue to date and have not been fully acknowledged. We see such calls in, among other texts, Frantz Fanon's writing, which has profoundly shaped decolonizing movements.

These attempts inform understandings of action in the present, but we may also go beyond that by asking proactively how we want to deal now with colonial legacies. In this attempt we may take inspiration, as de L'Estoile does, from the poet René Char, whose words he translates as 'our legacy comes to us without any testament' (De L'Estoile 2008: 270). De L'Estoile writes:

> Legacies are not simply 'handed down'; they are often claimed and negotiated, but also repudiated, selectively accepted, falsified or challenged. They involve various feelings, nostalgia and jealousy, remembering and forgetting, gratitude or bitterness. They may elicit contestation and negotiation, struggle for recognition and suspicions of illegitimacy. A legacy creates relationships (sometimes quite conflicting) between the various potential heirs: legacy at the same time divides and relates, as suggested by the double meaning of share, to divide and to have in common ('to perform, enjoy, or suffer in common with others', according to the *Oxford English Dictionary*). Dealing with colonial legacies points less to the 'bequest of the coloniser' than to the modalities of sharing, including through conflict, whatever remains of a long history of mutual relationship. (ibid.)

That is, a legacy is not binding, even if it is hard to shake off. This is because some legacies may be impossible to see, much less jettison. Scholarly as well as other work can identify colonial legacies and reveal their inter-weavings with current ways of knowing, being and doing. Such work can be and is carried out both within and beyond the academy. It may include reappraisals, including those aimed at epistemological and epistemic justice (discussed in chapter 4), repair, restoration, reparation or repudiation. Equally, following due consideration, some aspects may be deemed worth maintaining, albeit in more equitable ways.

Albert Memmi argued that while colonialism destroys the colonized, it rots the colonizer (2003 [1957]). We need not go so far, but it is important to acknowledge that colonialism was not something that happened only to the colonized; it also changed the colonizers and their very ways of being in, and knowing, the world (Nandy 1998 [1983]). Colonial legacies still inhere, often unexamined, in various metropolitan institutions, including universities, and in disciplinary engagements with the world. My own focus here is mainly the metropole. This book thus asks how the colonial past is narrated, justified and sanitized in the metropole, understood as a reluctant post-colony. How can anthropology in the metropole, along with cognate disciplines, enable a fuller and more just engagement with the colonial past and ongoing colonial legacies? How can anthropology shed light on resistance to such engagements or learn from and inform diverse attempts to build a better world? How can anthropological tools and methods be deployed in these attempts? Further, how can anthropology deal with its own colonial legacies and reform itself?

Colonial legacies of anthropology

Gopal argues that a sustained exploration of colonization and decolonization and a grappling with colonial legacies need to take place in the metropolitan university, which has been constituted in no small measure by colonial knowledge projects and extractions. This is also the case for disciplines originating in the colonial era, such as anthropology, which, at least in the Anglosphere, is located in the 'Westernized university' (Grosfoguel 2013). Dipesh Chakrabarty argues that, by their very constitution, the knowledge protocols of the university and university-based academic disciplines remain Eurocentric, generating what he calls a 'hyperreal Europe' (2000). This is not a real place, but it is one that exerts a powerful hold over the imagination and sucks all kinds of knowledge into itself, reframing and re-presenting it. Further, as 'the globality of academia is not independent of the globality that the European modern has created', European thought remains simultaneously indispensable and inadequate for describing non-western modernity (ibid.: 46). This, Chakrabarty writes, can either give rise to a politics of despair or motivate the provincialization of Europe. This latter strategy explores 'how [European] thought – which is *now everybody's heritage* and which affects us all – may be renewed from and for the margins' (ibid.: 17, emphasis mine; see also Mbembe 2021). In this sense, and as I will discuss later, some calls to decolonize are aimed at encouraging Europe to live up to the vision of itself that it has assiduously propagated and to share the world equitably *with* others whom it has long exploited and repudiated.

What are the colonial legacies with which anthropology has to contend and how does it constitute itself in relation to them? For now, we can divide them into three interrelated categories.

The problem of the West

A hyperreal 'West' – not quite a place, although loosely located now in Europe and the United States – haunts anthropology. Within and beyond the discipline, it is variously, often simultaneously, considered excessive and epidemic – absolutist, multiple and contradictory, and never fully expungable, recognized as both an aspiration and a threat, as a comparator and as malleable, potentially shaped by importing knowledges and ways of being from another hyperreal place – the 'non-West'.

What is anthropology's relation to the West? Can an academic discipline founded in colonial times and located in the modern university ever fully divest itself of its 'westernness'? In their edited volume *Who are 'We'?*, which unpacks the ways in which the 'we-ness' of anthropologists is imagined, based on disciplinary training and membership in a shared historically western intellectual tradition, Liana Chua and Nayanika Mathur argue that 'an element of ambivalence, if not outright antagonism, to their "own" (usually western) background has frequently characterised the activities of anthropologists, particularly those working within the anglophone mainstream' (2018: 2). Can anthropology, both located in, and critical of, a western intellectual tradition, pose an otherwise to a dominant and absolutist West? If yes, then from where and how? Does anthropology function as a kaleidoscope, revealing to the viewer dazzling possibilities that emerge from putting together fragments from all over the world to create a new image to which humanity can aspire, or does it function as a mirror, concerned with seeing the world in ways that do little more than reflect the West back to itself? Can anthropology escape the West? These questions are raised anew by those who seek to decolonize the discipline.

The problem of race

Race is hard to pin down. Peter Wade, who has worked on race in Latin America for well over two decades, writes, 'I still feel a deeply rooted uncertainty about exactly what "it" is and how to approach "it". This, I think, is no bad thing and guards against the over-simplification of something that, rather than being a single object, is a mercurial, shape-shifting and slippery set of ideas and associated practices, which exist always in relation to other phenomena' (2015: xi).

Most contemporary anthropologists are clear that race is a social construction and that epidermal or morphological differences do not translate in some biological or essential way to 'natural' or cultural differences between people. However, racialization has real social and material effects; it is, as Carolyn Rouse argues, a 'Durkheimean social fact' (2023: 362). This may take the form of asserting exceptionalism and of naturalizing inequality, both on the basis of race. Race is a relational category, and experiences of being raced vary across place and time. Racialization, and the experience of the self as raced, are affected by diverse variables, including historical factors, laws, class, gender, demographic patterns and location.

In 1991, Faye Harrison argued that neither mainstream nor radical/critical anthropology had made a strong contribution to our understanding of racism and the sociocultural construction of racial differences (2010 [1991]: 3). Although much work has since been done on these questions, including through a growing focus on whiteness, anthropology continues to struggle with how to think about and what to do with race. This is partly because race is a shifting category, and has been overlaid by other terms that also focus on difference – culture, ethnicity, religion, place of origin – in seemingly more benign ways, but which still carry the seeds of essentialism. Anthropologists have participated in this work, replacing race with other, often relativist, concepts that simultaneously emphasize equality and difference (e.g., Franz Boas and Claude Lévi-Strauss both foregrounded culture, albeit in different ways). But not talking about race does not eliminate racism; race muteness may reinforce it. This is something with which attempts and calls to decolonize are centrally concerned.

The body of the anthropologist – western and white?

When the figure of the West is personified, it is as a white man (the white woman occupies a more ambiguous position as lesser than the white man and needing protection from the West's others). It is he who purportedly can lay full claim to values understood as 'western', for example, freedom, rationality and detachment, or to competencies associated with the West, such as scientific or technological innovation, disinterested pursuit of knowledge, and the ability to create universal, rather than particular, knowledge. Where the West is valorized, its others are deemed lacking – perpetually needing intervention and education, and also often museumization. Where it is not, its others may be viewed more positively and as able to offer alternative ways of being from which the West can learn. Either way, the West's others are drawn into the purview of the West in ways that advance the interests of the latter. This is Edward Said's point in *Orientalism* (1978). Anthropology too has long been a player of this particular game.

The above three legacies have raised various questions within the discipline, two of which I will flag up here. The first is the whiteness of the discipline and the fact that researchers are often white and the researched non-white. This is a continuation of colonial patterns. The second is the legacy of a conceit of detached objectivity that ethnography and anthropology were (still are?) deemed to require. Thus, Harrison writes about Melville Herskovits's scepticism about African-American scholars' ability to conduct objective research on race and politics in Africa, and his consequent gatekeeping of African Studies in the 1950s (Harrison 2008: 14).

Both anthropology's whiteness and presumptions of detachment and separation from research subjects and sites have increasingly become a focus of attention and critique. Today, a growing number of anthropologists choose research topics on the basis of their political values, and they fully acknowledge the role of personal attributes in the formation of these values and the changes they hope anthropological work might help bring about. There are also growing numbers of non-white anthropologists, some of whom are choosing to conduct research among their communities of origin in ways that are oriented towards active and transformative care. This has given rise to calls to recognize the worth of this kind of action/applied anthropology and its contributions to anthropological knowledge and methodologies. It is clear that the discipline cannot continue to reward only work oriented mainly towards the production and furthering of anthropological theory, especially if non-white anthropologists are choosing more applied approaches to knowledge generation. A related question focuses on the status of the non-white anthropologist within the discipline. Various accounts (e.g., Uperesa 2016) also describe the experience of non-white anthropologists of being treated like 'marginal guests' or discuss their treatment as 'native anthropologists of home' as neither fully an anthropologist nor fully a 'native' but rather a sort of bridge between the two, or as an inconvenient insider-outsider who is taken seriously neither as anthropologist nor as native.

Anthropology, then, needs to do more as a discipline to build a better house in which different kinds of anthropologist/anthropology can flourish. As Daswani (2021) argues, 'simply including more Black, Indigenous, Brown, and Asian bodies' does not mean more inclusivity in practice (see also Gupta and Stoolman 2022). The 'we' of anthropology requires attention (Chua and Mathur 2018), as do questions of what anthropology looks like to people who are invested in the discipline in different ways and seek to shape it as a practice that extends itself virtuously while remaining recognizable to diverse participants.

Anthropology as a practice

My use of practice here follows the philosopher Alasdair MacIntyre. He defines practice as:

> any coherent and complex form of socially established cooperative human activity through which goods internal to that form of activity are realized in the course of trying to achieve those standards of excellence which are appropriate to, and partially definitive of, that form of activity, with the result that human powers to achieve excellence, and human conceptions of the ends and goods involved, are systematically extended. (MacIntyre 1981: 30)

Let us consider this in relation to anthropology. There are clearly recognized methods – participant observation, open-ended research questions, a hermeneutics of attention and acceptance, living with rather than looking at. There are shared understandings of what constitutes excellence – 'thickness' of ethnography, ground-up rather than top-down conceptualizations, the generation of knowledge through mutual interaction. To 'do' anthropology is to deploy these methods and accept these standards. But it is also to accept that other standards and methods may arise, as may other goals. MacIntyre writes: 'Practices never have a goal or goals fixed for all time . . . but the goals themselves are transmuted by the history of the activity' (ibid.: 33). They are also shaped by those who participate in the activity, bringing new reasons, protocols and goals to bear on it. This does not mean the abandonment of what makes it recognizably anthropological – the kinds of question anthropologists ask, the methods we employ, the kind of knowledge anthropological work produces. But these, as well as purposes and conceptions of excellence, are open to evaluation, disputation and extension.

New forms of thinking with and doing anthropology may come from new participants, hitherto overlooked participants or participants who straddle multiple academic or other practices. This can reshape the internal goods of anthropology – the sense that one has undertaken good research in ways that work for oneself as well as for the research subjects, has understood something, has changed something in the world – whether by positing a new way of thinking about something or opening up anthropology to different possibilities.

Attempts to systematically extend the practice of anthropology so that its conception of the relationship between ends and means is realized and the full participation of diverse actors is enabled require the exercise of virtues. Following MacIntyre, we might identify these virtues as courage, justice and honesty, among others. Brushing aside criticisms, from those who call for decolonization for instance, rather than engaging with them diminishes anthropology as a practice.

This does not necessarily entail agreement, but it must entail honest, rigorous and justice-oriented engagement. Sustaining the life of anthropology and extending it virtuously would also include conducting research in good faith, drawing from relevant knowledge and citing accordingly rather than instrumentally or narrowly, learning from just criticisms, whether from within or without, and refraining from shoring up the ramparts to reproduce privilege.

MacIntyre argues that practices wither or are corrupted when a focus on external rewards (renown or fame, status, promotions, differential salaries, invitations to speak and membership of exclusive 'clubs') overrides the internal goods of the practice. This is partly because external rewards are finite and can be cornered by a better-located or otherwise advantaged few. Further, although practices are sustained by institutions, they must not, MacIntyre warns us, be confused with institutions. That is to say, the university sustains anthropology, but its concern is not necessarily with the internal goods of anthropology or of any other academic discipline. Rather, like other institutions, it is necessarily concerned with external goods – money, accreditation, league tables, student numbers, post-study employment, quantitative markers of satisfaction. Institutions make possible the continuation of a practice, but in controlling access to rewards they can also corrupt that practice, privileging external over internal goods. Institutions, as I will discuss in chapter 6, can also tame just demands for change, bureaucratizing or otherwise blunting them. The discipline should, therefore, not make the purposes of the university its own.

Why does all this matter for a book on decolonizing anthropology? It matters for at least two reasons. First, recognizing anthropology as a practice means that we can also recognize its worth to us as participants while being fully aware that during the development of the discipline various inequities have arisen and been allowed to remain, which we as practitioners can move to redress or eliminate because we care about the discipline and its present and future. We can shift its horizons, its approaches and its methods. We need not throw out the baby with the bathwater. This book does not call for the dissolution of anthropology (unlike, for instance, Magubane and Faris 1985) because bad things have been done in its name or on the basis of anthropological work. Rather, it suggests that we take a long hard look at anthropology and ask how we can do better.

Second, we can interrogate the ways in which, over time, barriers have been put in place that limit full participation in the practice and confine the achievement of both internal and external goods of the practice to certain kinds of body, often in certain locations and consonant with extant asymmetries and hierarchies. What difference might it make to the practice to, as Mwenda Ntarangwi calls it, reverse the gaze (2010), that is, to approach the practice from the outside or from its marginal participants, laying bare its conceits and inequities as well as re-imagining its potential with a view to rethinking and rebuilding it, not beyond recognition, but more equitably and justly? After all, several of us came into anthropology precisely because it offered us much more lively ways of understanding, being in and acting on the world.

My journey into anthropology

I am female, born and brought up in India, in an upper caste and an upper-middle-class family. I have been in universities my entire adult life. I am now 53 years old and have been a UK-based anthropologist for over twenty-five years. I have taught at the University of Manchester since 2006.

I came to anthropology late, following an undergraduate degree in History in Madras (Chennai) and a Master's degree in the history of art at the National Museum in Delhi, both in India. For my Master's dissertation, I planned to focus on the iconography of Warli ritual painting. The Warlis are an Indigenous group in Western India (a 'tribe' as they are known in India) who make highly stylized ritual geometric paintings.

My research focus in the field shifted to a government development initiative that encouraged Warlis to paint on cloth and paper for sale. This brought money into Warli villages, but also other changes. Men replaced women as the 'artists' (almost everyone used the English word). They even took over ritual painting on walls, hitherto the province of older women. Compared with the more formulaic paintings on walls, those for sale were much more narrative in style, depicting various Warli activities, such as charcoal making, in vivid and interesting ways. I was puzzled that no one I met seemed to lament the exodus of women from the painting, but equally interested in the innovation and creativity that commodification seemed to have engendered. I returned to Delhi buzzing with questions. My supervisor, Professor Jyotindra Jain, who was the director of the National Crafts Museum, suggested that history of art would not allow me to ask the questions I now wanted to ask, and directed me to anthropology. I was hooked, reading voraciously (see Ntarangwi 2010 for a similar account of first encountering anthropology). When a scholarship was advertised for Indian scholars wanting to do a Master's degree in social anthropology, to introduce them to the discipline, I applied and was successful.

I was twenty-four when I moved to Cambridge, United Kingdom, leaving the Indian subcontinent for the first time. I completed my Master's degree in 1995 and began a PhD in anthropology at the University of Cambridge in 1996. I wanted to continue working in the field of craft development in India. My experience with the Warli painters had shown me how much development intervention, especially when supported by the state, could change things on the ground even in a short time.

I decided to work in Pattamadai, famous for its fine sedge mats woven by Tamil Muslims and the target of both governmental and non-governmental development interventions since the 1950s. I had three main questions: first, how were various development interventions shaping the weaving industry? Second, to what extent were colonial-era and postcolonial discourses used to promote and market 'traditional Indian crafts' informed by weavers' own understandings of their work? Third, did the identification of the weavers as traditional Indian craftspeople and of their objects as crucial to a Hindu ritual economy enable them to push back against the growing hostility to Muslims within Tamilnadu, and India? If so, how?

Here, I will talk about only two aspects of my doctoral work (Venkatesan 2009): Pattamadai Muslims' ways of approaching the rise of majoritarian Hinduism; and, relatedly, the ways in which they used their mats to help them find a valued place in the national narrative. First, relations on the ground are rarely captured in grand narratives of victims and oppressors. In Pattamadai, Muslims worked with resonances, ambivalences and a *longue durée* knowledge of others – local Hindus, development practitioners, state actors and so on – in sophisticated ways. They were, in Mattingly's terms (2014), researchers of and experimenters in their own lives and world, vulnerable to, but also the shapers of, others' visions of them. Binary understandings of politics and identity or oppressor/oppressed dichotomies do not, I think, quite capture the incompleteness and conviviality (Nyamnjoh 2017 [2015]), the moral experimentation (Mattingly 2014), 'the ordinary as an achievement' (Das 2012) and the frictions of lived life. Broader analyses of domination, hegemony and exclusion, especially on larger scales, are useful, but local understandings and practices complicate them (see Venkatesan 2012, 2019).

Second, I began to think about objects as agents, enabling the enactment of human intentions. Alfred Gell's *Art and Agency* (1998) had just been published, and it gave me a way of thinking with and against things as agents (see Venkatesan 2010). This led me to my next research project. Wanting to explore how things become primary agents, that is, fully and independently active in the world in human-like ways, I began work, also in Tamilnadu, with Hindu priests who transform statues of deities into living embodied gods (e.g., Venkatesan 2020). I thus began participating in major reappraisals of religion in anthropology. These involved moving away from understandings of religion smuggled in from Christianity, with its emphasis on immaterial entities (soul, spirit, etc.), to religion as a form of mediation (Meyer 2020), in which materials and things are crucial. We can call this a decolonizing thrust in the anthropology of religion.

During this fieldwork, I began to do something I call back-and-forth ethnography. I would discuss ethnographic texts I thought might interest the priests, to see how they understood and interpreted them. A discussion about renouncer expectations of reciprocity and soteriological freedom from Leela Prasad's 2007 book *Poetics of Conduct* with two Brahmin priests led me to think about freedom and how anthropologists have not focused much on this concept, neither theoretically nor ethnographically. James Laidlaw's 2002 article on ethics and freedom had already led to a new direction in the anthropology of ethics. That, along with this conversation with the priests, inspired me. Equally, since my Pattamadai days I had been thinking about the growth of populist majoritarian politics and the ways in which hitherto perfectly reasonable people could be persuaded by demagoguery cloaked in lofty concepts. Much work was being done in India on this, and I wanted to ask similar questions of England, where the populist right was surging, with freedom as its concept of choice.

I thus began work with (self-identified) economic and populist 'right-wingers' in England with the aim of understanding what kind of Britain the people on the right wanted to build and how they went about creating publics that supported this vision. I participated in activities, listened carefully, tried to understand their diverse points of view, and answered questions about my own politics honestly. They knew that my politics were very different from theirs, yet they still let me in. At no point did I feel responsible for furthering their aims.

I am outlining this brief history of my intellectual trajectory because I think it is important to show the kind of anthropologist I am. Much of my work is driven by theoretical developments in anthropology, and my fieldwork sites are chosen accordingly. I recognize the fairness of the criticism made by the Cambridge Decolonise Social Anthropology Society (DecAnthSoc) that 'our research interests and field sites have been glossed over as prerequisite decisions to serve as the foundation for more focused discussions about theoretical and methodological considerations.'[1] I agree that more than theoretical and methodological considerations should inform choice of research sites but argue also for the need to resist thinking about anthropological research with people in simple transactional terms – 'I get this and give you that' – or that it is the anthropologist's role to ally him- or herself with research participants' interests, or indeed that people are incapable of drawing boundaries in terms of how much they want to let an anthropologist in. I believe we ought to respect these boundaries – access is not a right.

In a related vein, I recognize the limitations of ethnography and have trained myself to speak not *for* people but *from* my experiences with them and from relevant reading and conversations. I have also had to teach myself that my worries, about the treatment of Muslims in India, for instance, are not the same as the worries of Muslims in my research site, who are much more nearly affected and who develop ways of working with and in the world as they find it. I can learn from them, but my understandings and my attempts to fight back are perforce different from theirs. In that sense, the distinction between self and other can be an ethical one. I am wary of big concepts – freedom, decolonization, liberation – and think we ought to approach them critically and carefully, asking who uses them, and how, and what their mobilization seeks to achieve. Indeed, even an aspiration to decolonize may not be benign. For example, the majoritarian Hindu movement in India have adopted the language, and sometimes the term itself, to block various progressive moves and criticisms (Baviskar 2023). This does not mean adopting a hermeneutics of suspicion. Rather, it involves careful engagement, thoughtful evaluation and positioned critique.

This is an anthropological approach, and indeed this book approaches decolonization anthropologically. It asks how the term has been used by different people in different places and times – the 'aboutness' (Duranti 2006) of the term, that is, towards what it is oriented and from where its impulses spring. My own initial understanding of decolonization stems from my particular situation as a female product of a nation that was once colonized by the British, my undergraduate training in history, and my growing up in a country whose post-colonial present has lived up to some promises and utterly failed in others, where many colonial-era laws still hold sway and confer power and oppression unequally, where English is still the language of status and opportunity in many domains, particularly in metropolitan elite universities, and where democracy and majoritarianism increasingly blend into each other. In the United Kingdom, I encountered decolonization differently, mainly but not only as focusing on race. I have had to learn what decolonization means to others with other histories and other bodies than mine. Indeed, even race plays out differently in my own experiences and those of people with subcontinental origins who were raised in the United Kingdom.

As to my politics, having been born around twenty years after Indian independence in 1947, and with a BA in history from India, I am anti-colonial. However, colonial legacies have not particularly adversely affected me personally; indeed, some have contributed to my own elite status and opportunities. I have had to learn what colonialism and its legacies mean to others much more adversely affected. I further recognize that although neo-imperial dispensations and asymmetries continue to shape the world, leading to the global North's political and economic subordination of the global South, past colonization and similarly patterned neo-colonial flows are not solely responsible for the ongoing immiseration of people. Inequalities within the post-colony merit critical attention. Equally, the restless and uncaring greed of late capitalism, supported by and enriching elites throughout the world, is not confined to the global South. This will, indeed already is, finding its way into and devastating both places and forms and viability of life in the global North. *Theory from the South*, as Jean and John Comaroff put it (2012), has tried to understand these devastations and, for its own survival, the metropole needs to learn from how people are trying to push back. I find Chandra Mohanty's (2003) nomenclature of the one-third and the two-thirds useful to recognize the presence of resource-capturing elites throughout the world and the consequent inequalities and oppressions that exist in unstable ways in both the metropolitan centres and former colonies. Greed, avarice and the desire to control are not confined to one kind of people. The language of decolonization, by too clearly identifying oppressors and victims along colonial lines, can flatten understandings and analyses.

Writing this book

Students are at the forefront of many calls to decolonize the university and anthropology in the United Kingdom. I thus decided to try to write this book with student input throughout. Such collaborative and experimental efforts are increasingly common, and I discuss some of these in chapter 7. In my case, I emailed single and joint honours undergraduate anthropology students at Manchester asking for volunteers to give me feedback on writing in progress. The University of Manchester released money to compensate them for this intellectual labour. Around twenty-five students responded, and a core of around fifteen emailed comments or showed up regularly to workshops subsequent to my circulation of drafts.

This was an extremely rewarding, if scary, way to write a book. The students queried things that did not make sense, pushed me to think harder and better, told me what worked, chided me for not following my own instructions to them on writing, sent me things to read and told me when I was being too cynical or sanguine. Megan, an incredibly careful reader, pointed out that I had used the word 'notwithstanding' nine times in two pages! She also followed up most in-text references and told me which ones needed more space in the text. Robin wrote:

> I am from Hong Kong, which used to be a British colony. Unlike a lot of colonies, though, I believe a lot of Hongkongers didn't actually wish to return to Chinese

rule in 1997 when Britain returned the colony to China. A lot of people emigrated because they were afraid of what Chinese rule would look like . . . Especially given what's happened in Hong Kong recently, people have even expressed the wish that Britain never had given up Hong Kong, or even that the territory come back under British rule . . . Have phenomena like this been discussed in literature on colonization and decolonization?

On language, Michaella wrote early on:

> The . . . paragraphs about the colonialism of the mind and the anecdote about your classmate reciting a work in Tamil reminded me a lot of the points Fanon makes about language in *Black Skin, White Masks* – especially the more psychological impacts/effect on an individual's self-worth. I agreed with [others'] points about including more anecdotes . . . but equally think it might be useful to make a reference to works like Fanon's just to give a sense that these anecdotes are not just incidental, and to reinforce the point that colonialism has psychological and academic detriments, so that the reader may have a better idea of why decolonisation is important.

In response to a somewhat unthought-through comment I had made about non-white authors not necessarily making alternative arguments, given substantially similar training, Isabel responded:

> Maybe it is less that authors with marginalized characteristics make alternative arguments, but that all people have racialized, classed, gendered etc. bodies, and their anthropological research is necessarily shaped through how their interlocutors engage with their bodies. A wide diversity of authors produces a wider variety of knowledge as some framings might align and intersect and some might not. Then it is less about 'quota-filling' diversification of reading lists and more about considering how an anthropologist's intersectional identity

plays a role in how/what/with whom they come to know their field site. But I also agree that these questions are not answered just through reading lists.

I felt vulnerable, supported and very, very grateful. The whole process has taken over three years; students came and went, some carried on their involvement even after graduation. The names of all the students are in the acknowledgements, and I hope they will recognize their role and contributions in what follows. The seven who stayed to the end were: Charlotte Antilogus, Florence Brown, Patrick Jones-O'Brien, Megan Riley, Isabel Sturges, Robin Tang and Hannah Wheeler. All mistakes and infelicities are, of course, mine.

Outline of chapters

The next chapter (chapter 2) critically examines the content and ramifications of the term 'decolonization' and its diverse usages. It introduces 'the logic of the colonizer' and explores the potential of alternative, yet complementary, terms and framings. These are disenclosure (Achille Mbembe, elaborated by Schalk Hendrik Gerber), motley (Silvia Rivera Cusicanqui) and domestication (Olúfẹ́mi Táíwò).

Chapter 3 focuses on anthropology's intertwined history with colonial expansion. I explore this relationship and the many complicities, collusions and collisions that have marked anthropologists' relations with colonial authorities and capitalists. The focus then shifts to attempts to decolonize anthropology and to associated publications, mainly from the United States from the 1990s. I outline and critically examine some of the aims of these scholars, especially Faye Harrison's pioneering work, particularly in relation to liberation and to shared purposes between research participants and anthropologists. The chapter argues that ethnography complicates the idea of anthropology as an agent for liberation. It makes a case for a more nuanced understanding of anthropology's role in the world.

Chapters 4 and 5 work as a pair, discussing the metropole and how it comes to know itself in particular ways. Chapter 4 draws on work by anthropologists, sociologists and feminist philosophers, as well as popular semi-autobiographical writing to focus on attempts to pursue epistemological and epistemic justice in relation to the colonial past and post-colonial present in the metropole. It argues that ethnographic work contributes to and complicates such projects, especially with regard to voice. Upholding the importance of ethnographic attention to detail, location and the diversity of voices within ascribed groupings, the chapter draws on the latest call from the United States to decolonize anthropology (Gupta and Stoolman 2022), to argue for the mutual provincialization of different anthropological traditions while maintaining critical conversations and collaborations. It emphasizes the importance of critique and disagreement among diverse participants in the practice of anthropology.

Chapter 5 continues this theme, this time focusing on the difference between activist theories of knowledge and anthropological approaches to knowledge. Drawing on the anthropology of ignorance, agnotology (the study of culturally induced ignorance), and critical race studies, the chapter argues that knowing in certain ways often requires active not-knowing or ignorance/ignoring. In this sense, ignorance is not something that is easily dispelled. It is ideological. This leads to an exploration of the workings of whiteness, from anthropological and activist perspectives. I ask what an anthropological and especially ethnographic focus on ignorance can contribute to attempts to bring about justice.

Chapters 6 and 7 also work as a pair. Chapter 6 focuses on the modern university. It draws on the work of curriculum and education scholars, mainly in South Africa, who participated in attempts to reshape university education after the end of apartheid and analysed these various attempts, including responses to calls to decolonize. The chapter situates their insights, particularly regarding curricula, to think about resistance and openness to change in universities. It makes the case for the deployment of anthropological methods and tools, including ethnography, to understand both the pushes and pulls of the metropolitan university, and the experiences and interactions of diverse university populations. Which calls to decolonize resonate and with whom; what do they miss?

Chapter 7 focuses on teaching anthropology. It places general calls to decolonize the curriculum in conversation with anthropological understandings of knowledge, the anthropological canon, and experiments in teaching. It argues for sympathetic yet critical engagement from a disciplinary grounding with general calls to decolonize.

The conclusion pulls together the book's various arguments, reiterating those about putting the anthropological house in order and the value of a decolonizing anthropology.

A final word

Before I end this introduction, I should say what this book is not going to do. It is not going to decolonize anthropology; that will always be a task in progress. Rather, this is an introductory volume whose goal is to highlight problematic colonial legacies in anthropology and diverse attempts to address them. It also suggests how we might use disciplinary tools to understand and undo the logic of the colonizer and rebuild our practice, defending aspects that need defence and redressing inequities. This last may not always lie in our power as individuals or disciplinary practitioners; the discipline is located in a world marked by inequalities and resource capture by powerful entities. It can and does speak truth to power, but not always effectively nor with consequent meaningful action, even internally, as recent scandals have shown. To critics who argue that this book focuses mainly on Anglosphere social and cultural anthropology from a British perspective, I say 'you are right!' As Carolyn Rouse argues, 'all anthropologists' concerns are shaped primarily by historical and political discourses in their own backyards' (2023: 365). If we accept that the strength of anthropology lies in speaking *from* the places the anthropologist knows best, then this book should not be otherwise. The intention is not for it to be parochial but rather a critical engagement with decolonization in, of and by anthropology from a particular location. I hope it will speak to, or inform, other located attempts to decolonize and to advance the practice of anthropology virtuously.

–2–
What is Decolonization?

'The postcolonial is a desire, the anticolonial a struggle, and the decolonial an ugly neologism.'
  (Silvia Rivera Cusicanqui, cited in Gago 2020: xiv)

Decolonization is one of the buzz words of the twenty-first century. Cusicanqui's indictment above and Leon Moosavi's reference to decolonization as a bandwagon (2020) indicate some ambivalence towards it. This is perhaps because the scope of the term is both wide and sometimes internally contradictory. Different invitations and injunctions to decolonize may:

- seek more equitable distributions of existing goods or better representation of under-represented groups in various arenas, including scholarship;
- focus on remediation, i.e., making up for denied access to valued goods;
- seek to promote social equity and justice;
- push for critical examinations of what is known and how it has come to be known and disseminated;
- seek epistemological and epistemic justice;
- require a reckoning of flows of wealth and consequent reparations;

- require the removal of objects and names that valorize colonizers and colonialism;
- demand the decentring of Europe and the proper recognition of other locations as central in their own right, rather than as existing only in relation to Europe;
- comprise projects of rejection and recovery; and
- demand radical change, including complete reorganization of social and political arrangements.

The above list is indicative, not comprehensive. When I began systematically thinking about decolonization, I felt that the term and injunctions to decolonize were often being stretched in too many directions, a bit like a metaphor we have in Tamil that roughly translates as 'like putting a G-string on an elephant'. And they seemed to involve some essential paradoxes: could one use the same term to make, often rightful, demands both for a bigger share of the pie and/or a seat at the table without shaking up the status quo too much *and* for radical transformation? Calls to decolonize sometimes appear illiberal and regressive (e.g., as used by some Hindu conservatives in India who argue that homosexuality was a colonial import). They may universalize problems that are place specific. Often, they generate binaries that ignore a basic entanglement of colonizers and formerly colonized, both of whom are products of colonization in complex and not easily soluble ways (see Nandy 1998 [1983]). There seem to be as many ways of thinking about decolonization as there are people calling for it.

Anye-Nkwenti Nyamnjoh argues that social movements can be significant in terms of the kinds of conversation they enable, rather than necessarily in terms of their clarity or achievement of objectives (2022: 3). In that sense, the 'decolonization turn' has opened up rich conversations and contestations wherever it has appeared. These are worthy of anthropological attention, revealing as they are of diverse diagnoses, aspirations and attempts to (re)claim the world and flourish within it. In this chapter, I work with three questions: What do people mean when they use the word decolonization? How do aspirations to decolonize play out in different places, whether former colonies or the metropole? Are other terms or a different language more suitable for specific ailments and aims?

In order to address these questions, I provide an indicative survey of diverse usages and valences of the term 'decolonization' and related variants. I show that the term spans various ways of understanding and dealing with colonial legacies. These can range from what can be described as individual-centred approaches to radical approaches that call for a complete dissolution of extant arrangements. I then turn to alternative, yet complementary, conceptualizations of the contemporary predicament and to potential solutions. Before I do that however, I outline a simple reason why decolonization may look different in different places: colonization took on different forms around the world and involved very diverse populations in very different kinds of colonial relations. As anthropologist Francis Nyamnjoh points out, 'since context matters, decolonisation cannot be articulated in abstraction. What is the context in which current clamours for decolonisation are inserted?' (2016: 129).

Types of colonialism

Historian Nancy Shoemaker identifies twelve types of colonialism, based on colonial intentions, although she points out that her list is neither exhaustive nor are different types mutually exclusive (2015). Equally, not all forms of colonialism are European in origin. I reproduce, slightly abridged, her typology for interested readers. If you already know this, you can skip it. But the key point is that even European colonialism looked very different in different places, and even in the same place at different times. For example, we can think of the many modes of governance under colonialism in the same broad region (reading Mamdani's 1996 *Citizen and Subject* on just South Africa is pretty mind-boggling). Given this diversity, how well do calls for decolonization travel?

> ### Shoemaker's Typology of Colonialism[1]
>
> **Settler Colonialism.** Large numbers of settlers claim land and become the majority. Employing a 'logic of elimination', they attempt to engineer the disappearance of the original inhabitants everywhere except in nostalgia.
>
> **Planter Colonialism.** Colonizers institute mass production of a single crop, such as sugar, coffee, cotton, or rubber. Though a minority, members of the ruling class might belong to an empire that enables their political, legal, and administrative control. Their labor demands cannot be satisfied by the native population, so they import African slaves or indentured laborers, as with the 'coolie' and 'blackbirding' trades.
>
> **Extractive Colonialism.** All the colonizers want is a raw material found in a particular locale: beaver fur, buffalo hides, gold, guano, sandalwood. The desire for natural history specimens and ethnographic artefacts could also be considered extractive colonialism. A slash-and-burn operation, extractive colonialism does not necessarily entail permanent occupation, but it often seems to follow. Extractive colonizers might destroy or push away Indigenous inhabitants to access resources but more typically depend upon native diplomatic mediation, environmental knowledge, and labor. Consequently, marriage 'in the custom of the country' is more common with extractive colonialism than with settler and planter colonialism.
>
> **Trade Colonialism.** Classic histories of the British North American colonies focus on mercantile capitalism's control over trading relationships. The colonial periphery feeds the metropole with raw materials, and the metropole manufactures guns, cloth and other goods to sell in its colonies. Tariffs and the policing of smuggling regulate trade to ensure that capital accumulates in the

metropole. Trade coercion also exists outside of imperial networks, as when the British Opium War concluded in 1842 with China's concession to open additional ports, besides Canton, to foreign trade.

Transport Colonialism. US pressure on Japan to open ports to foreigners in 1854 was not about trade but rather transport: Commodore Matthew Perry wanted safe havens for American whaleships. Transport colonialism includes hubs (the Azores, Hawai'i, and other island chains that became supply depots in the age of sail; steamship coaling stations; US-built airstrips and troop transfer stations on Pacific islands during World War II). It also entails route defenses, such as the US forts constructed on the Great Plains to protect American migrants on the Oregon Trail, and engineering projects that expedite travel, such as the Panama Canal. Transport colonialism does not mandate displacement of native peoples, but it does have a great impact on local economies and cultures by creating contact zones.

Imperial Power Colonialism. Sometimes the purpose of colonialism appears to be simply expansion for its own sake, to aggrandize domains. Imperial rivalry between France and Britain in eighteenth-century North America and the nineteenth-century Pacific involved settler, planter, and extractive colonialism but also inspired competition to amass territory ahead of the other empire.

Not-in-My-Backyard Colonialism. Colonizers sometimes want an empty place far away as wasteland for depositing convicts or conducting dangerous experiments. The British representation of Australia as *terra nullius* initially justified Botany Bay, a prison colony. France and Chile also established penal colonies on Pacific islands. In the twentieth century, US atomic testing relocated Marshall Islands inhabitants, much as settler colonialism might do, but not because anyone else would settle there. France also used distant colonies, first Algeria and then the Tuamotus, as atomic test sites.

Legal Colonialism. Through diplomacy or by force, one people might claim independent or superior legal authority in another's territory. In nineteenth-century treaties with peoples deemed barbaric, the United States assumed legal jurisdiction over American nationals. For example, the 1844 Treaty of Wanghia established extraterritorial courts administered by US consuls and, in the twentieth century, allowed for the US District Court of Shanghai.

Rogue Colonialism. Colonialism is not always a state-sanctioned enterprise. Filibusters and private companies can usurp foreign territory. The state might follow to protect and claim such interlopers as its own, as in the US annexations of Texas in 1845 and Hawai'i in 1898. Or the state might condemn its most freewheeling members to prevent diplomatic crises. The US government did not support filibuster William Walker in Central America. Britain disapproved of Edward Wakefield's New Zealand Company and used the 1840 Treaty of Waitangi to rein in such private land speculators. Rogue colonialism has some other colonialism (e.g., settler, imperial power) as its motivating rationale but raises critical questions about how individuals and the state interact in colonizing endeavors.

Missionary Colonialism. As private agents, missionaries could be considered rogue colonizers, but they deserve their own category for the distinctiveness of their purpose. They need native people to justify their existence.

Romantic Colonialism. Some colonizers want to escape to places that contrast environmentally and culturally with their permanent abodes. When Thor Heyerdahl took his newlywed wife 'back to nature' in the Marquesas (as he explained in 1974's *Fatu-Hiva*), he wished the islanders would leave them alone. More often, romantic colonizers – Paul Gauguin, Robert Louis Stevenson, and consumers of mass tourism – hope for native people to join in the fantasy as performers of local culture.

Postcolonial Colonialism. Former colonies cannot so easily shake off the colonial legacy. Economic dependency and entanglements continue, as do bonds of affinity. Fiji, nearly 100 years a British planter colony and independent since 1970, continues to bear the imprint of its colonial past in its multiethnic, multilingual citizenry; its unusual British-imposed, aboriginal-protectionist landholding regime; and the popularity of rugby among its people.

In the strict political sense, as discussed in the Introduction to this book, decolonization denotes the formal end of a colonizer/colonized relationship between nation-states, the recognition of the former colony as a sovereign political entity, and the transfer of institutional and legal control over territory to the new nation-state. However, even a quick perusal of Shoemaker's list should reveal that the political moment and what preceded and follows it will look very different around the world. Furthermore, even in the same place, different groups affected by colonization may have very different understandings of what decolonization would entail for them.

Indeed, the scope of the term 'decolonization' is constantly expanding. In his 2012 chapter, 'Decolonization: A Brief History of the Word', Raymond Betts found that from its early strictly political usage the term took on a fierce and angry urgency in Frantz Fanon's hands in *The Wretched of the Earth* (1963 [1961]). By the 1970s, Betts writes, there were around two dozen studies with 'decolonization' in the title, and its usage continued to grow. His Google search on '1 December 2010 listed some 750,000 sites for decolonization. Subsumed under this search word appear subjects as varied as decolonization and art, . . . music, and film; also decolonization of the imagination, decolonization and British literary canons, and "soul decolonization"' (Betts 2012: 33).

Soul decolonization

Intrigued by the last topic Betts mentioned, I went looking on the internet and found a 2019 blog post titled, 'Decolonising my Soul: My Journey to Reclaim African Spirituality', by Wangũi wa Kamonji,[2] an activist and regeneration practitioner in Nairobi, Kenya.[3] The author describes how she stopped being a 'staunch Catholic' in 2011 and embarked on a 'seven-year quest to discover, recover and live African spirituality'. This quest took her from the United States, where she was studying, back to her native Kenya, and to Brazil, South Africa and Vietnam, learning and experiencing diverse traditions of ancestor worship. She writes that '[a]ll of these elements were researched, reconnected to, reimagined, reconstructed, and welcomed into, and form a part of my practice today.' She describes the sorrow of her parents who keep hoping she will return to the church, and also what she gained: 'I'm at the point now where I introduce myself as a practitioner of African indigenous spirituality, no longer afraid to show up in my fullness.'

Wangũi wa Kamonji's quest is heartfelt, experimental and inventive in what appear to be deeply productive ways for her personally and for her professional and activist practice. She takes up ways of being in and knowing the world that rework her own relationship to herself, her ancestors, diverse planetary inhabitants and Africa. But her article does raise some questions. We see how different non-Christian traditions from very different parts of the world become resources in self-making here – can this be decolonizing or is it appropriation, however respectful? Further, what is the place of Christianity in Africa? For the author, Christianity became impossible when she recognized the Church's complicity in colonialism. This led her to undertake her spiritual quest to decolonize herself. But what of the millions of Christians in Africa: are they still colonized, and therefore de-Africanized? People do make this kind of argument, as is evident from Ghanaian philosopher Kwasi Wiredu's analysis that '[a]ny African who espouses Christianity without critical examination at some point of the truth or falsity of its propositions, or the validity of their supporting arguments, where there are any, must incur the label of being an intellectually colonized African' (1998: 20).

Wiredu goes on to argue that it is possible to be a non-colonized African Christian, but that a faith-based adherence to Christianity is insufficient: 'An African who espouses Christianity on due reflection may have to admit frankly, and with stated reasons, that s/he rejects the religion indigenous to his/her culture' (ibid.: 21). Further, 'ordinary common-sense dictates that one should not jettison what is one's own in favour of what has come from abroad' (ibid.). These are problematic statements for a number of reasons. For one, as anthropologists have pointed out, the boundaries between 'religion' and 'not-religion' are unclear. For another, how long before something becomes 'one's own', especially through processes of domestication? Indeed, as will be discussed in detail later, the relationship between decolonization and Africanization is contentious (Nyamnjoh, F. 2016; Nyamnjoh, A. 2022; Jansen and Walters 2022). Finally, does any academic have the right to ask for proof of proper commitment from people, especially selectively?

Two comments made in response to Wangũi wa Kamonji's article raise further issues. One person writes that the prayer Wangũi wa Kamonji says she chants 'was never to be uttered by women in Gikuyu society. Surely a returnee to "African Spirituality" would have come across this edict'. Another avers that she is happy to be Christian – the ancestors, she says, demand too much and people have died trying to appease them. Contra the author, who argues that she finally feels free, this woman writes: 'There is freedom in Christ and I wouldn't have it any other way.' Anthropologists have found this claim of finding freedom from oppressive social relations via Christianity in other places around the world, too.

Although the author describes her project as one of decolonization, would it be described as such by others equally invested in the term and its radical possibilities? Is it too focused on self-transformation? Let us turn to a position that eschews a focus on the individual, envisaging decolonization solely as the repatriation of lands and restoration of Indigenous sovereignty. I call this 'decolonization max'.

Decolonization max

US-based scholars Eve Tuck and Wayne Yang argue that 'decolonization is not equivocal to other anti-colonial struggles. It is incommensurable' (2012: 31). This is because 'decolonization brings about the repatriation of Indigenous land and life; it is not a metaphor for other things we want to do to improve our societies and schools' (ibid.: 1). Tuck and Yang argue that in settler colonies whose original inhabitants were partially exterminated, partially ousted, and then contained in smaller and smaller places (both physically and politically), turning decolonization into a metaphor can render settler colonialism innocent by replacing the claims of the original inhabitants of a place with those of other marginalized people, rendering the former invisible. That is, claims for national belonging by/for those oppressed due to their skin colour or place of origin further dispossess the original inhabitants, for example Native Americans in the case of the United States. In Tuck and Yang's words, 'the decolonial desires of white, non-white, immigrant, postcolonial, and oppressed people can similarly be entangled in resettlement, reoccupation, and reinhabitation that actually further settler colonialism' (ibid.).

These scholars' careful analysis of what they term 'settler moves to innocence' makes for uncomfortable reading, as does their unpicking of the idea of solidarity, which looks a lot less benign once they lay bare some of its implications in settler colonies. They rigorously articulate the challenges of non-metaphorical decolonization, unsettling comfortable convictions about conflating redistribution, racial equality or other such desired outcomes with decolonization.

Take Tuck and Yang's discussion of the Occupy movement from their decolonization perspective. This movement began in New York in September 2011 and spread rapidly across the world, including to 600 places in the United States. Among other things, it seeks to advance social and economic justice around the world. Its slogan, 'We are the 99%', points powerfully to the concentration of wealth in the hands of top earners comprising 1% of the population and, while not articulating any precise demands, seeks to change this imbalance.

The analogy of wealth with land (as seen in Figure 2.1) is, of course, problematic in a settler colony, as Indigenous scholar-activists were quick to point out. Settlers acquired land coercively from Indigenous peoples. Settler rights to land are illegitimate, whether claimed by the 99% or the 1%.

One Occupy site was in Oakland, California. Here, several Indigenous scholar-activists brought a memorandum to the Occupy General Assembly. In it, they called for the proper acknowledgement of Oakland as already occupied and as stolen land. Barker, one of the memorandum's presenters, documents the reluctance to engage with decolonization beyond the metaphorical:

> Ultimately, what they [settler participants in Occupy Oakland] were asking is whether or not we were asking them, as non-indigenous people, the impossible? Would their solidarity with us require them to give up their lands, their resources, their ways of life, so that we – who numbered so few, after all – could have more? Could have it all? (Barker, October 30, 2011). (Tuck and Yang 2012: 26)

The problem here is that, if non-metaphorical decolonization were to happen, it would not be the 99% who would

IF U.S. LAND MASS WERE DIVIDED LIKE U.S. WEALTH

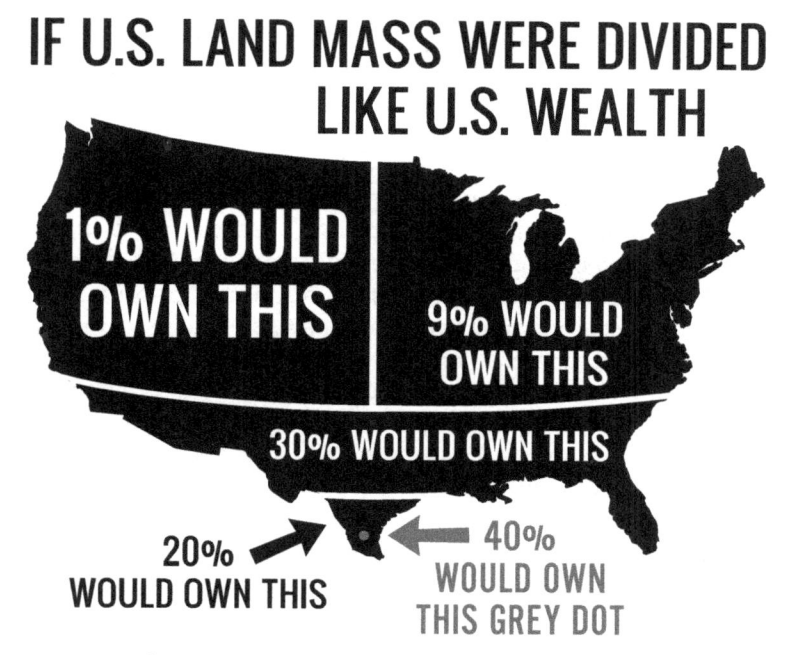

1% WOULD OWN THIS

9% WOULD OWN THIS

30% WOULD OWN THIS

20% WOULD OWN THIS

40% WOULD OWN THIS GREY DOT

Figure 2.1 If US land mass were distributed like US wealth *Source*: https://commons.wikimedia.org/wiki/File:If_US_land_mass_were_distributed_like_US_wealth.png

benefit from the redistribution; indeed, they would stand to lose what they already had, with the land being repatriated to its Indigenous inhabitants, however small their number now. Tuck and Yang write: 'For social justice movements, like Occupy, to truly aspire to decolonization non-metaphorically, they would impoverish, not enrich, the 99%+ settler population of United States. Decolonization eliminates settler property rights and settler sovereignty. It requires the abolition of land as property and upholds the sovereignty of Native land and people' (ibid.).

We begin to see why decolonization in Tuck and Yang's sense is not analogous to social justice or even to anti-racist work more broadly. Rather, the decolonization max position questions claims to landed property in the settler colony, not only of the original settler colonizer but also of those who were forcibly brought in or who came in the wake of settler colonization, however oppressed they may be. In the specific context of Occupy, both claims that it is decolonizing or demands to make it less 'white' on decolonizing grounds (e.g., Campbell 2012) simply fall away in the face of a non-metaphorical understanding of decolonization.

The decolonization max position pushes us to name much more specifically what we would change, for example, racism, inequitable distribution of resources, prioritization of wealth accumulation over wage increases, access to infrastructure and unequal access to and crippling debts from education. This may have the further advantage of enabling wider alliances around specific issues. Indeed, the language of decolonization can be alienating to some, who might see it as bound up with race or as an attack on the national past. Crucially, for Tuck and Yang, racial or other kinds of equity and equality, while important, do not mitigate the illegitimacy of the settler state nor constitute decolonization.

Modernity/coloniality/decoloniality (MCD)

Differing from Tuck and Yang's formulation, but also originating in the Americas, is the influential MCD framework. The Americas, of course, saw the earliest European colonial experiments and forms, beginning in the late fifteenth century, as well as the earliest formal decolonizations. However, decolonization and the formation of independent nation-states in Latin America did not see the end of the structuring of sociopolitical economic life and aspirations along colonial lines or racial inequalities privileging whiteness. In some regions, mainly Argentina and Southern Brazil, mass European immigrations continued well into the twentieth century. Thus, scholars are still debating the nature of colonization, and thus decolonization, in different South and Central American settings (see Gott 2007; Poets 2020). In this context, two terms have emerged from Latin America: coloniality and decoloniality.

Nelson Maldonado-Torres uses the term 'coloniality' to refer to

[l]ong-standing patterns of power that emerged as a result of colonialism, but that define culture, labour, intersubjective relations, and knowledge production well beyond the strict limits of colonial administrations. It is maintained alive in books, in the criteria for academic performance, in common sense, in the self-images of peoples, in aspirations of self, and so many other aspects of our modern experience. In a way, as modern subjects we breathe coloniality all the time and everyday. (Maldonado-Torres 2007: 243)

In other words, coloniality and modernity are understood as inextricably linked. If one is to be shed, so too is the other. Other scholars from the region see integral links between aspects of modernity, such as capitalism, and aspects of coloniality, such as racism. The positing of these fundamental links is inspired by Peruvian sociologist Anibal Quijano's 2000 theorization of what he calls the coloniality of power. According to Quijano, the Iberian colonization of America, from the late fifteenth century, fundamentally changed the world by doing three things:

1. articulating and solidifying the category of race as a basis for domination and exploitation (whiteness and its others emerge at this point as organizing categories);
2. beginning to systematically constitute labour around and in the service of capital, and with a capitalist character; and
3. connecting forms of labour relations to race – 'lower' races did lower-ranked and lower-paid work, if they were paid at all.

These changes were often enforced brutally. They were also turbulent and 'involved a long period of the colonization of cognitive perspectives, modes of producing and giving meaning, the results of material existence, the imaginary, the universe of intersubjective relations with the world' (Quijano 2000: 541).

Quijano argues that over time, and as Europeans began to colonize most of the world, we see European control shaping other arenas of social life. The resources and products of labour came to be increasingly controlled by capitalist enterprise; those of sex came to be controlled by the ideal of the bourgeois family; and those of authority by the ideal of the nation-state. Intersubjectivity, that is, the ways in which people understood themselves as particular kinds of people in relation to other kinds of people, came to be governed by the structural practices of whiteness.

Quijano suggests that Europe's domination of the world through this new model of power not only concentrated the world's wealth in Europe and in European hands, but also cemented the idea of Europe as the pinnacle of development and achievement in diverse spheres of life. Europe came to dominate the production of knowledge and even to define what counted as knowledge. This included the appropriation of extant knowledge that could be used for European advancement, the destruction of non-usable knowledge, and teaching, coercing or tempting the colonized to learn forms of knowledge that would be useful for colonial advancement.

Because modernity is indelibly linked to coloniality, Quijano and others of what is generally called the modernity/coloniality/decoloniality (MCD) group argue that what is required is decoloniality, which disclaims both coloniality and modernity/ies.[4] Walter Mignolo and Katherine Walsh write that decoloniality 'disobeys, and delinks from [the colonial matrix of power], constructing paths and praxis toward an otherwise of thinking, sensing, believing, doing, and living' (2018: 194). According to Sarah Trembath, '[d]ecoloniality . . . is a mindset or praxis; it is an orientation toward culture marked by a commitment to [root] out that which remains in culture, education, society, and so on from the colonial era' (2018).

I am restricted to English translations, but a number of scholars, including from or of the region, are not entirely convinced for various reasons.

Anthropologist David Lehmann (2022) suggests that decoloniality in this vein of jettisoning all vestiges of colonial influence may be the stuff of academic or privileged arguments. Many social movements in Latin America seek social justice

What is Decolonization?

and equality but not necessarily via decoloniality as articulated above.

Latin Americanist geographer Kiran Asher notes that many MCD scholars eschew engagement with post-colonial studies on the grounds that these themselves are caught up in the modernist project. This policing of boundaries and claimed purity means that the MCD project 'risk[s] resuscitating old binaries (theory vs. practice, structure vs. agency, and identity politics vs. anti-capitalist struggles) at best and simple reversals (modern bad and tradition good) at worst' (2013: 838).

Bolivian activist, scholar and intellectual Silvia Rivera Cusicanqui is more scathing, arguing that proponents of this framework have created 'a jargon, a conceptual apparatus and forms of reference and counterreference that have isolated academic treatises from obligations to or dialogue with insurgent social forces' (2020: 51). In doing so, they have built 'a small empire within an empire' (ibid.). I will return to Rivera Cusicanqui's own vision later.

While accusations of logocentrism and patterns of patron–client relationships (rather than genuine collaboration) between academics in elite universities and counterparts in the global South are common, Jonathan Jansen and Cyrill Walters identify the impenetrability of the high humanities language of the MCD framework, adding that the 'language of lament', and the 'uncompromising line of distinctions' (2022: 234, 235) caught imaginations but were not necessarily translatable into meaningful action, especially with regard to curricular change and institutional transformation.

Arjun Appadurai's critique of Mignolo and Walsh's 2018 book on decoloniality is that 'this vision is seductive, and it is hard to disagree with their notions of harmony and conviviality, but it also rests on a reversal of the historical impact of capitalism and colonialism. It seeks to return us to an earlier period of precolonial splendour' (Appadurai 2021). The subtext is: is this possible? I would add that the pre-colonial past may not necessarily have been splendid across the board. Neither power nor hierarchy is an invention of the colonizers, and colonial rule may provide hitherto unlooked-for opportunities for oppressed groups. I will return to this point.

Finally, some questions remain. In its forward-looking mode, decoloniality requires finding ways forward that are divested of the desires, oppressions and epistemes of coloniality-modernity. Is this possible, or even what people desire on the ground? Given that most parts of the world have been, perhaps irrevocably, shaped by colonialism, albeit unevenly, from where do imaginaries of a decolonial otherwise emerge? If they are to be found, how might they scale up or work elsewhere? Further, while some decolonial and radical thinkers argue that modern institutions by their very constitution play a role in maintaining inequality, many marginalized and disenfranchised people seek the reform and proper functioning of such institutions, particularly courts, to safeguard them from the excessive and extractive reach of the post-colonial state and corporation. They may seek entry into universities. In other words, they may not necessarily be imagining radically different arrangements, but rather ones that work more equitably. Many may even want to succeed within the current arrangements, which they have domesticated and rendered suitable to their own needs and aspirations (see, for instance, Moreno Figueroa and Wade 2022 on diverse types of anti-racist movement in contemporary Latin America).

As anthropologists, we might want to be cautious of overly prescriptive frameworks, paying attention instead to processes on the ground and across diverse scales, including struggle, resistance, recolonization, domestication and aspirations, that engage colonial legacies in different ways.

(De)colonization of the mind

It was 1981 or 1982, I was eleven or twelve years old and participating in a city-wide elocution competition for schoolchildren in Madras (now Chennai), South India. Competitors had each chosen a piece to recite and would be evaluated on memory, expressiveness, articulation and certain other criteria. I had picked a section from Mark Twain's *Tom Sawyer*. I loved the book and viewed Tom with a complex mixture of admiration and delighted horror. I played him with a swagger and rejoiced in my dungarees (so like my imagination of what Tom would have worn).[5]

Child after child went on stage and recited poems, passages and speeches (I remember being particularly struck by Martin Luther King's 'I have a dream', which I had never heard before). One girl recited a monologue from a 1959 Tamil film *Veerapandiya Kattabomman*, wherein the eponymous eighteenth-century chieftain questions the East India Company's right to collect taxes. It is a powerful speech. Kattabomman asks the company agent whether he has done any work in the fields, succoured the workers or tenderly cared for the women and children. Is he kin? No. He has done nothing, can make no claims and deserves nothing. The historical Kattabomman was hanged by the East India Company with the support of another local ruler.

Watching the film clip on YouTube now,[6] I go beyond the lurid colours and costumes, the theatricality and the still powerful words, and feel transported back to that open-air ground with its temporary stage and the shock of hearing someone recite in Tamil. It had not occurred to either me or the other children, judging from the stifled gasps, that we could recite in Tamil. English – the language of those Kattabomman was opposing, the language in which we were taught in school, the language that most of us had read from when we first began reading – felt like the natural language for such a competition. Was this ongoing colonization, and would the answer be eschewing English and turning exclusively to Indian languages? Let us turn to someone who advocates precisely that.

In his enormously influential book *Decolonising the Mind* (1987), Kenyan writer Ngũgĩ wa Thiong'o described what he called colonial alienation:[7]

> Colonial alienation takes two interlinked forms: an active (or passive) distancing of oneself from the reality around; and an active (or passive) identification with

that which is most external to one's environment. It starts with a deliberate disassociation of the language of conceptualisation, of thinking, of formal education; of mental development, from the language of daily interaction in the home and in the community. It is like separating the mind from the body so that they are occupying two unrelated linguistic spheres in the same person. On a larger social scale it is like producing a society of bodiless heads and headless bodies. (Ngũgĩ wa Thiong'o 1987 [1981]: 28)

So, in Ngũgĩ's terms, decolonizing the mind involves connecting the whole person to the world around them, body to mind, and members of society to each other through a common means of expression. It makes whole that which is fragmented by the violence, hierarchies and divisions of colonialism, and by the imposition and continued valorization of the colonial language. Ngũgĩ is especially critical of what he calls the English-speaking elite comprador class and its suppression of the authentic voices of the African-language-using peasants and workers. Only through reclaiming African languages and working with and in them, he writes, can the African overcome colonial alienation. Indeed, Ngũgĩ decided he would stop writing in English, first fiction and then anything at all: 'From now on it is Gikuyu and Kiswahili all the way. However, I hope that through the age old medium of translation I shall be able to continue dialogue with all' (ibid.: xiii).

One way of thinking about alienation and fragmentation is fairly straightforward. We can focus on the division of the post-colonial nation society into English (or other colonial-language-speaking) elites and non-English-speaking masses, with the former considered modern-bourgeois citizens and the latter as 'not yet citizens' at best and, at worst, irrational masses who hold back the nation from progress and development. These kinds of characterization are common among English-speaking elites in India. When this is compounded by a general understanding that English is essential for economic and social success, we see real dissonances and deprivations.

Working on schooling in Kolkata, India, anthropologist Henrike Donner shows how middle-class parents strive to ensure that their children are fluent in English, making all kinds of sacrifice, including preventing children from speaking Bengali even at home (2006). Schools recommend that educated mothers stay at home; a working mother would mean that non-English-speaking grandparents or servants would mind the child, hampering English language acquisition. However, things are changing and place matters. Turning to the Hindi heartland of Banaras several years later and in the context of a growing national confidence, chauvinism even, we see a somewhat different picture. Chaise LaDousa, in his ethnography *Hindi Is Our Ground, English Is Our Sky* (2014), discusses how many Banarasis want their children to learn English as it opens up employment opportunities within and beyond India. But the home language of Hindi retains its presence in diverse areas of public life, even acting as a check on bombastic anglicization. English here is domesticated; it remains a language that can open up certain opportunities, but not at the expense of Hindi, which remains the ground to English's sky.

But Hindi, albeit championed as the national language by India's current majoritarian populist government, is not accepted as such in various parts of the country. Like many post-colonial nations whose boundaries are a product of colonization, India has many mutually incomprehensible languages. Right from the onset of independence, there were struggles over choosing a national language (Agnihotri 2015). The proposed choice, Hindi, was fiercely opposed by southern states where it is not generally spoken. On independence, India's constituent assembly thus retained English as one of its official languages; this status continues, albeit losing ground in some parts of the country. Similar questions about a national language have arisen in other former colonies that boast multiple languages. They are tricky to resolve, especially given that the privileging of one language in the post-colonial state may involve the violent or otherwise coercive suppression of others.

There is another issue that is directly linked to decolonization and language, this time in somewhat sinister ways.

With the rise of Hindu majoritarian politics in India and the state's growing suppression of what is seen as 'un-Indian' dissent, criticisms voiced in English are increasingly dismissed as coming from so-called 'colonized Indians' who are out of touch with the 'real India'. Those so identified include intellectuals. Academic curricula are regularly purged of such writers, and careers are jeopardized. The pejorative term 'Macaulay's children' is evermore frequently heard. Macaulay, of course, was the moving force behind the English Education Act of 1835 (India), which made English the language of the colonial government and promoted English education in the country. Macaulay's Minute, which underpinned the Act, is infamous throughout India for its dismissal of Indian languages and knowledges.[8]

Although its intention is different, the contemporary invocation of Macaulay in India echoes Ngũgĩ's distinction between what he calls English-speaking elite compradors and the peasants, the authentic people of Africa who speak African languages. But can the mother tongue itself be oppressive for some?

Emancipatory and unificatory potential

Dalits, or former untouchables, have long recognized that English 'promises dignity, modernity and anonymity through an experience of language and subjectivity outside caste' (Saxena 2022: 63–4). Rita Kothari discusses an unpublished essay by Dalit bilingual (English and Gujarati) poet and activist Neerav Patel. Patel argues that standard Gujarati reflects caste-based hierarchies through and through; it marks as inferior, in its very vocabulary and usages, him and others like him. English, by contrast, does not bear the imprint of such oppression and discrimination. It does not carry the weight of memory, expectation and coercive emplacement of people. This foreign language, this 'foster mother', he writes, extends to the Dalit more justice and empowerment than his 'mother tongue' (Kothari 2013: 65; see also Saxena 2022: 65).

Dalit activist and thinker Chandra Bhan Prasad follows a similar line of thinking in his lauding of Lord Macaulay. He identifies first Macaulay's argument with Orientalists who saw everything Indian as virtuous (Prasad rightly disagrees with this viewpoint), and second his role in drafting the Indian Penal Code of 1860, which made all Indians equal before the law. This replaced Hindu customary law, which prescribed more severe punishments for a Dalit than for a Brahmin, even for the same crime (Prasad 2007). Offering more food for thought, Prasad makes similar claims for the emancipatory potential of capitalism, unyoked as it is from traditional economic systems that are inflected with caste-based hierarchies (ibid.)

Command of the former colonial language can also act as a bridge in multiple-language contexts. Kothari points out that English has acted as a common language with which Dalits from different linguistic groups in India have been able to organize around the commonality of their caste-based suffering and oppression. Similarly making the point about the importance of a common language, historian Ramachandra Guha (1999) writes about two progressive English journals that were established in colonial India and were widely read throughout the subcontinent: *Modern Review* (1907–65) and the *Indian Social Reformer* (1890–1953). These became vital fora not only for nationalists in India but also for progressives pushing for social reform, including against casteism. Indeed, Guha writes about how cricket, that once British sport, formed a staging ground for calls for anti-caste reform in the *Indian Social Reformer*. None of this, of course, negates the very real barriers to English-language acquisition in India, which still render it a vehicle for elite reproduction. But they do complicate the picture.

Finally, and Olúfẹ́mi Táíwò makes this point strongly with regard to Africa, the colonial language becomes domesticated in the places it enters (2022). Whatever the intentions of colonial educators, colonial-language education opened a window onto different worlds and possibilities for several anti-colonial thinkers and social reformists. The point is that people, once they encounter the colonial language and especially when they begin to read in it, go beyond what is prescribed. They begin to ask questions, including about why the values and political philosophies that underpin government in the metropole do not seem to apply in the colonies to colonized peoples. In that sense, a colonial education can provide the basis for radical claims to a shared, equal humanity and to an enjoyment of all that the world has to offer. We also see this in the work of, for instance, Stuart Hall and C. L. R. James, both of whom write about their colonial education in the Caribbean; in the case of James, cricket not only gave him a particular grasp of the world but also enabled him to turn a critical gaze on Britain and its hypocrisies (discussed in Lewis 2018, but see also James 2013 [1963] and Hall 2017).

In other words, the colonial language and the ideals, whatever their origin, that they disseminate, including via critical dialogue, are domesticated in the colonies and can give rise to new forms of life and thought that resist domination. The Haitian Revolution of 1791–1804 (discussed briefly in chapter 4) can perhaps be seen in this light, not as an outshoot of the French Revolution but as a domestication and a properly rigorous application of the ideals of liberty, equality and fraternity, which were betrayed in France at the outset. The language of domestication, then, emphasizes the agency of colonized peoples, unlike the language of decolonization, which continues to assume that all the power (including over forms of thought) remains with the colonizer. The story does not always have to look like a zero-sum game. We can be sensitive to when it is and when it is not.

What about Ngũgĩ's argument that writing in English enriches the English corpus but does little for the languages of Africa (or India, or other places)? There is no single or simple resolution to this, especially given that a host of people from former colonies (myself included) can write most expressively and fully only in the former colonial language. But, and I would argue this unreservedly, English is now an Indian language. Insisting that it is not denies the richness of Indian forms of domestication of English and the traffic between English and other Indian languages. This kind of domestication holds in other places. The Nigerian writer Chinua Achebe writes: 'I feel that the English language will be able to carry the weight of my African experience. But it will have to be a new English, still in full communion with its ancestral home but altered to suit new African surroundings' (1997: 349; written first in 1965).

Even as English is stretched, it too stretches other languages, becoming a part of them over the long period of mixture. Dipesh Chakrabarty writes:

> [I]t is only in Bengali – and in a very particular kind of Bengali – that I operate with an everyday sense of the depth and diversity a language contains . . . one becomes aware of how plural a language invariably is, and how it cannot ever be its own rich self except as a hybrid formation of many 'other' languages (including, in the case of modern Bengali, English). (Chakrabarty 2000: 21)

Olúfẹ́mi Táíwò (2022) makes a similar point about Yoruba and its accommodation and domestication of words and concepts from Arabic, Hausa, Nupe, Portuguese and English. It is also written in a variety of scripts, which inflect it in different ways.

In short, different people may engage the colonial legacy in very different ways when it comes to language, with some deciding on principle to stop using the colonial language (as Ngũgĩ did) and others embracing the possibilities it opens up for participation in global capitalist enterprise (as Donner's and LaDousa's interlocutors do, albeit in rather different ways). Those marginalized by co-language speakers may recognize its emancipatory potential (as Chandra Bhan Prasad and Neerav Patel do), and others may conflictedly yet emphatically embrace the language while seeking new centres and new relationships to self and the world, as is clear from Achebe's words above. Throughout is the recognition that colonialism and coloniality shape more of our worlds than we can ever fully grasp; and not necessarily always negatively, as the emancipatory potential of English for some

Dalit writers, and also a focus on domestication, reveal. Decolonizing the mind by abstaining from the colonial language is more complex than it looks. Similar points were raised by members of the large audience at Ngũgĩ's public lecture in Manchester in 2023.

Returning to the recitation competition, the real problem was not that I had chosen a text in English to recite, it was that it had not occurred to many of us that we could have selected something in Tamil. That is partly down to Macaulay, of course, but it is also down to diverse choices made in and by members of multilingual independent India, especially elites. Of course, I may still have chosen to recite from *Tom Sawyer*. English, like Tamil and later Hindi, are all fully part of my world, and, at eleven, Tom Sawyer's exploits clearly fired my imagination.

Questioning decolonization

In *Against Decolonisation*, Nigerian born and raised, and now US-based, political philosopher Olúfẹ́mi Táíwò cautions against the indiscriminate injunction to 'decolonise this!', especially within the academy. He argues that what he calls 'decolonisation$_2$' has moved far beyond the original political sense of the term, becoming a 'catch-all trope, often used to perform morality or authenticity' (Táíwò 2022: 5). He questions the conflation of the general project of human emancipation with decolonization, and further contends that 'many of the tasks that "decolonisation" is supposed to help us with are already being, or can be, carried out without invoking this buzzword and . . . without the histrionics that often go with it' (ibid.). Having read this, I went back and checked the index of Dipesh Chakrabarty's *Provincializing Europe* (2000). I did not find the word.

One of Táíwò's problems with 'decolonisation$_2$' (and he has many!) is the ways in which some versions that insist on a return to roots or nativism set up what he calls a Manichaean contrast between colonizer and colonized. This, he argues, belies the traffic between them, as well as ignoring the long pre-colonial contacts between parts of Africa and Europe. Further, he argues, colonized people's creative and selective domestication and repurposing of things from the colonial culture for their own societies and purposes then go unrecognized. In this narrative, the colonized remain perpetual victims. They can turn only inwards, either to the past and/or to some authentic untouched-by-colonialism reclaimed self. But is this possible? And even if it were and some people chose that option, would this invalidate other choices, such as to use English or other European languages, and/or build on, domesticate or refine conceptual frameworks articulated in or via the metropole? Although I do not fully follow Táíwò in his somewhat polemical argumentation, I think there is value in paying attention to several problems he raises. In particular, and with specific reference to academic work, I paraphrase a set of questions he suggests are worth asking before attempting the task of decolonization:

1. Is X created, caused, determined, conditioned or influenced by colonialism? The nature of this relationship determines whether X is a candidate for decolonization.
2. Once it is determined that X is a candidate for decolonization, what effects of colonialism must be eliminated?
3. Táíwò gives the example of Juju, a Yoruba musical form whose genesis dates to the colonial period and which has at its core non-African musical instruments. Can it be meaningfully decolonized? What essential character of Juju might change if it is 'decolonized'? Has X endured in the post-colony because the people themselves have embraced it for reasons of their own? These reasons may be assessed on their merits and demerits and on their effects, but the agency of those who might be retaining colonial languages, ideas, usages, institutions and so on cannot be gainsaid.
4. Finally, does the colonial genealogy of a discipline or of ways of thinking or doing really matter, if the practice has transcended or seeks to transcend its problematic history? This question, of course, sits at the heart of various arguments about anthropology.

Thinking with these four questions, argues Táíwò, enables us to see why calls to 'decolonize this!' in the academy must be made very carefully. He indicates the risk of cutting off aspects of certain ways of thinking or being, on the grounds that they have been colonized. This can lead to the impoverishment of scholarly engagements with the world and the world's engagement with the breadth, depth and diversity of scholarly and other responses around the world to colonization, and grapplings with colonial legacies. Finally, it may lead to censorship and a shutting down of knowledge acquired through scholarship.

During a panel at an anthropology conference a few years ago, a graduate student outlined how a lecturer had described the demand for English-language education in Nigeria. The student said he had objected to the description, saying that English was forced on people by the colonizers. Apparently, the lecturer had agreed. He had argued that it was also the case that several people had actively sought to learn English for various reasons. The student was firm that the lecturer, a white man, had no right to tell him, a Nigerian, about what went on in Nigeria. He was displaying such a colonial attitude, the student said. We need to decolonize education.

Reading Táíwò reminded me of my discomfort at the time, and the deference that was shown to the student's claim. Here was a clear example of how the language of decolonization can shut down debate and eliminate diversity and nuance. Does this stance do justice to the pushes and pulls of language acquisition, revealed by scholarship among other things? Does it do justice, for instance, to the complexity of Achebe's statement about English – 'I have been given the language and I intend to use it' (1997 [1965]: 348) – and his subsequent domestication of the language for his own purposes?

Disenclosure and motley

Táíwò's stance is that it is possible to be fully alive to the diverse evils of colonialism, and thence be anti-colonial, without subscribing to 'decolonisation$_2$'. Indeed, others have argued that the real problem lies not necessarily with colonial artefacts and remnants, but in a particular logic perfected during colonial rule that encloses modes of being and becoming. Thus, Gerber (2018) argues that one of the challenges facing post-colonial states is that of moving beyond the logic of the colonizer. This logic, which he argues has dominated and enclosed the world, comprises 'a (pseudo)universalist perspective that became incarcerated in various oppressive political, economic, social, and intellectual practices and institutions' (ibid.: 2). At the heart of this logic is domination through a claim to the Unity of Being, contained in and reaching its apogee in a particular figure. This central figure (or centre) identifies with itself all that is good, true, right and valuable in universalist terms, that is, the quality of being true in and appropriate for all circumstances. Everything else is defined and dominated by the centre according to similarity with or difference from it, generating hierarchies. This is often done by force, but not solely.

Europe once claimed the centre, setting in place a hierarchy with the figure of the European white man at the head and everyone else facing various degrees of imperfect assimilation, expulsion or extermination. It is now possible to see similar claims to the centre in post-colonial states with the figure of Europe replaced by the nation, a particular religion or race, or a similar universalizing figure or 'social body'. Those who either do not accept the claims to universality of this new central figure or who are understood as its other may suffer a similar fate to colonialism's others. In the worst case, they may be treated as the *damné* – the subject who is forged in the non-ethics of war (Maldonado-Torres 2007) – or as problematic and hence requiring surveillance, control and education. Formal decolonization here may end up with a 're-enforcement of the logic of the colonizer', just with a different figurehead (Gerber 2018: 1). It is this very logic of the colonizer that requires dismantling.

Gerber's hermeneutic inspiration comes from 2015–16 student protests in South Africa, where he is based (ibid.:

endnote 1). And it is to African thinkers, particularly Achille Mbembe, to whom he turns as he tries to answer the question of how to build a world that is not based on a logic of dominance from an acclaimed centre.

In *Out of the Dark Night: Essays on Decolonization* (2021), Mbembe argues that the immense promise of formal decolonization is lost when it becomes mired in a metaphysics of difference, in nativist or other exclusionary claims, or in expulsion of the other – whether in the person of the colonizer or the ideas, institutions and things identified with the colonizer. Then decolonization is caught up with that which it seeks to expel. It is concerned with boundaries and with policing them. Instead, Mbembe suggests, drawing on the work of French philosopher Jean-Luc Nancy, that the philosophical aim of decolonization can be summed up in one phrase: disenclosure of the world (*déclosion du monde*), which denotes the opening of an enclosure, the raising of a barrier. What emerges from disenclosure neither follows the logic of the colonizer (domination and subordination from a centre) nor constitutes any of the following, 'Africanization [Mbembe is mainly concerned with Africa], indigenization, or endogeneization' (2021: 56), all of which continue to enclose.

For Mbembe, disenclosure offers the possibility of claiming one's place in the world with others and sharing in the creation of a world in common from the shared colonial past. It is a will to community, but a will that is based on pluriversality rather than on claims to universality or the subordination of multiplicity to a single logic. Mbembe does not fully explain the term 'pluriversal', but I read it etymologically as combining the Latin words *plur* (more) and *vers* (to turn or transform). The pluriverse, then, is a shared world with multiple meaning-making locations, each capable of transforming, folding into and pushing back against the other. In the pluriverse, one does not take it for granted that there is one authorized way of knowing, being or doing. Rather, these things are left open, and people work out how best to create common cause and meaning with each other. They may not always agree. A commitment to pluriversalism may be destabilizing but, as Gerber argues, it opens up a space for an acknowledgement of our existence as always being-in-the-world *with* others and sharing that world without collapsing differences.

Similar to, but also different from, disenclosure is Silvia Rivera Cusicanqui's notion of motley. She writes that motley, translated from the Aymara concept *chi'ixi*, refers to something produced by juxtaposition. Like the grey that we can see from countless spots of black and white placed together, it is neither the one nor the other, nor the product of physically mixing the two. The motley, then, 'expresses the parallel coexistence of multiple cultural differences that do not extinguish but instead antagonize and complement each other' (2020: 66). Again, we see resistance to capture and an openness to both creation and conflict on the basis of difference that is never collapsed into a single entity or universalizing centre. Rivera Cusicanqui argues that the motley can be a basis for a different politics – 'a notion of citizenship that does not look for homogeneity but rather for difference' – and on that basis enables 'legitimate and stable forms of coexistence . . . creating a homeland for all' (ibid.: 66, 68). I cannot claim to fully understand Rivera Cusicanqui's vision – her work has not been much translated[9] – but, like Mbembe's disenclosure, it resists centres, purity and assimilation, calling instead for the building, from and with difference, of a grounded yet less categorically defined and hence more widely liveable and lively world.

Disenclosure is a positive proposal, leading to the opening up of the centre. Doing so can lead to stabilization of the motley principle, that is, a world that is created in common and which promotes flourishing in ways that build on differences but without necessarily tying them to identity, existing political forms or legacies. Rather, the thrust is towards emancipation based on responsibly, albeit provisionally, articulated ideals and actions that help realize a collectively made and shared equitable world. This is, by definition, always a task in progress.

Decolonization, disenclosure and the motley in the metropole

Colonization has also shaped the metropole in diverse ways. Unsurprisingly, then, decolonization, in the sense of the formal end of colonies, has also had profound effects on the metropole. Former colonizer nations have had to come to terms with the loss of colonies. At least in theory, they have had to engage with formerly subjugated peoples as equals, or negotiate new forms of engagement. And they have striven, by various means, to maintain their economic and political dominance in a changing world.

The demographic effects of colonialism have also been massive. In the case of the British Isles, for instance, Niall Ferguson estimates that around 20 million people left to make new lives in the colonies between the early 1600s and the 1950s (2004: 53).[10] Only a fraction returned, most remaining to form settler colonies that gained different kinds of independence from Britain from around the end of the eighteenth century to, sometimes, well into the twentieth century. Some of these colonies went on to become metropolitan centres, continuing to maintain close ties with the 'mother country', albeit on different terms. Settler colonies such as the United States saw huge forced flows of people as slaves from the African continent from the very beginning. Faye Harrison describes these populations as forming internal colonies to signal that they have never received equitable treatment or social justice even after formal decolonization. In that sense, and also for Indigenous peoples in the Americas and elsewhere, the logic of the European colonizer is alive.

Formal decolonization continued to see flows of people into the metropole. Betts highlights two kinds of migration into Europe after colonies gained independence (2012). The first was the reverse migration of Europeans. The second was the flow of people from former colonies who came to Europe seeking economic betterment, education or refuge, or in response to active invitations to assist in post-war recovery. Between 1948 and 1980, 1.5 million people from various parts of the former empire found their way to the United Kingdom; in the 1970s, 237,000 people moved to the Netherlands from its former colonies; and, between 1945 and 1990, 514,400 Moroccans went to France (ibid.: 32).

These migrants were not always welcomed, notwithstanding their long-standing relationship with and contributions to the colonial centres, making these latter what they were and have now become. With the growing flow of non-white people from former colonies into Europe, racism took on new forms in the metropole. This ranged from outright discrimination ('No blacks allowed') to the rise of political parties that framed immigration and immigrants as a threat to the nation and national culture, as well as more invidious forms of exclusion and oppression. These in turn gave rise to diverse progressive endeavours that emphasized inclusion and respect, often with a focus on the benefits to the receiving nation from the migrants. In this vein, the term 'decolonization', as used in the United Kingdom at least, has often focused on combating racism, on celebrating the contributions of migrants and on insisting that institutions and the public civic sphere foster and support ethnic and racial diversity in their make-up. This has involved challenging racial and other colonial hierarchies and forms of exclusion that materially and affectively structure the world.

What might the conceptual languages of disenclosure and motley add to that of decolonization in and of the metropole? In the former colonies, formal decolonization opened up avenues for re-imagining and rebuilding the self and the nation-state. This perforce involved the whole or partial dismantling of colonial forms of centring; the resulting empty space has been the site of contestation, and new forms of life have emerged that continue to be disputed. In that sense, (perhaps only ever partial) disenclosure, domestication, and hopes for a stable and inclusive politics of the motley continue to play out and be sought in diverse ways in former colonies. What about in the metropole? As Nandy (1998 [1983]), Gopal (2021) and Mbembe (2021) among others argue, the metropole has found and continues to find it hard to relinquish the centre, but it needs to if it is to live equitably *with* others, proximal or distant. This process may be harder than for former colonies because it requires different kinds of reckoning, and the acknowledgement of colonialism as conquering without being in the right (Mbembe 2021: 223). What processes of disenclosure must the metropole undertake to open up the centre and promote forms of life that, based on the motley principle, enable various kinds of person to share the national and other spaces equally? These are the challenges of decolonization in the multiracial, multiethnic metropole.

Conclusion

If nothing else, the survey above of different usages of the term 'decolonization' must show us that the concept does different work in different formerly colonized places, ranging from calls to return land to acts of jettisoning colonial legacies and replacing them with other ways of knowing, being, governing or of finding oneself. Indeed, the diverse debates about decolonization emerging from Africa in particular reveal the complexity of the post-colonial situation and even the basic difficulty of understanding both what exactly colonialism did in diverse places and to diverse peoples and how to move beyond its harmful legacies while trying to build, participate and flourish in a shared world. For me, two exchanges illuminated the difficulty of comprehending colonialism and its effects, including with reference to race. The first is a series of emails between Dipesh Chakrabarty and Amitav Ghosh, beginning with Ghosh's commentary on *Provincializing Europe* and moving on to questions of memory and justice (Ghosh and Chakrabarty 2002). The second is a conversation between Margaret Mead and James Baldwin on race, responsibility and a host of other issues, in which each struggles with the other's viewpoint even when they are broadly in agreement (Baldwin and Mead 1972). When even some basic questions about race, oppression, responsibility and memory, for instance, are hard to fully grasp, grasping what is meant by decolonization should be equally difficult. Debates and conceptual framings that problematize claims to a moral high ground or to uncompromising distinctions between good/bad, victim/oppressor, North/South are valuable as we think through decolonization in caring and careful ways.

I thus endorse Gerber's (2018) suggestion to adopt an attitude of reticence and dissidence to calls to decolonize, especially where it looks like they may reproduce the logics of enclosure (dominance, separation and/or essentialization). We can pause before accepting that decolonization is the answer to a particular problem, instead examining critically why the term is being invoked and what work it is doing in any given situation. What exactly does a call to decolonize demand? We might or might not want to run any call to 'decolonize this!' past Olúfẹ́mi Táíwò's questions. But it is worth asking whether such calls may constitute a form of elite capture, that is, control over agendas and resources by a group's most articulate people (Olúfẹ́mi O. Táíwò 2021),[11] or whether they close off or direct attention too narrowly or in morally freighted exclusionary ways. An attitude of reticence and dissidence would also involve asking whether social justice and equity might be served if the language of decolonization, where it was used, was put aside in favour of other frameworks that could help build alliances across ethnicities, languages or other things that divide us. In this chapter, I have introduced some complementary terms – disenclosure, motley and domestication – and will work with them as well as with decolonization in what follows as we turn our gaze first to anthropology and then to the metropole and its institutions, mainly the university.

–3–
Colonialism–Anthropology

Anthropology, like several other academic disciplines, came into being in its current form in Europe in the colonial period, and more specifically from the latter half of the nineteenth century. As such, its early flowering is imbricated through and through with European and colonial epistemologies and enterprises. Kathleen Gough has described anthropology as a 'child of Western imperialism' (1968: 403) and it has also been variously depicted as the handmaiden of colonialism, a tool of colonialism and a child of colonialism, leading to critical, even denunciatory, scrutiny that has extended well past formal decolonization and into present-day calls for decolonization. For example, see Zoe Todd (2016) for a discussion of anthropology's, and specifically the academy's, continuing colonial praxis and, conversely, Herbert Lewis (2014, 2021) for a strong critique of such characterizations, mainly with regard to North American anthropology. These depictions have become almost slogan-like in their take-up in some quarters, notwithstanding the careful way in which Gough, at least, discusses the matter with reference to the geopolitics of the time, inflected by the Cold War.

This chapter explores the relationship between anthropology and colonialism, touching on anthropology both during colonialism and in a post-colonial world in which diverse colonial legacies still obtain. It asks to what extent the discipline's colonial roots affect the underpinnings, concerns and practice of contemporary anthropology. It also selectively engages the large and important literature on the anthropology of colonialism, which saw an efflorescence in the 1980s and 1990s. This body of work involved critical and between-the-lines examinations of the archives in combination with fieldwork to re-examine colonial relations on the ground. The 1980s and 1990s also saw critical examinations of the practice of anthropology, including a focus on representation, positionality and presumptions of the 'timelessness' of the ethnographic 'other'. Among these are Clifford and Marcus's edited volume, *Writing Culture: The Poetics and Politics of Ethnography* (1986) and Johannes Fabian's *Time and the Other* (2014 [1983]). Important critiques also came from Africa, including Archie Mafeje (1998a; 1998b), who asks 'where is African anthropology by Africans [?]' (1998b: 103) and raises searching intellectual and theoretical questions including about ethnography, epistemology and the place of alterity in anthropology. I will not discuss these in detail here, as they have aroused significant critical attention and evaluations, including by the authors themselves, and already inform most anthropologists' background knowledge, finding their place in reading lists throughout the Anglosphere and beyond. Collectively, this body of work is attributed with opening up new directions, including anthropology at 'home', auto-ethnography, reflexivity and growing attention to change – from internal and external sources. These have arguably always existed, especially in the work of pioneer African-American scholars who have gone unrecognized and uncredited (Harrison and Harrison 1999).

This turns the chapter's attention to Faye Harrison's work aimed at reviving and centring the work of African-American pioneers and providing new directions for anthropology with the explicit aim of decolonizing the discipline. Acknowledging the importance of Harrison's solo-edited volume *Decolonizing Anthropology* (2010 [1991]),

I nonetheless critically engage the book's subtitle, *Moving Further Toward an Anthropology for Liberation*. I argue that a central tension in contemporary anthropology needs resolution. Is it an academic discipline that contributes to the understanding of diverse aspects and forms of human social life, or an interventionary discipline wherein understanding is always tied to actively and directly tackling ills in the research site, which may also be the anthropologist's 'home' community? If it is both, what does this mean to how anthropologists do their work? This is a long-standing question, which remains alive, about the purposes of anthropology. Thus, in the 1995 debate between Nancy Scheper-Hughes and Roy D'Andrade on the pages of *Current Anthropology*, Scheper-Hughes (1995) argued that anthropology should be a 'militant discipline', while D'Andrade (1995) maintained that moral and objective models should be kept distinct. These debates and the published comments, as well as countless other discussions, including from different national traditions (see, for example, Baviskar 2023), reveal that anthropologists can and do disagree about what anthropology is, should be and can do.

What the decolonization discussions add to this tension is the experience and treatment in anthropology of 'native' anthropologists in the metropole who may be simultaneously informed by a commitment to making a positive difference to their own communities, making scholarly contributions including to methodologies, and to changing the practice of anthropology – its standards, values, approaches and horizons. Some scholars in this vein further argue that anthropology should be an explicitly anti-racist and decolonizing discipline and that anthropologists need to be activists who pursue these aims both in relation to and beyond the discipline. Whether we agree with this latter point or not, and indeed I argue that academic understanding based on ethical research does itself count as a contribution and that the anthropologist does not also have to be an activist, it is clear that the discipline needs to set its house in order in important ways.

This chapter is not a history of anthropology. Rather, it works through selective case studies and gradually widens its gaze to explore the points and questions raised above, almost entirely speaking from and with the anglophone literature. This is not to deny or marginalize anthropology from elsewhere; rather, it stems from the fact that it is hard to do justice to these rich traditions when working only with translated texts.

Anthropology and British colonialism – some case studies

In *Anthropology and the Colonial Encounter*, Talal Asad dismissed 'wild remarks about anthropology being merely the handmaiden of colonialism' (1973: 16). Notwithstanding this dismissal, more than one article in Asad's well-known edited volume, which focuses on British social anthropology in the early twentieth century, reveals that some anthropologists actively served colonizing imperatives. Other papers in the collection reveal more complex dynamics – alignments, partings of ways, compromises and complicity. Key members of the early British tradition – Bronisław Malinowski, E. E. Evans-Pritchard, Alfred Radcliffe-Brown and Max Gluckman – find their place in the volume along with governors, administrators and other colonial functionaries who adjudged the relevance or not of knowledge produced by anthropologists. Anthropologists variously sought to 'sell' the discipline's usefulness to governance projects, were seen as threats to colonial enterprises, criticized colonial practices (not always because these were exploitative; sometimes because they were based on ignorance!) and accepted the inevitability of colonization, seeking only to mitigate some of its effects.

Much of this work is a product of what Peter Pels calls the anthropology of colonialism. He argues that this is also an anthropology of anthropology because, 'in many methodological, organizational, and professional aspects the discipline retains the shape it received when it emerged from – if partly in opposition to – early twentieth-century colonial circumstances. Studying colonialism implies studying anthropology's context, a broader field of ethnographic activity that existed before the boundaries of the discipline emerged and that continues to influence the way they are drawn' (Pels 1997: 165).

The case studies below of anthropological entanglements with colonial governments reveal that anthropologists, described by Chris Fuller as 'official anthropologists' (2017), were employed by the state to produce knowledge that would aid colonial governance (1: The ethnographic state and its afterlives), clashed with the colonial state and other colonial actors even as they sought support (2: The Rhodes–Livingstone Institute) and helped 'invent' or systematize aspects of local governance to enable colonial governments to institute indirect rule, that is, colonial rule via highly managed 'traditional' leaders and structures with later anthropologists accepting these systems as fact (3: Reification and refinement), and domestication of colonial imports by local people in ways that baffled importers and exceeded their control (4: Domestication).

Together, the studies reveal the diversity of anthropological engagements with British colonialism and also the domestication of colonial projects and imports by local people. Finally, they reveal how knowledges produced during and of colonialism have afterlives that continue to inform projects in the post-colony. The case studies draw strongly from British colonialism and the Indian material because that is the history I know best. But my choice is also based on Fuller's remarks on India's near absence from, and the lacuna this has created in, anthropologies of colonialism and of anthropology (Fuller 2014). This is puzzling, given the importance of India to Britain, the world's biggest colonial power between approximately 1800 and 1950, and Dirks's description of the colonial state in India as the ethnographic state (2001: 43). The rich and thought-provoking colonial,[1] post- and anti-colonial, and critical scholarship from India rarely features in more strident calls for decolonization (although see non-anthropologists Rivera Cusicanqui 2020 and Olúfẹ́mi Táíwò 2022). Anthropologists who already know these things may wish to skip these case studies. They might, however, ground the above points for students.

Case Study 1: The ethnographic state and its afterlives

The colonial state in India embarked on several massive projects employing anthropologists to 'know' the populations it was governing. Each project raised discussions and further refinement of categories, methods and so on, which in turn made contributions to early anthropological theory and methods.

Herbert Risley of the Indian Civil Service was one such official anthropologist, who directed the ethnographic survey of India from 1901. Risley 'sought to apply to Indian ethnography the methods of systematic research sanctioned by the authority of European anthropologists' (Risley, cited in Fuller 2017: 606). Further, the questionnaire that Risley prepared along with Sir Denzil Ibbetson and John Nesfield, who were also engaged in official ethnographic studies, drew inspiration and even some questions from *Notes and Queries on Anthropology* (BAAS 1874), the classic field methods text published by the British Association for the Advancement of Science. Risley also consulted anthropologists Edward Burnett Tylor and Henry Maine, among others, who were supportive of his efforts. Risley's *The People of India* (1908) is an astonishing publication, containing information on physical types, social types, caste, marriage and other themes. It attracted criticism almost from its publication, including with regard to the attention paid to caste and the links that Risley makes between caste and race. Notwithstanding this, official ethnographic studies continue to shape Indian self-understandings and governance projects. Indeed, the Indian government still employs official anthropologists in the colonial style (see Jenkins 2003; Shah 2017).

One of the many features of these copious colonial-era studies was the ways in which they were used by Indians to shape colonial ways of knowing. Kapil Raj (2000) shows how elite intellectual collaborators – learned Brahmins, Islamic scholars and others – shaped British officials' understanding of the land they sought to govern by teaching them about, for example, 'Indian' laws and customs. In other words, elites used these studies to reaffirm their privilege. Critical scholarship on colonial-era studies, too, has been appropriated by groups seeking to maintain privilege. For example, Cohn's work on the censuses and the fixing of caste (1987) is increasingly used to argue that caste was a colonial artefact and thence mobilized to discursively 'purify' Hinduism of casteism in India, and enable upper-caste capture of the subaltern position outside, particularly in the United States (Chakravarti 2019).

Case Study 2: The Rhodes–Livingstone Institute (RLI)

The RLI was set up in 1937 following lengthy negotiations between the governor of what was then Northern Rhodesia and the Colonial Office in London. The RLI's first director was anthropologist Godfrey Wilson, who was appointed as a 'functional anthropologist' following checks to discover anything to his discredit (Brown 1973: 186). The stated role of the institute was to discover and apply knowledge of African society to aid in the governance of the territory, but its work and remit were severely circumscribed from the outset. Settlers, especially mine bosses, were adamant that they would not be governed by anthropologists (ibid.), and that the work of anthropologists should not hamper their highly profitable extraction or promote dissidence among (the highly exploited) labour. It took only three years for Godfrey Wilson to resign his post. His research agenda for himself and for Max Gluckman (appointed in 1939) roused unrest among the settlers, particularly mine bosses, because it proposed a focus on African mineworkers, African residents of urban and industrialized areas (a category that was not recognized or permitted in the territory but which nonetheless existed) and Africans who moved back and forth between urban and rural areas. The research would have resulted in an understanding of Black lives and aspirations in this rapidly industrializing and extractive territory. None of this was considered 'safe' in terms of maintaining the status quo in white–Black relations in Northern Rhodesia and particularly in the Copperbelt, where Wilson faced huge barriers to conducting research. His initial research there in a mining town, Broken Hill (now Kabwe), was stopped after strikes, first by white and then by Black miners, in 1940. The governor's intervention to enable Wilson to resume research was fruitless because company bosses thought his 'methods . . . might cause discontent and unrest besides undermining the African respect for the European mineworkers' (cited in Brown 1973: 192).

When Max Gluckman took over the RLI directorship, he tried to maintain its independence from the Colonial Office and the settlers by insisting, against strenuous opposition, that the preliminary training and the writing up of research by RLI anthropologists would be at British universities. Nevertheless, the pressure from the Colonial Office and the settlers continued, as Richard Werbner shows in his discussion of A. L. Epstein's ban from continuing fieldwork in a mining township and his labelling as a 'subversive' by the Chamber of Mines (Werbner 2020: 123). Epstein then applied to begin new research in Papua New Guinea in 1959, but his security record followed him and his application was turned down, only later being granted after much diplomatic work behind the scenes. Likewise, there was an attempt to ban Gluckman from Papua New Guinea. This was after he had moved to Manchester in 1947 to start up the anthropology department there.

What this discussion of the RLI reveals is that anthropological work was potentially seen as useful, but equally could be seen as subversive and dangerous by colonial authorities and non-state colonial actors. Fredrik Barth's 2005 survey of British anthropology reveals the amount of work that went into establishing anthropology as an academic discipline in British universities between 1898 and 1970 in ways that separated it from an applied discipline in the service of colonial or other governments. This was not entirely successful, of course, as governmental permission, funding from both government and colonial enterprises, and the bulwarking of anthropological research on the back of colonial expansion continued to influence the discipline. Notwithstanding this, it seems that independent-minded anthropologists, especially those with an eye to full careers in the burgeoning academic field of anthropology, far from being 'run' by colonial authorities or settler populations, were likely to get the backs up of those whose interests lay in maintaining the highly problematic status quo. However, it remains important to note that, as Asad points out, 'The colonial power structure made the object of anthropological study accessible and safe – because of it sustained physical proximity between the observing European and the living non-European became a practical possibility' (1973: 17).

Case Study 3: Reification and refinement

In Fiji, following formal colonization in 1874, various Fijian chiefs participated more or less enthusiastically in British attempts to systematize land rights to create a 'neat, simple and beautifully structured system' that formed the basis of governance and also specified rights to land according to patrilineal clan (Clammer 1973: 204). That this system was more or less invented did not seem to bother too many people at the time, including anthropologists (ibid.), who accepted it as fact. Indeed, Clammer discusses the work of anthropologists, such as W. R. Geddes and G. K. Roth, who reified the system in their anthropological writings in diverse problematic ways.

The advent of large numbers of Indians, transported to Fiji as indentured labour in the late nineteenth century, brought further innovations and the solidification of the chiefly system. In this regard, anthropologist John Kelly (1995) discusses the slow and somewhat experimental ways in which race came to be an organizing factor in Fiji. He argues that racial and essentializing thinking emerged as governance tools, including protecting native Fijians from land grabs by sugar corporations and other white settlers, and as a way of managing and containing relations between Fijians and Indians. In the second quarter of the twentieth century, labour movements were increasingly everywhere, including in British India. Colonial authorities worried that Indians might spread these among Fijians. This meant drawing up ever-tighter boundaries along racial lines between Indians and Fijians, and also between certain kinds of missionary (e.g., Jehovah's Witnesses and Hindu Arya Samaj), suspected of harbouring dangerous 'communist' tendencies, and the Fijian and Indian populations.

The afterlives of colonial knowledge-gathering exercises for the purposes of governance and anthropological reification continue to affect post-colonial social and political life. In Fiji, for instance, as Lorenzo Veracini (2008), Stephanie Lawson (2010) and Patrick Leonard (2019) argue, they continue to adversely affect the political and social agency of Indo-Fijians. In relation to the preservation of chiefly power in colonial and post-colonial Fiji, Lawson also argues that:

> although discourses of resistance to either colonialism or neocolonialism may be radical in some sense, they can also be highly conservative when aimed at preserving traditional modes of authority and legitimacy, especially where these in turn support social and political privilege. We may also question whether the 'anticoloniality' that underpins many postcolonial approaches – not just in historiography, but in anthropology, politics, geography, literary and cultural studies, and so on, may sometimes be too hospitable to indigenous hegemony and all that this entails. (Lawson 2010: 313)

A simplistic understanding of the colonial oppressor and colonized oppressed and a consequent uncritical acceptance of the 'emic' voice may end up reaffirming privileges, including those gained in the colonial period. It may prevent a careful understanding of internal hierarchies and hegemonies and a focus on rank-and-file movements for justice and equity.

Case Study 4: Domestication

Jean and John Comaroff's monumental two-volume publication *Of Revelation and Revolution* (1991 and 1997) pays close attention to a hundred years of records to explore Tswana–missionary interactions in what is now the northern part of the Republic of South Africa from the early nineteenth century onwards. It thus traces incipient to full-blown globalization, modernization and colonization over the *longue durée*, showing how the conversion of the Tswana to Christianity played a crucial part in this process by altering not only Tswana consciousness but also whole ways of life over time. It is no exaggeration to say that these two volumes are key forerunners of the now thriving field of the anthropology of Christianity, including a focus on missions and their cultural and hegemonic effects.

The publications also sparked important conversations that focused on the agency of the colonized and on the domestication of new ideologies to the extent that they became hegemonic but not in ways that were under the control of the bringers of these ideologies. Thus, historian of settler colonialism Elizabeth Elbourne argues that, although the Comaroffs convincingly show the success of the British non-conformist missions, they pay less attention to:

> [t]he rapidity with which Christianity was out of the hands of the missionaries and settlers who brought it, the corresponding importance of non-Europeans in the spread of Christianity, the multiplicity of uses to which diverse interest groups of all ethnicities put Christianity as both a language and a practice, and the political and cultural complications of regions with multiple power players. (Elbourne 2003: 444)

In other words, various African groups were key players in missionization, and they domesticated Christianity in ways that perplexed European missionaries. This did not, of course, protect them from the iniquities of political colonialism, which was to follow these early missions.

This limited set of discussions both about anthropology during British colonialism and from the anthropology of colonialism reveal more multifaceted relations on the ground than straightforward understandings of oppressor and oppressed. Tensions between different kinds of colonial agent (government, missionaries, planters, settlers and so on) further complexify the picture, as does an attention to local elite practices and the take-up of colonial-era imports. This should not, of course, blind us to the real suffering endured by various colonized groups during colonialism. It also remains the case that formal decolonization did not end colonial-era hierarchies, unequal distributions of resources and subordination of various groups especially, but not only, on the basis of race. The normalized patterns of white generators of knowledge and non-white objects of knowledge, cemented during colonialism, also continued more or less undisturbed, at least in the metropole. This last point, Barth argues, 'must not be sidelined as political critique of the practices of a handful of anthropologists, but needs to be reframed as a major topic of social analysis' (2005: 51). This challenge would be taken up in the United States, where one year before Asad's 1973 volume, Dell Hymes's edited collection *Reinventing Anthropology* (1972) raised similar questions while also charting new directions for the discipline. (For a critical evaluation of both volumes, please see Mafeje 1998a.)

Indeed, by the 1970s, the centre of anglophone anthropology had shifted to the United States (Barth 2005: 57; Silverman 2005: 346). There are a number of reasons for this, discussion of which lies outside the scope of this book, but see Silverman's brief history (2005: 257–348). The first specific call to *decolonize anthropology* came from Faye Harrison in the United States (Rouse 2023: 361). It is to Harrison's call that I now turn. Before I do this, let me discuss the often invoked and unmarked 'we' of anthropology because it is pertinent to this discussion.

Opening up anthropology

When we think of an anthropologist, what kind of person comes to mind? Usually white, I imagine, and in the past, male, although now increasingly also female, and 'shored up by various structural mechanisms and inequalities that striate the contemporary academic world system' (Chua and Mathur 2018: 2). One aspect Chua and Mathur identify as marking the hegemonic figure of the anthropologist is a fascination with alterity, embodied in, ideally, a racially, geographically and/or socially distant other with whom affinity can be built through ethnographic research.

This fascination with difference and affinity produces a particular figuration of the anthropologist – one who uproots themselves, goes away, is transformed and is able (or, at least, seeks) to transform. Such a figuration of the anthropologist arising during colonialism remains hegemonic and dominant in anthropological imaginations of who 'we' are and what 'we' do. This has the effect of denying or stunting the development of other kinds of anthropology or anthropologists who do not cut such a figure nor share a similar fascination with alterity. They may be deemed other to anthropology and not 'other enough' to research subjects to undertake 'proper' anthropological research.

This idea that the anthropologist *must* be different in some crucial way to research participants means that the insider-anthropologist, that is, one who works with their own people, is often not taken as seriously as the, usually white, stranger who comes in from the outside. The insider-anthropologist may even be taken as a native informant who speaks 'our' – anthropological – language but is not fully one of 'us'. This not only marginalizes the insider-anthropologist, but it impoverishes the discipline. Research projects that arise from intimate knowledge over a lifetime and from occupying the same kind of body as one's research subjects and thus being subject to similar stresses and strains, from racialization for instance, are overlooked. Equally overlooked is work by non-hegemonic scholars and intellectuals that can, by showing how colonialism's others saw and understood the world, destabilize the dominant white centre and expose its blind spots to provide new and more equitable directions for the discipline.

Thus, a growing number of anthropologists have argued and continue to argue that the discipline needs to rethink its fascination with alterity. It needs to properly engage and address its own assumptions about the figure of the anthropologist and support the many different values and purposes that drive anthropological research (for a rich discussion of these points, see St Clair Drake 1980).

Other approaches to research, including the purposes of research, have also garnered attention among those who seek to transform anthropology. Chief among these is Linda Tuhiwai Smith's *Decolonizing Methodologies: Research and Indigenous Peoples*, which focused on research among Indigenous peoples (1999; revised and expanded second edition in 2012). In its second edition, Tuhiwai Smith – an Indigenous New Zealander herself and Professor of Education and Maori Development – addresses the understandable suspicion with which Indigenous people view researchers, perhaps especially anthropologists. The answer, she argues, is not less research but better and more respectful research with and for the benefit of Indigenous peoples. A second strand of the book focuses on the promotion of research by Indigenous scholars and activists in ways that acknowledge their barriers, constraints and opportunities. Tuhiwai Smith recognizes the very real issues Indigenous peoples face around the world, including disenfranchisement, dispossession, high mortality and morbidity rates, lack of infrastructures and substance abuse. The question she poses is: how can research among Indigenous peoples, whether the researchers are Indigenous or not, benefit research subjects' communities? Although Tuhiwai Smith's book is not aimed at anthropologists or anthropological research, it now sits on many an anthropologist's bookshelf and informs visions of what research can and should aim for.

Rethinking and refiguring anthropology

Faye Harrison's influential edited volume *Decolonizing Anthropology: Moving Further Toward an Anthropology for Liberation* was first published in 1991, with multiple subsequent editions. I worked with the 2010 edition. In her Introduction, Harrison presents various problems with anthropology:

- that it has not sufficiently theorized race and hence does not have the tools to tackle racism;
- that academic anthropology (in the United States and Europe) remains predominantly white and that the work of African-American and other Black anthropologists has been insufficiently recognized, leaving many of them to work in the periphery rather than the centre of the discipline, despite the significance of their work to enduring questions, which have also thus been sidelined;
- that anthropology has likewise ignored the work of non-western radical thinkers to its own detriment and that of the people of the world;
- that anthropologists have, since the post-modern turn, squandered the discipline's critical potential by focusing too narrowly on the problems of representation rather than engaging in political struggle; and
- that anthropological writing and concerns are not sufficiently broad or accessible to those who might be interested.

Harrison outlines the goal of the book as the subversion, decolonization and transformation of anthropological inquiry 'to encourage more anthropologists to accept the challenge of working to free the study of humankind from the prevailing forces of global inequality and dehumanization and to locate it firmly in the complex struggle for genuine transformation' (Harrison 2010 [1991]: 10).

Decolonizing Anthropology continues to resonate within the discipline. Its papers are rich and thought-provoking, touching on ethical issues in ethnographic research and wider politics, on the ways in which particular places or people come to be understood as problems, and on the bodies and positions of the researchers, and inclusions and exclusions thereof. In her Introduction, Harrison discusses the neglect of race in anthropology, both as an object of study and in the discipline's own practices of citation and support, which have consistently sidelined Black scholars and their work, neglecting their ability to contribute to grounded engagements with race. Harrison thus gives African-American scholars their due place through an analysis of their contributions to critical inquiry, particularly in exploring the mixed racial settings of the United States and the Caribbean with special regard to Black lives.

Harrison's work revitalized anthropology in the United States and beyond, spawning numerous supportive critical engagements. Thus, in 2016, Jafari Allen and Ryan Jobson published a paper on what they call 'the decolonizing generation', to assess, among other things, its effect on rethinking anthropological theory and questions of race in anthropology. The same year also saw contributions by different scholars to a multi-part online discussion on 'Decolonizing Anthropology' (edited by McGranahan and Rizvi 2016) on what was the *Savage Minds*, now *anthro{dendum}*, blog. This collection shows clearly that anthropological approaches to decolonization are diverse, differing across locations and the specific concerns of the anthropologists, based on, among other things, their own bodies and identities.

However, these publications all share a core concern in attempting what can be identified as multiple forms of disenclosure. As I discussed in chapter 2, for Achille Mbembe disenclosure involves the opening of barriers that prevent flourishing. It offers the possibility of claiming one's place in the world with others and a sharing in the creation of a world in common from the shared colonial past. It is a will to community, but a will that is based on pluriversality rather than claims to universality or the subordination of multiplicity to a single logic. What then are the attempted forms of disenclosure in the literatures discussed above?

The first of these is the foregrounding, especially in anthropological understandings of race and problematizations thereof, of the work of Black scholars, especially those who have historically been relegated to the margins of the discipline. In doing so, a different trajectory of anthropological thought is imagined.[2] Allen and Jobson, for example, suggest that anglophone anthropologists think about race with the ideas of Haitian anthropologist Anténor Firmin, as contained in his book *De l'égalité des races humaines* (*Anthropologie positive*), published in Paris in 1885. Firmin held that 'Anthropology has been the discipline which can best provide answers to the great problem of the origin and nature of man and the question of his place in nature' (cited in Fluehr-Lobban 2005: 3).

Importantly, and unlike many others at the time, Firmin began from a position of the equality of the races. Perhaps unsurprisingly, his work did not make its mark in European anthropological circles of the late nineteenth century when colonial expansion and wealth depended on denying such equality and thence justifying exploitation. Allen and Jobson ask what anglophone, Euro-American anthropology would have looked like had Firmin been taken seriously, with his work forming a base for subsequent theory, methods and practice in the discipline. Drawing on Kamala Visweswaran, they suggest that the discipline may well have steered clear of the emphasis on culture that sidestepped careful anthropological attention to race, theoretically as well as in terms of lived experience and as anti-colonial praxis. This shortcoming, they argue, was systematically addressed only well into the twentieth century by the decolonizing generation. This kind of thinking with hitherto marginalized scholars constitutes a moral and experimental re-imagining of the discipline, with potentially far-reaching effects, including decentring the whiteness of the discipline and dismantling the hegemonic figure of the anthropologist.

A second form of disenclosure involves removing the barriers in writing between a professional self and personal attributes – race, gender, sexuality and nationality, for instance. Greater attention is paid to who is able to do what and why, and relationships before, during and beyond fieldwork. This, the authors in the *Savage Minds* collection argue, leads to a more engaged and politically aware anthropology. The conceit of a detached anthropologist is shed, with the anthropologist working with, among and for others, rather than claiming a neutral, value-free position.

A third form of disenclosure, also seen in this literature, calls for a greater openness of anthropology to cognate disciplines such as Black Studies and Indigenous Studies, with a subsequent decentring of anthropology itself. Scholars emphasize here the importance of learning, from activist and other epistemologies, ways of being and interventions in the world. The call is not so much to dismantle anthropology but rather to shape a new anthro-politics.

A final form of disenclosure is the opening up of research to imperatives other than knowledge production. How, the decolonizing generation asks, can anthropology actively benefit research subjects rather than only generate understanding and theory that is not directly oriented towards action?

Alonso Bejarano and colleagues' book, *Decolonizing Ethnography* (2019), is a good example of this last aim. The authors describe how two anthropologists – Daniel Goldstein and Carolina Alonso Bejarano – had designed a project that combined researching the securitization of undocumented migrants in New Jersey, United States, with activism on their behalf. They write that two assistants who joined them, Lucia López Juárez and Mirian Mijangos García,

> evolved from research assistants to collaborators to full-fledged ethnographers while continuing to work as activists for immigrant rights and immigration reform. In the process, they took the work of ethnography and activism – two linked yet parallel elements in the project's original conception – and fully integrated them, such that the ethnographic research became indistinguishable from the activism. As they conducted research about work accidents and wage theft, Mirian and Lucy not only learned about and collected data on these problems. They also used the research encounter to inform injured workers of their rights, to deliver services directly to them, to exhort them to become active in demanding benefits under the law, and to recruit them to join a local immigrant rights organization. At the same time, the knowledge they gained through research made them more effective activists. Through interviewing and participant observation, Lucy and Mirian developed broader and deeper perspectives on workplace abuses than what they knew from their own experiences or from talking in isolated and unsystematic

ways with victims of abuse. These efforts contributed to an expanded understanding for all of us on the research team. Armed with data to support our claims, we could argue more forcefully for the rights of undocumented workers while empowering those workers to take up their own defense. (Alonso Bejarano et al. 2019: 10–11)

This not only made the project richer and more robust in terms of data, they write, but it also demonstrated the utility of anthropological tools in self-empowerment, public advocacy and personal transformation. Here, we see two forms of disenclosure: first, by making anthropological tools available to research assistants to use as they see fit, the anthropologists are lifting barriers between themselves and those they direct as assistants. In turn, this serves to dissolve the boundaries between the academic learning and publication-oriented aspects of the project and its activist aspects. Anthropologists and research assistants now do both parts of the work on what sounds like equal terms, albeit based on the motley principle that recognizes and builds on differences in training, experiences and aims of differently positioned members of the team.

Anthropology has come a long way since the 1990s, but some issues that Harrison and her co-authors raise continue to apply. Take, for instance, the controversy around the setting up of the editorial board for a journal, discussed by Giulia Liberatore in her book *Somali, Muslim, British* (2017). Liberatore opens chapter 2 with a brief account of the 2015 launch of the *Somaliland Journal of African Studies*, which did not have a single Somali scholar on its board. Safia Aidid, a Somali who was at the time a Harvard PhD student and is now a historian at Toronto, queried this, using the hashtag #CadaanStudies (whiteness studies). An anthropologist on the journal's editorial board responded that no serious scholars of Somali origin were available. When this was refuted, he claimed that Somalis in the diaspora with access to higher and high-quality education were simply not willing to put in the work to become academics. Following the ensuing acrimonious discussions feels like a journey into anthropology's dark past, replete with tropes of the lazy native.³ In that sense, and rather shockingly, the calls to reform anthropology still resonate. Indeed, it is unsurprising that Akhil Gupta's 2021 presidential address to the American Anthropological Association focuses squarely on anti-racism and decolonization, including the need to change the culture of the discipline (Gupta and Stoolman 2022). Although these authors are mainly addressing US anthropology, many of their points resonate more widely, and Faye Harrison is clearly an inspiration. I will return to Gupta and Stoolman in the next chapter.

For liberation?

The subtitle of Harrison's edited volume *Decolonizing Anthropology* is *Moving Further toward an Anthropology for Liberation*. It may be understood as proposing a charter for the discipline in two ways: first, that anthropology should be liberated from its colonial antecedents and logics, enabling the discipline to critically engage and challenge oppressive conditions, particularly those emerging from racialization and racism; and, second, that anthropological work should explicitly focus on the liberation of research participants from oppressive conditions. The second of these aims, to paraphrase Max Weber (1946 [1919]), gives us a vision of an anthropology that exhibits an ethics of conviction and also an ethics of responsibility. The former refers to the conviction that a particular position or action is right and good, the latter to the ways in which one might take responsibility with others for enacting this conviction. Where research participants and the anthropologist agree about oppressive structures and inequities, and the anthropologist has specific competencies to help bring about positive change in ways that work for research participants, there can be few quibbles with the second aim. However, the vision of anthropology as 'for liberation' requires some thought before its acceptance as a charter for the discipline, especially in terms of research aims.

Liberation is a complex term, and one person or group's idea of liberation may entrap or exclude another's, sometimes actively and at others unintentionally, as is clear from diverse ethnographies. Naisargi Davé's *Queer Activism in India* (2012), for instance, details the various schisms and disagreements between different lesbian activist groups and between male homosexual activists and female lesbian activists in the early 2000s in India. A key disagreement hinged on whether decriminalizing homosexuality should foreground the distinction between private and public. Doing so, it was argued, would be good for well-off gay men but could continue to criminalize poorer men who had no private spaces of their own and ended up in parks or other public places. It would also, it was argued, trap women for whom the public/private distinction posed a real danger. Similar disagreements arose about whether the law criminalizing homosexuality ought to be repealed or read down – limited in its scope – and whether activist groups ought to cater to particular constituencies or be maximally inclusive. Further, we see in the book how the women's movements in India explicitly distanced themselves from lesbian movements, arguing that fighting for basic rights trumped activism around sexual desire.

Davé, who explicitly identified herself as queer lesbian in her book, was accepted by and worked with several activists, including volunteering (e.g., working on a phone helpline set up by one organization). But she was also occasionally treated with suspicion, partly because the groups were mutually suspicious and tensions sometimes ran high. Importantly, the Indian women in the book try to work out for themselves what they ought, and want, to do in the situations in which they live and towards which they have somewhat different approaches. They also recognize that some concerns from abroad, of North American lesbians, for instance, simply do not make sense to them. Furthermore, partly because the Indian government claims decolonization as a way of maintaining the heteronormative and patriarchal status quo, they try to avoid too much foreign involvement. Thus a British activist who had completely relocated to India and worked from the outset with one of the lesbian groups was asked to leave a solidarity circle formed of lesbians at a hostile women's conference because she was white. Her presence, some worried, might lead to the dismissal of lesbian activism in India as western-led.

Also focused on lesbian activists, specifically feminist separatists in London in the late 1980s, is Sarah Green's book *Urban Amazons* (1997a). The book is one of the saddest ethnographies I have read. It begins so hopefully with the funding of various lesbian and gay collectives by the Greater London Council, and the setting up of the Lesbian Archive and Information Centre, but ends rancorously with disputes about race on one side and sexual desire on the other. One half of the Archive collectively ended up suing the other half in the High Court of Justice. Reflecting on this fieldwork, with its intense debates, conflicts, challenges and changes within feminism and for feminists, Green writes:

> Repeatedly, women I spoke to said they felt something was changing, but they weren't quite sure in what direction, except that it felt like a fragmentation of something, that things were cracking at the seams somehow. Some spoke of a siege mentality, referring to the ongoing battles about identity politics, particularly concerning race, but also about lesbian sexuality and sexual desire, prompted by the increasing number of women whom many separatists labelled 'libertarians'. The name was intended to indicate that such women were profoundly anti-feminist and were promoting forms of sexual expression amongst lesbians that were . . . precisely the kinds of sexual relations which separatism, based either on radical or revolutionary feminist ideas or a combination of both, argued were the foundations of heteropatriarchy. (Green 1997b)

Again, we see that liberation is not so easy to define; 'libertarians' wanted to enjoy lesbian sex in ways that the separatists could not condone. The anthropologist here tries to understand what is at stake, how things come together and how they fall apart. Importantly, Green's work, like Dave's, reveals that good intentions may not be enough. We see this kind of thing over and over again in the development literature also (see, for instance, Venkatesan and Yarrow 2012), and we need to learn from it rather than assuming that anthropology can further liberation, even where the anthropologist is broadly sympathetic to the liberatory aims. The anthropologist may well have their notions of what might constitute liberation, but these may not map onto research subjects' notions of emancipation. Furthermore, different research subjects may disagree among themselves on what constitutes emancipation or how it may be best achieved. An anthropology *for* liberation, then, is perhaps better understood here as an anthropology *of* liberation.

In the cases discussed above, the anthropologist's job is to sympathetically understand, describe, analyse and critique diverse ways in which people strive to create, in Das's words, an ordinary everyday that they can inhabit (2012) or to recreate their worlds by transcending or challenging mores that they identify as problematic. Here, anthropological work involves the recognition that people are the researchers of and experimenters with their own lives (Mattingly 2014); it is crucial to respect that without the anthropologist's own ideas about liberation getting in the way. This is also Saba Mahmood's point in *Politics of Piety* (2011). Further, people who live permanently in a place might be compelled to consider on-the-ground contestations and the need for compromise in ways that the academic may not. Even the anthropologist working 'at home', by virtue of education and employment, may not face the same familial, financial, governmental or societal pressures that research participants do.

Finally, as Kirin Narayan points out in her article 'How Native is a "Native" Anthropologist?' (1993), as academics we straddle multiple worlds, striving to generate knowledge from interactions with research subjects. This knowledge may be scaled up, becoming knowledge about the world as it is currently organized. Anthropological knowledge speaks *from* the experiences and concerns of research subjects, but also from other kinds of knowledge. Thus, Paul Farmer links the terrible human suffering on the ground in Haiti to broad geographical and deep historical processes (1996). He shows that Haitian suffering is produced by structural violence, some of it originating in Haiti, much of it spread across the globe. Producing broader understandings of social and cultural patterns and dynamics by interrogating phenomena across multiple scales is a scholarly concern not necessarily shared by people on the ground.

For these reasons I advocate sympathetic resistance and dissidence to the identification of anthropology as a discipline for liberation. Rather, by showing how subjects are always in formation in processes of struggle, anthropologists can reveal the provisionality of diverse emancipatory moves. This does not mean eschewing any participation in struggle, but it does mean recognizing that struggles can themselves generate unsettled motley politics on the ground and that there are often no single or easy paths to emancipation.

Disagreements

Reticence and dissidence are perhaps especially required when studying up (working with elites; Nader 1972) or studying sideways (working with people who are not that dissimilar in structural terms from the anthropologist; Ortner 2009, 2010). David Mosse writes honestly, openly and thoughtfully about objections raised by some of his research subjects to the analyses in his book on international development policy and practices and the ways in which project 'success' is produced and represented (2006). Mosse had worked for over ten years in a project run in Western India by the British Department for International Development (DFID). As an anthropologist-consultant, he contributed to the project in diverse ways. DFID, he writes, subsequently 'decided to support a study of the project experience from my particular anthropological perspective' (ibid.: 935). A draft of his study, which Mosse planned to publish as an ethnographic monograph, was sent to former colleagues at DFID and in India and drew their ire. He writes:

> Those of my project colleagues who raised these objections sought to interrupt the publication process and to ensure that many parts of the book were rewritten. In April 2004 I was called to defend my ethnography in front of angry informants – international experts and Indian project managers – in the presence of professional colleagues. The move to publication had strained and broken valued relationships of fieldwork. (Mosse 2006: 935–6)

In the end, Mosse did publish his substantially unaltered ethnography, but not without much soul-searching about the whole process. Two things stand out.

First, Mosse makes it clear that he was writing generally about aspects of development policy and practice *from* his work with this project. He was not writing about this project per se but about certain systemic features of international aid. His co-workers, however, saw his work as evaluating and judging them personally with, they claimed, consequent effects on both their professional reputations and careers, and the project itself. Disagreements like these are not easily resolved, especially in cases such as these where 'ethnography offers another means of public engagement with powerful institutions whose knowledge systems constantly organize attention away from the contradictions and contingencies of practice and the plurality of perspectives' (ibid.: 938). The anthropological contribution in such cases may result in the multiplication of objections, including by some research participants.

Second, the anthropologist's account is neither wholly objective nor wholly subjective; it is, however, always *positioned*, both in terms of the anthropologist's social relations with other diversely positioned actors in the field and in relation to other accounts, textual or otherwise. Given that research subjects may, as here, disagree with the knowledge produced by the anthropologist, it remains important that we as authors take responsibility for published work (Strathern 1987) and remain accountable for our work in multiple ways and to diverse constituencies.

Of course, research informants may not even be particularly interested in the ethnographic text or analysis. This was the case with my own doctoral work. One trader who was very adroit at public relations for himself and the weaving industry told me, when I offered to translate the text for him, that 'some people may be interested; just make sure my name is in there'. Others placed copies of my book (2009) in pride of place when I took them back as gifts but mainly focused on the photographs. A development practitioner whose work was coterminous with, and with whom I shared a house during, fieldwork read it in detail and mostly agreed with my analyses, including about the failure of one of her projects, despite her careful and extremely competent work (Venkatesan 2010). She was frustrated that, having analysed the workings of craft development in India, I had no solutions that would improve it. She did, however, accept my explanation that my interest and expertise lay in working out and analysing how complex interventions played out on the ground and in making my work available to anyone who would find it useful. We remain good friends, occasionally collaborate and act as each other's sounding board.

Although research subjects may co-write or edit ethnographic accounts to rich effect, as in Alonso Bejarano et al. (2019) discussed earlier, the multiple-authorship format as advocated by Gupta and Stoolman (2022) to decolonize anthropology thus may not always be appropriate. What remains is the importance of ethnographic outputs being justifiable and justified and of anthropologists taking responsibility for their positioned analysis. This is rather different from furthering liberation or from shaping mutually beneficial purposes. It is no less critical though, especially when anthropologists' fieldwork takes them into professional organizations that put a lot of effort into managing representations of their work, as Mosse found. As the range of ethnographic sites expands, including through studying up, and studying sideways, the objections may increase, and power asymmetries may go in the opposite direction to that commonly understood within the discipline. Publishing, then, may inform but also open up diverse objections from research participants and others, which need to be engaged but may not find satisfactory resolution.

Inappropriately engaged?

When is an ally not an ally, and how does scholarship become the site of dispute? Importantly, what is the role of, and effects of, critique? Jeffrey Tobin (1994) discusses long-standing disagreements between two scholars in Hawaii: Jocelyn Linnekin at the Department of Anthropology of the University of Hawaii and Haunani-Kay Trask, director of the university's Center for Hawaiian Studies. Tobin describes Trask as a Native nationalist active in Hawaiian sovereignty campaigns.[4] Linnekin is 'one of the anthropologists most involved in working for Native Hawaiian land rights' (1994: 115). The women have much in common regarding their education and critical interests, yet they 'consistently oppose each other on political and scholarly issues' (ibid.). Linnekin, the cultural constructionist, takes issue with aspects of Hawaiian nationalism, and Trask, the Hawaiian Nationalist, likewise with cultural constructionism (ibid.: 115–16). The problem, Tobin writes, is not that they do not understand one another. Having consistently been reading and responding to each other over decades, 'each understands the other only too well' (ibid.). They disagree, however, on the relationship between culture and politics in ways that matter in Hawaiian politics: Is culture political or politicized? What constitutes a proper understanding or expression of culture? Whose voice counts in matters of political import?

The first of these three questions matters enormously in Hawaii, where campaigners, including Linnekin and Trask, oppose certain US military activities, including the use of an island – Kahoʻolawe – for naval target practice. The campaign group to which Trask belongs argues that Kahoʻolawe has always been a sacred site for Native Hawaiians. Linnekin argues that the sacredness of Kahoʻolawe is probably a recent invention (she does not commit either way). Further, she argues that the assertion of its sacredness is a response to US

Navy bombings. Kahoʻolawe, then, for Linnekin, serves as an example of how nationalist movements formulate tradition and use it for political ends. Trask disagrees. Her argument is that Hawaiians oppose the bombing of Kahoʻolawe because it is sacred. Politics has not made the island sacred; rather, Hawaiian culture has become politicized because of the US colonization of Hawaii, and this extends to Kahoʻolawe. In sum, Linnekin argues that politics produces culture while Trask argues that culture is politicized. Why does this argument matter?

In 1977, five members of the Protect Kahoʻolawe ʻOhana were arrested for trespassing on the island. They were convicted on the grounds that their motivation was political. This overrode their own claim that as Hawaiians they were motivated by *aloha ʻaina*, or love of the land, a key Hawaiian spiritual and cultural concept. A government anthropologist was called in as an expert witness and was critical to the conviction. Kahoʻolawe continues to motivate the disagreement between Trask and Linnekin.

The Native Hawaiians' claim here became something that the anthropologist was asked to expertly analyse and endorse or challenge. It is in this light that Trask argues that 'Hawaiian culture is determined by Hawaiians. The truth of a cultural claim is, to a great extent, determined by membership in the Hawaiian community' Tobin 1994: 121). It is not open to questioning by others, no matter how well intentioned or based in scholarship. Doing so aids the colonizing enterprise, suppressing Native rights to speak about Native culture and matters. This extends to anthropologists, however much they understand themselves as allies. Indeed, Tobin points to an instance when the US Navy used Linnekin's published work to denounce Hawaiian assertions about Kahoʻolawe. Cultural constructionists, that is, those who argue for culture as process rather than as essence, can become co-opted. Even when the anthropologist actively supports the Native, the former's voice is assigned more authority than the latter's. It was in this vein, Trask says, that the Protect Kahoʻolawe ʻOhana ended up asking Linnekin to write to the US Navy about the island. Indigenous scholar and poet Alice Te Punga

Somerville makes a similar point in her discussion of settler-colonial studies and its relationship to Indigenous Studies, stating that some disciplines are given not only more weight but also more status in conversations within, but perhaps particularly beyond, academia (2021). This concern can equally apply to anthropology.

I have drawn extensively on Tobin's discussion of the disagreement between Trask and Linnekin because he points to an important tension that underpins anthropological demystifications of nationalism and essentialism in an emancipatory and inclusionary vein (drawing on arguments that emphasize cultural constructionalism or the making of culture) and disciplinary engagements with Native nationalism. Is it possible to be critical in this vein and be an ally? In *Decolonizing Anthropology*, Harrison strongly argues for the desirability, even necessity, of anthropologists engaging with native, particularly radical native, scholars. But what form should these engagements take? As Tobin shows in his careful analysis, there are no clear answers to this question. Should the anthropologist who demystifies nationalist arguments in one context refrain from doing so in another? On what grounds? When is critique appropriate and when is uncritical endorsement? Lawson's point in relation to Fijian chiefly discourse, discussed earlier, may also be subject to similar questioning.

Tobin, who was taught by both scholars, both of whom were aware of his paper pre-publication, largely ends up on Trask's side while nonetheless acknowledging Linnekin's careful, thoughtful scholarship and sympathy and work for the Hawaiian cause. He concludes that 'if we acknowledge that critique can be a weapon, then we must accept responsibility for the weapons that we produce' (1994: 133). But does this resolve the dilemma? Is taking responsibility enough or should Linnekin cease publication on Hawaiian politics and culture? What of her commitment to her scholarship and to larger debates into which it enters beyond the Hawaiian context?

One way of answering these questions is to ask who has more to lose, the anthropologist who can, after all, turn to other research, or the Native nationalists who are fighting for everything they hold dear and for whom these discussions have existential import? This, of course, is yet another question; indeed, my point is that this kind of issue defies easy resolution, going well beyond a moral commitment to engaging the work of Native scholars, intellectuals and activists.

When we turn to Davé's and Green's work discussed earlier, the situation is compounded by the fact that all parties involved are 'native' and cannot agree with one another. Under such circumstances, the anthropologist's role, rather than being *for liberation* or being straightforwardly able to endorse one view over another, looks more like Weber's early twentieth-century description of that of the social scientist (discussed in Burawoy 2016). That is, although the particular object that the anthropologist chooses to study is dependent on their values – i.e., is not value-free – it is not for the social scientist to prescribe particular aims or courses of action based on these. Rather, the objective is to understand how particular aims become meaningful and articulated in particular spaces and times, and to explore the implications of different ways of achieving them as well as the barriers to their achievement. This is one way in which anthropology can be of use to interlocutors and others in this kind of situation. At the level of the individual anthropologist, this has to be up to each of them to work out – with due regard to scholarly integrity, robustness of argumentation and relations with research informants and others – what to say, and how to say it, when and to whom. There can be no simple or straightforward answer from or for anthropology, and there may always be situations where the anthropologist is viewed with mistrust and anthropological forms of critique as problematic.

I suggest, therefore, that while it is crucial that anthropologists ensure the integrity of the practice (preventing abuse of various forms in institutions and beyond, producing careful and thoughtful analyses based on available evidence, opening up methods and publications to objection, giving proper credit that goes beyond narrow citational norms, etc.), and eschewing racism and other forms of discrimination or sidelining, a vision of the discipline as being 'for liberation' requires critical questioning. This is particularly the case when research participants and anthropologists do not share a common politics or goals.

The 'repugnant other'

The year 1991, in which *Decolonizing Anthropology* was published, also saw the publication of Susan Harding's article titled 'Representing Fundamentalism: The Problem of the Repugnant Cultural Other'. Harding underscores the point that the anthropologist may not always sympathize with the aims (political or otherwise) of research subjects, nevertheless arguing that the latter's 'repugnant' views deserve critical and sympathetic attention, perhaps because they are prevalent in the public sphere or influential in important ways or because those who espouse them are problematically cast outside the pale of the public and civic space.

Harding's own focus is on the production of Christian 'fundamentalists' in the United States by modern discursive practices, which position them as 'opponents of modernity, progress, enlightenment, truth and reason' (1991: 375). This is not unlike charges levelled at colonialism's 'others'. The difference here, though, is that few anthropologists feel moved to apply anti-colonial or anti-orientalizing tools to contextualize and explain the life-worlds and choices of these close others who are considered repugnant. Indeed, anthropologists working with people with 'distasteful' views may themselves be treated with suspicion because of their choice of research subject. Harding writes about the continuous inquiries by her colleagues about her own background and her motives for choosing this and not some other object of inquiry. I also have encountered this kind of questioning over my own research in England among libertarian Brexit-supporting right-wingers. I have lost count of the number of people who have asked me how I can bear to work with 'these people'. No one has ever asked me about the views on gender, some of them repugnant to me, held by my research subjects in Tamilnadu, India, who share my own Tamilness and Indian upbringing and are generally understood as 'worthy research subjects'.

Why is this kind of research important? Stigmatizing groups whose politics are 'distasteful' (Pilkington 2016) and refraining from ethnographic research with them means the discipline does not produce systematic ethnographic knowledge either about why they hold such views and seek to enact them or about how they perceive their projects as ethical or necessary and recruit people to their cause. This leaves anthropology unable to explain the rise of populist and exclusionary far-right politics and its alliances with soft-right politics, and of diverse, including oppressive, responses to the late-capitalist world in which we find ourselves, instead leaving such knowledge production to investigative journalism and oppositional activist groups. Condemnation, then, replaces explanation. This research requires epistemic reflexivity of a different kind to research conducted among people whose politics the ethnographer shares. This is not about redemption, even though it humanizes those who are dismissed as beyond the pale, but it does important work in enabling an understanding of the growth of regressive politics (see Pilkington 2016: 13–36).

In terms of decolonization, it makes sense to understand and engage those who seem bent on reproducing, or deepening, inequalities. Following Harding, Grace Carey argues in her summary of a 2019 round table on these questions, that '[w]e should ask ourselves as a discipline why posturing ourselves in opposition, struggle even, with the "bad guys" of the world constitutes "good" anthropology' (2019). Indeed, studies of whiteness, including of white supremacy, increasingly form part of attempts to further understandings of the persistence of racialization and racism in different parts of the world. Anthropologists have much to contribute to these attempts, not just from the perspectives of those affected but also by working with those who perpetuate inequities. If the problems originate in specific spaces (bureaucracies, courts, scientific establishments), studying these is important (as a number of anthropologists do). One might discover surprising things, change could be wrought, and at the very least dissenting points could be put forward or analyses produced that might herald desired results.

Conclusion

The decolonizing impetus of the 1990s, as well as related developments earlier and later, have altered anthropology in various ways. This has included a reckoning with anthropology's imbrications with colonialism, and the diverse ways in which anthropology and anthropologists helped produce and build on colonial knowledges and benefited from colonial rule, even while some of them resisted colonial imperatives. Importantly, work such as Harrison's showed how the discipline reproduced colonial logics and disregarded the work of African-American and other non-white scholars, thus eschewing fruitful and more equitable directions. Critical scholars also systematically dismantled the myth of the detached disinterested anthropologist, and therefore of objective anthropological knowledge. Anthropologists' bodies and affiliations, this work showed, matter in important ways – both within academia and in research relations. This requires acknowledgement and a reshaping of the discipline along disenclosing and motley forms of belonging. New ways of working with research participants emerged that engaged and furthered their aims. This not only produced new forms of knowledge but also sought positive change in the world. There is still a way to go to realize the visions of these moves, particularly within academia, but there is no gainsaying their importance.

However, as I have argued, building a better anthropology is not the same as promoting an 'anthropology for liberation'. As the ethnographies and controversies I have discussed reveal, liberation is a complex term and people may disagree with each other about what it is and how to achieve it. Statements such as 'we need to support native or third world intellectuals or peoples' are too simplistic. Further, as we have seen, the work of the anthropologist may come into direct conflict with that of activists or research participants. This is perhaps particularly the case with decolonization.

At some level, decolonization always addresses the nation – either to argue for the rightness of certain nationalist projects or to demystify the nation or another bounded entity to enable full belonging of those considered its others. Critical work, however careful, sympathetic and even perhaps decolonizing, may undermine decolonizing nationalist projects based on primordial or essential claims. Such work can also willy-nilly be co-opted by those who deny such claims. Given this, there perhaps will always be situations where the anthropologist and anthropological work are held in suspicion or are reviled. This might be the case even when the anthropologist and local decolonizers, including scholars, share key political aims; or where research participants and the anthropologist have worked closely on the same projects for a long time.

There is no satisfactory resolution to these kinds of conflict or disagreement, nor can they be straightforwardly understood in terms of colonizing oppressor or colonized oppressed. It is important to recognize that we cannot know what someone will do with our research or publications, nor might it be possible to satisfy research participants and also reveal structural problems with, say, international development projects. There will be some spaces where the anthropologist and anthropology may always be suspect, and not just by governments or others who seek to control what is known and how. Even decolonization as currently conceived may not allay all suspicions about anthropology and anthropologists. Taking due care and responsibility and remaining accountable for one's work remain essential.

In light of the above, I suggest that a key responsibility of all scholarship, decolonizing or otherwise, is the promotion of epistemological and epistemic justice. This is the subject of the next chapter.

–4–
Epistemological and Epistemic Justice

Few books are as devastatingly angry as Frantz Fanon's *The Wretched of the Earth*. Written shortly after the wave of newly created independent nations following the Second World War, Fanon's work lays bare Europe's material dependence on the colonies:

> [I]n a very concrete way Europe has stuffed herself inordinately with the gold and raw materials of the colonial countries: Latin America, China, and Africa. From all these continents, under whose eyes Europe today raises up her tower of opulence, there has flowed out for centuries toward that same Europe diamonds and oil, silk and cotton, wood and exotic products. Europe is literally the creation of the Third World . . . So when we hear the head of a European state declare with his hand on his heart that he must come to the aid of the poor underdeveloped peoples, we do not tremble with gratitude. Quite the contrary, we say to ourselves: 'It's a just reparation which will be paid to us.' Nor will we acquiesce in the help for underdeveloped countries being a program of 'sisters of charity.' This help should be the ratification of a double realization: the realization by the colonized peoples that it is their due, and

the realization by the capitalist powers that in fact they must pay. (Fanon 1963 [1961]: 102–3)

This chapter heeds Professor of Postcolonial and Decolonial Studies Gurminder Bhambra's call for epistemological justice in the social sciences, that is, a commitment to asking searching questions both about how knowledge about the self and the other is constructed in the metropole, and about the forms such knowledge takes – usually, a valorized colonial centre and a lacking or needy colonial periphery (Bhambra 2021, 2022). This then leads us to questions of epistemic injustice (Fricker 2007), which ask how and why some voices, and some kinds of narrative, are considered unworthy of attention.

I begin this chapter with selected projects within the academy that promote epistemological and epistemic justice. I show how they seek to reshape metropolitan understandings of colonialism and the direction of flows in ways that run counter to popular understandings. I then show how this kind of scholarship informs work undertaken beyond the academy to promote semi-autobiographical projects of epistemological and epistemic justice and disenclosure. This can be a rich resource for teaching and can help us think about work in anthropology that begins with the self rather than the other. Next, I turn to questions of epistemic privilege and suggest that epistemological and epistemic justice in anthropology, particularly in ethnography, require a clear distinction between speaking *for* and speaking *from* and *about*, even when the anthropologist is an insider. Indeed, what do the terms 'insider' and 'outsider' mean – in research sites, but also in disciplinary usage – and why might they need opening up, especially, but not only, in relation to race? How are self and other mobilized in projects to decolonize anthropology and in relation to 'outsiders-within' (Harrison 2008)? How do these questions play out in anthropology as a disciplinary practice? I engage these questions partly through a critical examination of Gupta and Stoolman's call to decolonize US anthropology (2022). I conclude by suggesting that it might be useful to think about anthropology as a community of critics and a place of productive disagreements therein (Strathern 2006). This relies, of course, on there being equitable relations within the discipline, which is something that needs sustained attention.

Epistemological and epistemic justice

When we use the term 'epistemology', we are asking meta-questions about knowledge. How do we know what we know? What do we consider important to know? What do we leave out when we decide what counts as knowledge? Epistemological justice seeks to redress the fact that, in a given field, what is considered knowledge and who counts as a legitimate knowledge producer is a function of power. If my understanding of a topic leaves out germane points, leading me to construct a particular understanding of myself or the world, and I have the power to claim that this understanding is the right one, I am committing epistemological injustice. The pursuit of epistemological justice, then, demands a reappraisal of not only what counts as knowledge but also the processes of knowledge production in situations where injustice is recognized as having prevailed. It requires a critical examination of what is taken into account and what/who is left out.

Epistemological justice is closely related to what feminist philosopher Miranda Fricker calls 'epistemic injustice', or a situation in which 'someone is wronged in their capacity as a knower' (2007: 1). In other words, epistemic justice becomes impossible when certain people are deemed incapable of producing what counts as knowledge. This may be on the basis of their particular bodies, their social positions or their inability or unwillingness to speak in acceptable ways. As with epistemological justice, bringing about epistemic justice has to go deeper than simply listening. It requires a fundamental re-examination of self and of injustices perpetrated by knowing self and others in certain ways. The two, then, are closely linked.

Fricker differentiates between two kinds of epistemic injustice. Testimonial injustice occurs when prejudice causes

> ### Epistemological and Epistemic Justice
>
> Epistemological injustice results when germane information is either wilfully ignored or when research does not move beyond established ways of knowing that are a reflection of existing power relations. Redressing such injustice requires us to ask how we know what we know, and what has been left out. Projects of epistemological justice can reveal other histories, other ways of knowing colonial rule and its legacies – both in the colonies and the metropole – thus enabling us to ask how new understandings can enable fresh responses to issues in the present. New understandings cause us to know the past and the present differently and may help bring about better futures. Epistemological justice requires the promotion of epistemic justice and the dismantling of epistemic injustice.
>
> Epistemic justice refers to attempts to recognize and redress the injustices that occur when someone is wronged in their capacity as a knower, either because they are deemed incapable of knowing or because there is no framework to make their experiences knowable, sometimes even to themselves. In that sense, epistemic justice is a subset of epistemological justice. It pays attention to voice, whereas the latter pays attention to diverse bases of knowledge, not only in terms of knowers and their experiences that are denied the status of knowledge.

a hearer to give a deflated level of credibility to a speaker's words. A corrective to this is caring and careful listening to a person/group so wronged, recognizing them as knowers of not only their own lives but also the world from their particular positions. At a more theoretical level, this involves paying attention to the relationships between epistemic trust and social power, and between social disadvantage and epistemic disadvantage. It requires asking in a patterned way why some kinds of people are consistently believed and others are not. Examples of this are the police's disbelief in a Black person's claim about ownership of a car, and a middle-class white person's disbelief that the police would target Black car-drivers by stopping them and asking them to prove ownership.

The second kind of epistemic injustice is hermeneutical injustice, which occurs when a gap in collective interpretive resources puts someone at an unfair disadvantage when it comes to making sense of their social experiences. Fricker's own example is of suffering sexual harassment in a culture that lacks that critical concept (2007: 1). We can also think about experiences of racism in a national, institutional or social setting that denies it is racist or operates through colonial logics, instead locating the problem in particular individuals (victim or perpetrator). These constitute instances of both epistemological and epistemic injustice, and rightly come within the scope of disenclosure, and thence decolonization, because they define the centre and enclose it.

Promoting epistemological justice in the academy

Entry into academia of people from former colonies and of non-European origin has been steadily increasing. This, coupled with wider reappraisals of colonial and other forms of archive, subaltern studies approaches and innovative methods, has generated fresh critical appraisals of colonialism. Scholars from diverse disciplines have meticulously substantiated Fanon's claim. This scholarship points to the fact that, contrary to popular narratives about self-driven advances in Europe and the flow of benefits from Europe, it was contributions from the colonies/the colonized that enabled the massive economic, technological and industrial development of the metropole. These contributions also affected citizen–state relations in the metropole. Money from colonial extraction, whether by private persons or the state, could and did fund diverse welfare programmes in the metropole without increasing taxes. Deploying soldiers from colonies in wars reduced the need for conscription. People in the metropole questioned colonial expansion and had to be reassured of its importance for them. These reassurances reveal much about the colonizers' priorities.

Take a speech in 1895 by Cecil Rhodes, British colonialist of Southern Africa: 'You must remember that your "Little Englander" says, and very fairly: "What is the advantage of all these expansions? What are the advantages of our Colonies?"' (cited in Stead 1902: 166). Rhodes goes on to point out that the great advantage of retaining and expanding colonized territories is to ensure markets for British goods, as well as to ensure the flow of raw materials for British factories.

In line with Shoemaker's argument that colonialism varied in detail, if not in its overall thrust to control and expropriate, I provide below a brief discussion of work on British colonialism to give an example of the kinds of flow mentioned above. The reader well acquainted with this scholarship may choose to skip it, but the case study's main purpose is to flesh out Fanon's point that the metropole always needed its others. It was always Nation+.

By Nation+, I mean that the metropole, notwithstanding its mythologies, did not achieve what it did by itself. Contributions from the colonies, including forced or voluntary flows of people, supplemented its resources and made its growth possible in ways that were crucial to its formation. Its others, then, were woven into its very fabric. Recognizing this has implications for projects promoting full and homely belonging of the metropole's others in the national space.

Case Study: Growth at Whose Cost?

Economic historian Aditya Mukherjee in his 2010 article, 'Empire: How Colonial India Made Modern Britain',[1] shows how at every stage of British colonialism in India huge transfers of wealth were made from the colony to Britain. His argument is trenchant: the latter enriched itself at the expense of the former and, importantly, empire shaped the development of capitalism and industrialization in Britain from early on.

Dividing British colonialization of India into three stages – the merchant-capital stage, the free-trade or industrial-capital stage, and the finance-capital stage – Mukherjee shows how, in each of these, wealth systematically extracted from the colony fuelled industrialization and capital accumulation in the metropole. Thus, in 1801, at a crucial stage of Britain's Industrial Revolution, unrequited transfers to Britain from India swelled British domestic savings for capital expenditure by 30%. In that same year, the sum of unrequited transfers to Britain from other colonies including the West Indies almost doubled this amount to 84.06% of British capital formation out of domestic savings (Mukherjee 2010: 76).[2] In lay terms, this means that the money put aside in the British national economy for investing in national infrastructures and other wealth-generating projects was massively supplemented by wealth from the colonies. This advanced British industrialization and fuelled British economic growth and productivity. The colonies also acted as gigantic markets and, as such, were not permitted to industrialize or to compete with British manufacturing interests. In 1800, the Indian subcontinent had a 19.7% share in world manufacturing output, but under the British this had declined to 1.4% by 1913 (ibid.). This, as many scholars have argued, was a direct result of British policies.

All the British colonies paid for Britain's wealth and economic development. West Indian historian Eric Williams identifies the West Indian plantations as central economic dynamos for the English economy and politics of the seventeenth, eighteenth and nineteenth centuries. This was recognized by commentators at the time (see Williams 1994: 51; see also McCarthy and Sealey-Ruiz 2010: 77).

> The trend continued. In 1884, of the £203 million at the disposal of the British state for general government, £89 million came from the United Kingdom, £74 million from India and £40 million from the rest of the empire (Bhambra 2022: 11). That is, over half of the money spent on and in Britain, including on welfare, was extracted from the colonies. After 1945, the few remaining colonies were made to tie up funds 'in order to give Britain cheap credit' and 'to subsidize Britain's post-war standard of living' (ibid.: 12).
>
> The gains from colonies were not only economic; they also shaped citizen–state relations in the metropole. Bhambra (2022) argues that, over the nineteenth century, revenues from India as well as Indian military personnel enabled Britain to build up its role in the world without requiring British citizens to bear the costs, either financially or in terms of conscription. She cites Martin Daunton who argues that, unburdened by the costs of a nation at war, 'the [British] working class was assimilated to the state rather than viewing it as coercive or exploitative' (cited in Bhambra 2022: 6). The wave of revolutions that convulsed continental Europe from 1848 onwards did not occur in Britain. Rather, they happened across the empire and were firmly suppressed.

Teaching this history very concretely in the United Kingdom can potentially open up discussions about what is owed to members of former colonies whose ancestors have enriched the United Kingdom over generations. It can also open up new ways of thinking about the foundations of the British welfare state and re-channel conversations about migrants benefiting from it without having paid anything in. Should aid to former colonies be properly reconceptualized as the repayment of debt? Who, precisely, should repay this debt, given that the gains from colonialism and also the harms of colonialism were not felt equally by colonizing as well as colonized populations? This last question leads us further into scholarship that seeks epistemological and epistemic justice, even if it may raise uncomfortable questions about oppression and how the oppressed in one place or in relation to one group may become oppressors in other settings and vice versa. I will return to this.

Not just material benefits but also radical questioning?

But it was not only wealth that flowed from the colonies. Other things, including ideas and ideals did too. In chapter 2 of their book *The Dawn of Everything* (2021), anthropologist David Graeber and archaeologist David Wengrow focus on an essay competition, organized in 1754 in France, which posed the question: 'What is the origin of inequality among men, and is it authorized by natural law?' (2021: 48). This puzzles them. Why would eighteenth-century French essayists wonder whether inequality had an origin rather than being the natural order of things? After all, France at the time was a profoundly hierarchical and unequal society, where hardly anyone had any experience or expectation of equality. They thus ask of France: 'What are the origins of the question about the origins of social inequality?' (ibid.: 51).

Graeber and Wengrow argue that European, specifically French, encounters with Indigenous North Americans from the seventeenth century onwards and the dialogues between them about their respective forms of life and clashing ideas about authority and liberty generated European questions about ideas such as freedom and equality. Indigenous Americans asked challenging questions of missionaries, trappers and soldiers, including about why anyone should accept another's authority over them, and why property, status and control were prized so highly. These kinds of question, the authors argue, had effects on Europeans' understandings of their own societies and of taken-for-granted assumptions. Jesuits were startled, too, by the reasoned counterarguments with which their attempts at persuasion to Christianity had to contend and by the openness of discussion among Indigenous groups: 'It was only over time, as [indigenous] Americans learned more about Europe, and Europeans began to consider what it would mean to translate [indigenous] American ideals of individual liberty into their own societies, that the term "equality" began to gain ground as a feature of the discourse between them' (ibid.: 76).

Graeber and Wengrow tell us that writings by missionaries, in particular, about their encounters with Indigenous Americans from around the beginning of the seventeenth century went on to become bestsellers in Europe, sparking discussions and generating ideas to think about and with. Thus, they argue, values long considered as originating in Europe were in fact a product of European encounters with Indigenous Americans who showed Europeans that people could be free and equal, that establishing consensus was crucial and that concern for property was not universal. It was in North America that Europeans realized that 'there were clearly societies in existence that did things very differently' (ibid.: 61). This provided a sense of social possibility. The process feels almost anthropological. It provides a counterfactual of the kind that anthropologists tend to like.

Graeber and Wengrow's argument has attracted critical attention. Kwame Anthony Appiah picks out some important problems with it (2021), showing that several of these kinds of conversation were already present and circulating in Europe independently of 'Indigenous critique'. This latter was indeed present, and even earlier than Graeber and Wengrow claim. Appiah thus discusses a *c.*1580 essay by Michel de Montaigne about the reactions of three Tupinambá brought from South America to the French court. He cites Montaigne: '"there were amongst us men full and crammed with all manner of commodities" while others "were begging at their doors, lean and half-starved with hunger and poverty". The Tupinambá wondered that these unfortunates "were to suffer so great an inequality and injustice, and that they did not take the others by the throats, or set fire to their houses"' (2021: the essay is Montaigne's 'On the Cannibals' [2003]).

Graeber and Wengrow may be exaggerating the effects of Indigenous critique on Europeans, but the point was that it existed and was being heard – long before the seventeenth century, in spaces where inequality, justice and so on were already being discussed. However, it seems clear that European thinkers were thinking with and learning from colonized/to be colonized peoples, even as European powers were inflicting great atrocities. This dialogic movement of ideas continued throughout the colonial period, as Priyamvada Gopal shows in *Insurgent Empire* (2020). The book tracks anti-colonial sentiment in Britain throughout the colonial period and reveals how much of this was informed by protest, dissent and criticism from the colonized, especially in the rebellions in India (1857) and Morant Bay in Jamaica (1865).

The wide coverage in England of the 1865 Morant Bay Rebellion saw, in some quarters, a growing recognition of the similarities between the struggles of white workers in England and those of Black workers in Jamaica. Gopal writes that 'labour leaders and trade unionists called for common cause to be made, not least because the Tories could do to the English working classes what they had done to the Jamaicans' (2020: 88). Importantly, she argues, this sympathy and support was partly a dialogic response to the claims put forward by the rebels in Jamaica. Thus, liberal ideas about humanity, dignity and fairness in the metropole were shaped and sharpened by their breach in the colonies, by both the claims of the rebels and the brutality of their suppression. Sympathizers in England learned from the rebels' language and declarations what unfreedom might look like and why freedom was important. Workers, in particular, could see how much worse their own conditions could become, based on what was happening in the colonies.

Unsurprisingly, then, maintaining the idea that proper values could come only from authorized European sources was crucial to colonial control. Much effort was expended to prevent alliances between disaffected members of different colonies or between colonies and the metropole. Indeed, the worry about solidary labour and nationalist movements travelling between colonies and to Britain and from Britain to the colonies, causing instability or jeopardizing capitalist and colonial interests, was very real in the late nineteenth century, as discussed in chapter 2. Similar fears had also accompanied the independence of Haiti in the early nineteenth century, leading to the more or less full-scale erasure of Haiti's revolution that still continues in some quarters.

Scholarship of the kind I discuss above is growing and attracting critical attention that is enriching and nuancing it further. Autobiographical works that seek epistemological and epistemic justice are also drawing on this kind of work, as well as on personal experiences and histories. These bring the gist of this scholarship into the public domain and in doing so potentially reshape ideas about who can claim full and 'homely' belonging (Hage 2000 [1998]) in the metropole. It demands anthropological attention. I discuss one such work below: *Empireland* (2021) by Satnam Sanghera, a Punjabi Briton.

Claiming full belonging

'Imperial amnesia' is the name Sanghera gives to the selective ignoring of the fact that hundreds of thousands of non-white Britons call the United Kingdom their home, having been in the country in some cases for generations or even centuries, *because* of Britain's imperial ventures across the globe over the last few hundred years. They/we are all here, as Sanghera titles his chapter, 'because you were there' (2021: 64–84).[3]

The problem with this imperial amnesia, this forgetting that non-white people have been in Britain for centuries *because* of colonialism, is twofold, says Sanghera. First, it perpetuates the existence of a defining political narrative that non-white immigrants are aliens who arrived in Britain without permission, with no links to Britain, to abuse British hospitality. This has become a leading contributor to the fantasy of a white Anglo nation and its eternal outsiders-within. Second, the ways in which British history is taught in schools mean that even non-white Britons often do not know this long history of a multi-ethnic country.[4] Sanghera writes, 'If I had been taught about these amazing characters, instead of endlessly being fed the idea that my family and I were some sort of novel social experiment, interlopers in a white country, it would have made a huge difference to my sense of belonging' (2021: 80). He goes on to reveal how his own school and university education and wider reading was shaped by colonial attitudes in its assumptions and omissions. It was when he read Edward Said's *Orientalism* that he recognized how he had learned/ been taught to view the non-western world, including his own Punjabi heritage, 'through patronizing Western eyes' (Sanghera 2021: 171).

Sanghera, like other non-white Britons, is told by people 'to go home' when he voices criticisms about contemporary Britain or its past. But there is no other home. Or he is told to be 'grateful' for what Britain has given him. But why should someone feel grateful for the benefits and rights extended by a state to its citizens, of whom he is one? In a footnote, he does, in fact, tell his reader what he is grateful for, but he adds, 'I *was born here*, not India. I am British, I am as entitled to comment on my home nation as the next man and the endless insistence that I display my gratitude is rooted in racism. Racism, which is, in itself, rooted in the fact that the children of imperial immigrants born here are not always seen as fully British' (ibid.: 189, emphasis in original).

For me, the most remarkable aspect of Sanghera's book is that, in order to write it, he went, as he says, from knowing little to nothing about Britain's colonial past to thinking systematically about it and its implications both for people like him and for the British nation itself. This is very encouraging for those who seek to promote epistemological and epistemic justice through scholarship. Like Bhambra, Sanghera argues that a fuller understanding of the role of empire in the making of the metropole can transform the metropole. This may be described as a pursuit of epistemological justice, a way of filling in gaps in wider understandings of the constitution of modern Britain – the place of empire in this story – and of how Britain has, for several centuries, been Britain+ in ways that matter. It also furthers epistemic justice – the author claims a voice as a Briton who will not be denied national belonging. Finally, it is an act of disenclosure, breaking down a white-centred and compartmentalized understanding of Britain and revealing it as Britain+ from the very outset of colonialism. In Mbembe's words, work like this can 'lift closures in such a way that what had been closed in can emerge and blossom' (2021: 61). And it is a generous book, unflinching in its appraisals but also appreciative of diverse aspects of the Nation+ story.

I have spent some time on Sanghera's *Empireland* for three reasons. First, I think it is a fantastic teaching resource for a first-year anthropology course in the United Kingdom. It wears its scholarship lightly and raises various issues that could be explored in seminars: the imagined nation, national belonging, forgetting and silence, identity, power, education, multiculturalism, intergenerational change and the power of critical work that begins with the self and extends outwards. Given the ways in which the book weaves scholarship with personal experience, different kinds of student from the United Kingdom or elsewhere may be able to bring to the classroom their own experiences and understandings of belonging or not. This, and work like it, can enable more experience-near teaching, enabling productive estrangement and expanded understandings of the imperial-national past and present. This may help promote work towards more just futures and a 'homely nation' for all. Indeed the text has been widely and positively reviewed, even in the right-leaning press. Second, it reveals the epistemic possibilities of claiming a full place in the shared world *with* rather than *in spite of* difference. Finally, work like this offers other kinds of resources than ethnographic work and programmatic texts for anthropologists interested in decolonization.

Ethnography and the question of epistemic privilege

Sanghera speaks for himself to claim full belonging in Nation+. That is, he claims epistemic privilege as someone who, from his ascribed position as a not-quite-full Briton, can explain to others how they have misrecognized the workings of the nation they share. Anthropologists rarely

> ### Epistemic Privilege
>
> Epistemic privilege is the understanding from standpoint theory that certain individuals or groups by virtue of their oppressed position are better able to understand the workings of society, going beyond the claims of that given society to fairness and so on.

claim epistemic privilege in this way. Rather, they attempt to produce accounts that work from an assumption of epistemic privilege on the part of research participants to then promote epistemological and epistemic justice. This does not mean disclaiming the anthropological voice, but it does mean separating it from those of research participants. I show this here through a discussion of two ethnographies.

Nathaniel Roberts's ethnography *To Be Cared For* (2016) is set in a Dalit ('untouchable') neighbourhood in the southern Indian city of Chennai, which he calls Anbu Nagar (neighbourhood of love). Roberts shows how Anbu Nagar residents refused to identify themselves in terms of caste, even though their caste in large part informed and justified both their neglect by city authorities, who failed to provide even the most basic sanitation and water facilities, and negative evaluations by others. Rather, they described themselves as 'poor' and insisted on their common humanity with others. This casteless humanity was morally freighted by two commitments: to care actively for others; and to understand oneself as being worthy of care. Caste, they argued, was based on a denial of shared humanity; this is immoral and hence so is Indian society, which upholds caste distinctions. This is why they imagined a special connection with foreigners, also casteless and therefore capable of caring for fellow humans in ways that Anbu Nagar residents valued. This raises an interesting dilemma with regard to epistemological justice. Is Anbu Nagar residents' knowledge about foreigners acceptable as 'true knowledge'? If not, what is its status? For the scholar, is some knowledge good to think with, without the necessity of committing to the truth of it?

Let us turn to questions of voice. Anbu Nagar residents speak for themselves in diverse ways throughout the book. Importantly, they refuse to think or speak about themselves in terms of caste. This is notwithstanding the importance of caste-based logics in their oppression. Epistemic justice here requires accepting their voicing of their experiences and predicaments and learning from them. But it also can involve speaking from this to larger issues. Indeed, Roberts does speak to the literature on caste and hegemony *from* his work in Anbu Nagar. His focus on conversions to Pentecostal Christianity, especially by married women who see in it avenues to seek and proffer valued forms of care, also challenges the moral panic around religious conversions in India. In showing how 'slum Christianity integrated the slum community *as a whole and irrespective of religious affiliation*' (2016: 11, emphasis in original), he also questions an 'emergency law' enacted in Tamilnadu in 2002 banning religious conversions, partly on the grounds that they cause conflict. In other words, Roberts's work promotes epistemological justice by challenging dominant evaluations of Dalits and promotes epistemic justice by focusing on their own understanding of their situation, including denial of caste. But it also goes beyond what Anbu Nagar residents themselves want from him, that is, to care for and be cared for by him. Underscoring their insistence on a shared humanity, he speaks *from* them to wider anthropological and political questions. His anthropological voice is consistently and ethically separated from his research participants' voices.

Anthropological work can also complicate a straightforward understanding that shared ascribed identities lead to common politics. Anbu Nagar residents' denial of caste might frustrate more politically active Dalit groups who fight for rights and recognition *as* Dalits. The point is not about who is right or wrong. Rather, anthropological work can show that there are many ways of understanding predicaments and means of finding resolution to them. These understandings may militate against each other. Ethnographic attention, then, reveals that shared ascribed identities – whether based on caste, race or another category – do not necessarily lead to identical understandings or action. I suggest that this is important for decolonization not only of the world, but also in relation to the internal workings of anthropology within and beyond national boundaries. I will return to this point.

Roberts also engages very thoughtfully with the insider/outsider distinction. He is not Indian and does not look Indian. Anbu Nagar residents do not, then, slot him into oppressive caste hierarchies that have perpetuated and continue to perpetuate injustices on Dalits, nor mistake him for an Indian government agent or NGO fieldworker, who instructs, assists and admonishes, thus continuing to reproduce the status quo. However, he writes, 'Simply being a foreigner, and hence in their view, a theoretically casteless person, was not enough. It was as if I had to perform my castelessness at a bodily level before they could fully accept it' (2016: 34).

Could I have done this same research? Unlikely. My birth into a Brahmin family, socio-economic class and the specific location of my family home in the same city mean that even though, or more accurately *because*, we share a language and a cultural framework that emphasizes caste, my immediate identification as a 'rich person' would have made my acceptance difficult and the tests more stringent, if they were carried out at all. Bodies matter, and insider/outsider statuses do not straightforwardly map onto shared race, nationality, gender, mother tongue or cultural framework.

For the growing number of graduate students who begin verbal accounts of their proposed research with the almost guilty preface, 'As a white person . . .' or, conversely and more assertively, 'As an insider . . .', Roberts's chapter on fieldwork (2016: 13–46) can provide fruitful thought, as can the following discussion of Pilkington's work among English nationalists, who emphasized their whiteness and made it central to their activism (Pilkington 2016). This work with 'distasteful' proximal, not-quite others also pursues epistemological and epistemic justice, this time focusing on people who are simultaneously oppressors and oppressed.

Hilary Pilkington conducted ethnographic research with activists of the English Defence League (EDL), a populist, right-wing, anti-Islam and anti-immigration movement

(2016). She joined demonstrations, meetings and protests, attended court proceedings, conducted interviews and spent time with EDL activists in their homes and elsewhere for over a year. Her ethnography details the companionship and affective satisfaction provided by activism and the sheer joy in violence felt by some activists. But it also reveals the troubled life circumstances of several activists, the effects of the shrinking of public services, the lack of housing, jobs and opportunities, the workings of class and the existence of a two-tier justice system that sees EDL activists sentenced more harshly than South Asian British counter-protestors, even when the charge is the same (2016: 169; see also Smith 2011: 24 for an account of differential treatment in another setting). Pilkington is clear that levels of poverty and deprivation are higher among ethnic minority populations in the United Kingdom, but she engages the question of white suffering sympathetically and carefully to understand the growth of white victimhood and the accompanying racism. Racism here is inflected by colonial logics, but other things, including despair, also produce it. Work such as Pilkington's and Smith's can shift the conversation, not necessarily away from decolonization, but towards more informed understandings of how oppressed people become oppressors and how race comes to matter afresh under certain political-economic conditions.

Fricker argues that the work of promoting epistemic justice may be described as the cultivation of ethical-intellectual virtues that would improve our lives as both subjects and objects of knowledge. In ethnographic work, these virtues include listening with attention and care, even when accounts seem garbled, wrong, counterintuitive, aggressive or based on exclusionary claims to belonging. Listening does not have to entail agreement, but it does involve attentive engagement. It also involves being, doing and experiencing things together. Promoting epistemological justice, too, demands these virtues and also involves questioning settled accounts, including asking whose knowledge counts and what kinds of things are deemed constitutive of, and contributing to, particular knowledge practices. I turn now to considering these questions with regard to the internal workings of the practice of anthropology.

Resonances and possibilities

I have told the story above in a way that maps onto the development of anthropology. Wealth, ideas and things flowed from the colonies, enriching the metropole, including supporting the formation of new academic disciplines such as anthropology. Ideas, unlike wealth, flowed back and forth, generating new ways of knowing in metropole and colonies, often to the detriment of the latter. However, dissidents in the colonies and the metropole gathered allies and inspired each other, even as the colonial juggernaut rolled on. Following formal decolonization, while some things changed, old patterns endured, notwithstanding reappraisals and professions of good faith. The quests for epistemological and epistemic justice continue, especially initiated by people from former colonies. The ignored, marginalized or reviled others of colonialism question settled narratives and claim proper acknowledgement for contributions. In the metropole, those understood as eternal outsiders demand proper and homely belonging. Anthropology, too, has seen similar struggles and concerted efforts to destabilize and disenclose in order to shape better relations within, and directions for, the discipline. Questions that have been asked and continue to be asked include: can racial justice be achieved, and how? Can knowing differently, especially by revivifying forgotten or marginalized voices and histories, forge new and more equitable directions? What kind of practice emerges when everyone who is part of it can claim recognition and membership without having to constantly justify their very presence, or participate in ways deemed acceptable by those who claim unquestioned belonging? How are responsibility, ownership and the distribution of credit and benefits to be reconfigured? How is epistemological and epistemic justice to be achieved? How is epistemic privilege to be understood?

It is in light of these kinds of question that Akhil Gupta and Jessie Stoolman made their clarion call to decolonize US anthropology (2022). I will not dwell on their arguments, especially with regard to race and the United States, as they have attracted copious commentary, much of it readily available.[5] Instead, I will selectively focus on one aspect of their call – the importance of not collapsing diverse experiences and projects into one overarching framework or in terms of the concerns of a dominant centre. Gupta and Stoolman argue that 'mutual provincialization among extremely disparate forms of domination and exploitation leads to a more powerful overall picture than does tying them together to tell a singular story' (ibid.: 779). Like Amita Baviskar and Carolyn Rouse (both 2023) in their responses to Gupta and Stoolman, I will argue for a similar mutual provincialization of different national and regional traditions of anthropology and also projects within/or with reference to anthropology in ways that militate against the formation of a single centre, especially with regard to decolonization. In doing so, I emphasize the importance of continued disenclosure and the promotion of motley forms of belonging that aspire to provisional stability within the practice of anthropology, such that it retains its vitality and rigour.

One way to think about national/international yet regional traditions of a discipline such as anthropology, without being overly methodologically nationalist, is to ask what kinds of question are understood as pressing in particular places with particular histories, colonial and post-colonial legacies, and contemporary situations. How do they shape both hopeful action and anthropological interests in, and with regard to, that place? This is to accept certain premises: first, that the decolonization of US anthropology would look rather different to that of British anthropology or indeed, to that of the Indian, Russian, South African or Latin American anthropological traditions, with their converging and also diverging histories, inequalities, asymmetries and experiences of privilege, more generally and within the academy. Second, and therefore, although these different traditions speak to one another, they also speak past one another and maintain diverse internal conversations, not all of which may be accessible elsewhere (partly because of language barriers). Finally, teaching too – content and style – in each national tradition will vary, especially on undergraduate anthropology programmes that endeavour to teach students to think about the world immediately around them in critical ways, as well as to learn from other places and ways of knowing and doing. Students do not arrive as blank slates; they are already socialized into knowing the world and their own places in it. Teaching, then, needs to respond to the particular demographic make-up and the 'knowledge in the blood' (Jansen 2009) of specific student populations, including attending to and supportively challenging blind spots and prejudices. None of this constitutes an argument for parochialism, but it does argue for a discerning responsiveness that is oriented to the contexts within which one learns, is heard, works and hopes to make a difference. It thus makes perfect sense for Gupta and Stoolman to call for the decolonization of *US anthropology*. They provide food for thought for other anthropological traditions, but reticence and dissidence remain important.

So, too, does slowness in response to calls to decolonize, especially when the majority come from one or two centres that are already dominant. This is perhaps particularly the case in the Anglosphere. There is the ever-present risk of recentring the discipline from the United States, and to a lesser extent the United Kingdom, because the best-resourced universities of these countries have access to the largest array of publications, both in terms of publication and consumption. Scholars located in richer nations also have greater access to research grants, thus shaping research directions (see Baviskar 2023). Further, anthropologists in the United States, the United Kingdom, the Commonwealth and other former British colonies, as well as diverse other countries, publish in English, partly because of the external rewards of publishing in prestigious international journals, many of which are in English. Selected work in other languages is translated into English; untranslated work goes unnoticed. The hyper-production of anthropological writing in the English language and the speed of circulation of ideas mean that new forms of epistemic injustice can emerge. Everything becomes grist to the mill of anglophone anthropological production, enabling a sort of recolonization and a demand that work speak to other work already familiar in anglophone centres, multiplying particular discourses. Thus, Silvia Rivera Cusicanqui writes about having been asked by the editor of an English-language journal to 'correct her sources' and cite Anibal Quijano, even though her own work on decolonization had followed an entirely different trajectory (Rivera Cusicanqui 2020: 62).

Indeed, the continuous stream of programmatic publications – each emphasizing its theoretical novelty and cementing its position – that come from the almost industrial academic machines of the richly resourced sites may actually prevent the kind of scholarship and work that change on the ground in different places requires. In such a situation, it is worth keeping in mind Rivera Cusicanqui's description of how she and others in Bolivia encountered texts: 'Having few books, in contrast with the "current hyperaccessibility," demanded of us that "we make use from our own vantage point of the texts we had, but also that we make fragile the certainty of our thought starting from reality"' (cited in Gago 2020: ix–xx).

It is also worth keeping in mind the potential of ethnographic work. The openness of engagement may well be something that anthropologists can carry into decolonization projects focused on anthropology itself and its diverse practitioners. This is not only because ethnographic research can complicate binaries, adding texture and nuance. It is also because ethnographic work is never fully exhausted; it is always open to re-engagement and relies on the maintenance of relationships that themselves change as people and situations do. Differences emerge from *within* the spaces of ethnographic engagement and they may not be the same as those at the outset. The opposite of difference here is not sameness but the creation of a shared ground of recognition and mutual – if partial – understanding. In her response to Gupta and Stoolman (2022), Rouse presents a conversation between five anthropologists and sociologists from different countries, which reveals their rather different understandings about colonial legacies, the post-colonial condition and ways forward, both in terms of diagnoses and required action (2023: 362–4). This should give us pause for thought. Claims to epistemological and epistemic justice demand recognition and care, not the erasure of difference and the re-enclosure of the centre. This is particularly important in projects to decolonize; they must not recolonize.

Keeping a space open for critique

This leads us to another question. Even as differently historied and positioned people and standpoints are increasingly participating in the practice of anthropology, on what/whose terms are they doing so? Gupta and Stoolman write about the problems of 'white-norming' anthropology departments in the United States and the continuous reproduction of 'a structure of alienation in which BILPOC [Black, Indigenous, Latinx and People of Colour] faculty, students and staff will always be the ones who do not fit in' (Gupta and Stoolman 2022: 786). Setting aside the obvious issue with lumping together the experiences of such a disparate collection of people, it is clear from diverse posts on sites such as *anthro{dendum}*, as well as in various publications and in conversations, that anthropology has a problem. The problem simply put is as follows: many anthropologists feel unable to speak up or out to their colleagues, especially about decolonization, and this complaint comes from almost every kind of (although not every single) anthropologist, whatever their ethnicity, race, gender or other attributes. A hermeneutics of mistrust may result in mutual enclavement, which serves neither the practice of anthropology nor individual participants.

I thus agree with Gupta and Stoolman that the culture of the discipline, and more specifically of departments, needs to change, given the case that specific kinds of anthropologist feel persistently unsupported and their very presence challenged in both their own departments and anthropology more widely. A whole set of things clearly needs to happen within departments and in spaces where anthropologists come together: complaints properly investigated and action taken; remarks from students or other academics about 'diversity hires' firmly dealt with; summary dismissals of positions and claims, and the treatment of colleagues as 'native informants', or indeed, as 'white supremacists', called out; professional courtesy modelled and expected in all interactions including, and perhaps particularly, in disagreements; and non-disclosure agreements or similar legal attempts to silence people banned. These are basic, and that we are still talking about them in the breach is deeply worrying.

But, beyond this, are there certain things that every anthropologist has to agree with or to? Can we, should we, expect a common politics for the discipline? Or do we try to build a motley space that enables full belonging *with* difference that is based on the ethos of friendship. Davé describes this ethos as 'a kind mutual estrangement . . . the commitment, or at least willingness, to be strange to oneself and *to* and with another, such that the ground for ethics is not the rational/categorical, but only the immanent' (2015: emphasis in original). I suggest that critique and disagreement are crucial to this ethos of keeping open the immanent, and of keeping the space rigorously open for different modalities of participation in the ever-extending yet recognizable practice of anthropology. To do this, I draw on Marilyn Strathern, who writes:

> A discipline is a body of data, a set of methods, a field of problematics; it is also a bundle of yardsticks, that is, criteria for evaluating products and maintaining standards. Knowing that the canons may be constantly changing and that outcomes are uncertain can be taken as a sign of life as much as the reverse . . . the aim of criticism in research is to re-multiply, re-divide, the outcomes of any one particular argument.
>
> Criticism bifurcates; it makes a single account multiple again . . . More emphatically, disciplines look

to disagreement as points of growth ... the researchers' (academics', scholars') hope, that there will be an outcome to their labours, is given impetus through practices of disagreement. In looking to colleagues for criticism, they look for life. For the instruments of self-renewal, the papers they write and the books they generate allow disagreement to remain unclosed. The disagreement, the opening out to further futures, can be left just as that. (Strathern 2006: 199–200)

We need to take this approach to disagreement and critique into discussions about decolonization – what it is, how location and histories matter, and how to accomplish the diverse and various aims that fall within its broad remit. The imperatives of epistemological and epistemic justice are best served by the cultivation of ethical-intellectual modes of engagement in the institutional settings in which anthropologists are located and teach, and based on careful scholarship on issues that matter in the diverse places in which anthropologists conduct research. Defining decolonization with reference to the concerns of a dominant centre does disservice to the diversity of anthropological projects and anthropological modes of attention. This means that the space of productive disagreement, including about what constitutes decolonization, needs to be kept open.

As to what constitutes worthwhile anthropological research, this too needs to be kept open. Applied and engaged research are important, but so too is work that is oriented towards theoretical or intellectual contributions or to explanation. All proposed and actual work should be subject to engaged critique about diverse aspects. Critique here is not something that encloses participants to pre-decided spheres or reproduces centres. Its purpose is to enliven and expand horizons rigorously and with a concern for just and equitable scholarship. A generous and engaged culture of critique between practitioners, accorded equal status as colleagues, keeps the immanent possibilities of the practice open and generates new directions. Disagreements will always exist, and so will broader inequalities that the discipline alone cannot address, but the intention must be to build the practice virtuously based on the logic of the motley, that is, by building on and living well *with* difference to generate a 'community of critics' (Strathern 2006). Such a community must accept that anthropologists participate in the practice of anthropology in multiple ways and for diverse purposes, while holding such work to agreed-upon disciplinary standards and yardsticks. All these forms of participation advance the practice and extend its horizons. Thus, I fundamentally disagree with Walter Mignolo's argument that:

> [y]ou could certainly be a Maori and an anthropologist and by being an anthropologist suppress the fact that you are Maori or Black Caribbean or Aymara. Or you can choose the decolonial option: engage in knowledge-making to 'advance' the Maori cause rather than to 'advance' the discipline (e.g., anthropology). Why would someone be interested in advancing the discipline if not for either alienation or self-interest? (Mignolo 2009: 172)

Amita Baviskar writes, with regard to the realities of research funding, expectations of publication and governmental interference in academia, that 'Indian anthropologists maintain two lists in their minds: projects we are doing and projects we would rather be doing' (2023: 5). It is not much of a stretch to think this is the case for most anthropologists. The question for the discipline is how it can enable different kinds of anthropologist to do the projects they would rather be doing while holding them accountable to standards of epistemological and epistemic justice.

Conclusion

Arguing that all scholarship be judged by its promotion or not of epistemological and epistemic justice, this chapter has focused on diverse ways in which anthropological and other scholarship, as well as autobiographical projects, promote such justice through reappraising the colonial past and thence disenclosing and re-visioning the world in more equitable ways. Not all oppression is colonial in origin, and I argued that ethnographic attention to diverse forms of suffering and attempts to refashion the world give us other ways of thinking about what it might mean to do 'good' anthropology. This includes not restricting anthropological work to research subjects with whom we can agree or whose causes we support. Doing so diminishes the scope of anthropology and ethnography to produce scholarly insights about the world. Working with others requires the separation of the anthropological voice from those of research participants. This is an ethical imperative. Likewise, no one speaks *for* anthropology only *from* particular anthropological traditions and histories. Criticisms of anthropology and the related need for decolonization, then, look different in different places. Thus, I turned to Gupta and Stoolman's 2022 paper, building on their argument for mutual provincialization of diverse anthropological traditions in ways that nevertheless keep open traffic and critique between them.

My argument throughout is that, regardless of long-standing inequalities and the continued presence of colonial logics, we are anthropologists because we choose to be. Something about the practice attracts us, even as aspects repel us, and we participate in it accordingly. The question, then, is how do we shape the practice of anthropology in ways that properly recognize diverse forms of participation in it? I have given some suggestions, and they are, of course, open to critique.

The next chapter focuses on what is often understood as the opposite of knowledge – ignorance. It argues, following recent anthropological work as well as that of philosophers and critical theorists of race, that ignorance is more than not knowing; it also encompasses not wanting to know for all kinds of reason. Thus, projects of epistemological and epistemic justice need to consider the role of ignorance in maintaining inequalities.

–5–
Ignorance and Ignoring

In *Man in Motion*, a children's novel by Jan Mark, two teenage boys – Lloyd and Keith – are out and about in their ethnically diverse English city. They see a South Asian woman pushing a pram, and Lloyd helps her bring it down some steps. As the woman walks away, Keith says, 'during the war, there weren't any of them' (1991: 110). This is not the first disparaging remark he has made about non-white people, and Lloyd is deeply uncomfortable with his racism. In this instance, had Lloyd known not only that there were South Asians in Britain well before the Second World War but also that the British Indian Army contingent numbered 2.5 million men by the end of 1945, he would have had the means of refuting Keith's ignorance and assumptions about who has claims to or belongs in the United Kingdom (if only by virtue of participating in the wars of 1914–18 and 1939–45). Sanghera (2021), discussed in the previous chapter, makes a similar point.

Anthropological studies of how curricula are devised, and of their aims and their effects on knowledge/ignorance, can help us understand how ignorance is manufactured. What kind of schooling, we may ask, produces what Canadian Professor of Education and Indigenous scholar Shauneen Pete describes as a situation of 'national ignorance' (2018: 181)?

We might also want to insist, through our associations, on anthropological input in school curricula if this is not already happening.

But ignorance may not be dispelled by new knowledge. This is because ignorance may take many forms, 'including ideologically inspired false consciousness, the innocence of blank slates, and the inability [or unwillingness] to comprehend some information' (Gershon and Raj 2000: 3). Indeed, the new information may be decried as a distraction or as ideologically motivated. Thus, in 2020, British actor Laurence Fox, who is now a figurehead of 'anti-wokery', deplored what he understood as 'the institutional racism of forcing diversity' on audiences by the inclusion of a Sikh soldier in *1917*, Sam Mendes's film about the First World War.[1]

Fox's outburst saw a deluge of information about Sikh (and South Asian) soldiers in the First World War being made available in the public sphere, including stinging rebukes from Sikh associations. Perhaps perversely, publicly aired desires for ignorance can have positive outcomes. Hardeep Singh, deputy director of the Network of Sikh Organisations, argued in an article that the backlash against Fox's comments increased general awareness of Sikh contributions to both world wars and ended up being good for British Sikhs.[2] The now widespread public knowledge that Sikhs made up 20% of the 1.5 million-strong British Indian Army contingent in the First World War brought forth a partial apology, with Fox nevertheless insisting that the inclusion of non-white soldiers 'was somewhat incongruous with the story'.[3] Clearly, he would rather not have to see non-white soldiers on the British side, even though they were there! That is, he would rather that ignorance was maintained.

Fox's stance is comparable to that of one of my research subjects, a member of the UK Independence Party (UKIP), which identifies itself as the 'only truly patriotic political party in the United Kingdom'.[4] The first time we met, he told me that he would never hear a bad word about the British Empire because it was fundamentally a good thing. I wondered about the many things I could say to counter this view and decided on the massacre of a peaceful gathering in Jallianwala Bagh under the orders of General Dyer in April 1919, and a personal anecdote about my great-uncle who was a pilot in the British Indian Air Force. I had been told that, following a successful sortie somewhere near Singapore in the Second World War, my great-uncle was barred by the colour of his skin from entering the establishment into which other officers went to celebrate. Were these good things?, I demanded. My research informant paused. 'No, but most of it was good, and anyway we were better than the Belgians and the French.' Again, new knowledge is quickly contained and ignorance reinforced through comparison.

This chapter argues that a focus on epistemology and epistemological justice warrants a focus on ignorance and on its more active form of ignoring. This is because ignorance is much more than a simple state of not knowing. The growing interest in ignorance in anthropology (Hobart 1993; Gershon and Raj 2000; Dilley 2010; High, Kelly and Mair 2012) and philosophy (e.g., Proctor and Scheibinger 2008; Mills 2017) reveals that ignorance and ignoring are powerful tools, deployed by diverse people to various ends. Proctor identifies three forms of ignorance that are pertinent to us (Proctor 2008: 3): ignorance as native state (or resource), ignorance as lost realm (or selective choice), and ignorance as a deliberately engineered and strategic ploy (or active construct). These are not dispersed by rectification, he argues, because ignorance actively does things in the world. Michel-Rolph Trouillot, of course, was an early theorist of ignorance in his discussions of the production of history and the erasures therein that led to widespread ignoring of the Haitian Revolution in ways that actively fashioned ignorance and furthered European myth-making (1995).

Anthropology and ignorance

In their edited volume, *The Anthropology of Ignorance: An Ethnographic Approach* (2012), Casey High, Ann Kelly and Jonathan Mair argue that anthropologists, like other academics, value knowledge. After all, this is our stock-in-trade. We generate data, analyse them, and on that basis produce and disseminate explanations and critiques. This pursuit of knowledge, Mair, Kelly and High write in their Introduction to the volume, '[e]ntails an ethics: knowledge is the value that justifies all aspects of academic activity, whether it is desired as a means of promoting other goods (health, happiness, well-being) or as an end in itself' (2012: 1).

As anthropologists, we are trained to take the knowledge of others seriously, drawing on it and speaking from it to generate disciplinary knowledge. Such an enterprise is predicated on both the knowledge ethnographic participants are understood to possess and our ability to learn from them what they know. We produce knowledge by 'cataloguing, preserving, translating and explaining' that of other people (ibid.). We also produce knowledge by drawing on knowledge from other sources – anthropological mainly, but also other related scholarship. We strive to show that our ethnographic subjects are very knowledgeable indeed. This is often conceptualized as 'more holistic knowledge', for example, the refusal to differentiate between human and non-human, thing and person, or nature and culture. This can stem from a kind of western pessimism, which many anthropologists, both budding and professional, evince. Indeed, as I have argued elsewhere (Venkatesan 2021), such claims are often explicitly oriented towards self-transformation. That is, 'we' have become ignorant or have learned to know the world in harmful ways. 'They' can help dispel this ignorance and teach 'us' to live well.

Indeed, Mair and colleagues argue, ignorance – either on the part of the ethnographer about their ethnographic subjects or that of the West about other ways of being in the world – has always preoccupied anthropologists. There are, of course, the regular 'arrival and settling in' stories, which often present the anthropologist as the ignorant yet well-meaning outsider who has to be instructed in local forms of courtesy and behavioural expectations. Over time, the anthropologist learns from his/her research subjects not only how to behave appropriately in their world, but also their ways of knowing, and their knowledge and wisdom. At least, this is the ideal. These accounts hold even for anthropologists 'at home'. After all, research is predicated on recognizing one's own ignorance about something that is knowable and deserves to be known. Implicit within our project is also the assumption that our ethnographic subjects value knowledge, too, and seek to increase their fund of knowledge. This gives us a model for anthropological work wherein researcher and research participants come to know things together for shared purposes. This last way of thinking about knowledge fits into the decolonizing rubric.

However, anthropological accounts also and often rely on the ignorance of ethnographic subjects in order to present their own 'expert knowledge' about their subjects' lives and the effects of multiple variables and factors that are not fully discerned or discernible in the thick of things. This is justified on the basis that the anthropologist, as an outsider, has an overview of the entire social structure, unlike those who are actually living these lives. The anthropologist can see the forest as well as the trees. Indeed, Eduardo Viveiros de Castro goes so far as to argue that this assumption of 'epistemological advantage over the native' is inherent to a certain kind of anthropology. He suggests that, in this kind of anthropological endeavour, '[t]he native's illusions are taken as necessary in the double sense of inevitable and useful; they are, to hijack a phrase, evolutionarily adaptive. It is this necessity which defines the "native" and distinguishes him from the "anthropologist": the latter may be wrong about the former, but the former must be deluded about himself' (2003: 3).

Viveiros de Castro intends this as a criticism, of course, and it is an important one. But what if the preservation of certain forms of life requires self-delusion and the suppression of uncomfortable knowledge, that is, requires active ignorance? This chapter thus follows Mair and colleagues in their argument that not knowing/ignorance is worthy of anthropological attention because it might be productive in avoiding, creating or maintaining relationships, and may even be constitutive of personhood (Mair, Kelly and High 2012: 19). It also follows insights from agnotology, the study of deliberate culturally induced ignorance, and from critical theorists of race that ignorance merits attention as an active form of being in the world. I draw on these to engage the growing anthropological attention to whiteness. In particular, I focus on activist theories of knowledge that are normative in orientation, seeking to dispel ignorance in order to transform social relations marked by privilege-based oppression, and contrast these with anthropological modes of attention to ignorance. Throughout, I argue that attempts to decolonize merit attention to ignorance as much as to knowledge.

White ignorance

Philosopher of race Charles Mills explores the multiple manifestations of what he terms 'white ignorance' and its role in ongoing forms of racism and racial inequalities in liberal settings (2017). Mills, like Fricker (2007), argues that epistemology in philosophy has focused on the individual knower rather than on social forms of knowing. However, people do not know in isolation. Ways of knowing are shaped by socialization as well as by social positionings based on, among other things, class, gender and race. Mills's particular interest is in the dependence of social knowing on forms of not-knowing or not wanting to know. He thus argues that we need to pay attention to 'group-based cognitive handicaps, i.e., an epistemology of ignorance' (2017: 51) and, further, that white supremacy is based on cultivating such an epistemology of ignorance. The question then is: how do we 'pin down' the 'idea of an ignorance, a non-knowing, that is not contingent, but in which race – white racism and/or white racial domination and their ramifications – plays a crucial causal role?' (2017: 55).

Mills provides a ten point demarcation and clarification of his position (2017: 56–9). I will briefly summarize these in a list and return to relevant points as I go along.

1. The need to historicize white ignorance as a cognitive phenomenon.

2. Differentiating white ignorance from general patterns of ignorance in which race plays no determining role.
3. The difficulty of adjudicating when specific kinds of non-knowing are categorizable as white ignorance or not.
4. Whether resulting in active racism or outright race-based dominance or not, white ignorance serves to suppress knowledge of white privilege.
5. White ignorance is confined not only to white people; the power relations and patterns of hegemony can mean that it may be shared by non-white people to a greater or lesser extent.
6. White racial ignorance can produce non-white racial ignorance – forms of Black supremacy, for instance, that invert claims of white racial superiority.
7. The need for a concept of moral ignorance, which comes within white ignorance. That is, 'not merely ignorance of facts with moral implications, but also moral non-knowings, incorrect judgements about the rights and wrongs of moral situations themselves' (2017: 58).
8. White ignorance is not the only kind of privileged-group-based ignorance.
9. Even though we might speak about white ignorance generally, it does not follow that it is uniform across the white population. For various reasons, some white people will overcome it.
10. The point of trying to understand white ignorance is not merely sociological. It is normative. Change is desired and actively sought.

Whiteness studies

Mills thus gives us a concept of white ignorance that strongly links it to white supremacy, and a project that seeks to map an epistemology of white ignorance to reformulate an epistemology that generates authentic and transformative knowledge. This is a similar aim to that espoused by whiteness studies. Anthropologist Katharine Tyler summarizes whiteness studies as follows:

> Historically, race and ethnicity studies have focused on the lives of the oppressed, that is, minorities who are racially and ethnically marked by the White majority. Whiteness studies set out to invert this by examining the formation of White ethnic and racial identities . . . The contemporary reproduction of White privilege and dominance is intimately entwined with colonial practices, representations and nuances. White power has always been visible to those people that have been enslaved and colonized by Whites. Whiteness studies build on their perspective to challenge the idea that matters of race and ethnicity are just Black issues. The effect of this is to contribute to ongoing critiques of racism and postcolonialism. (Tyler 2009: 40)

Whiteness studies explains, among other things, the racial interests of whites and links them collectively to a position of racial dominance (Hartigan 2005; see also Alcoff 2015). It works to show both how racial inequality is structured, and also how white people who benefit from such inequality wilfully fail to see their own position and privileges as deriving from racialized and racist practices and structures that subordinate, impoverish or marginalize non-white people. That is, they practise self-affirming ignorance.

Whiteness studies offers a compelling lens through which to think about and explain racialized global and, where applicable, national inequalities – in wealth, incarceration rates, access to infrastructures, expectations of safety and justice, life expectancy, and educational and other awarding gaps. Closer to the ground, it asks how white people are socialized to ignore their own disproportionate presence in high-status, well-paid or decision-making roles, learning instead to speak in terms of 'meritocracy', 'hard work', 'competence' or even the agent-avoidant term 'luck'. It also encourages questions about forms of white silencing (it's not nice to talk about things that make people uncomfortable) and 'white-norming', a term Gupta and Stoolman use (2022). Finally, whiteness studies addresses hegemony: how do non-white people, especially those who aspire to or have achieved class mobility, come to accept or even reshape themselves to fit dominant norms?

Not every white person who benefits from structural racism is consciously reproducing white supremacy. This makes such privilege no less problematic or less based on forms of ignorance and ignoring (one group still disproportionately benefits, usually runs things and shapes what is both possible and sayable). It can be the case, and perhaps often is, as Katharine Tyler argues, that white privilege and power are reproduced unintentionally and without malice (2009: 41). Let us ground the above in an ethnographic discussion.

It's not nice to talk about race

In a paper based on ethnographic research in two schools in a US urban school district in Arizona, Angelina Castagno (2008) explores teachers' practices of silence and silencing which, she argues, reproduce whiteness *and* hamper students' abilities to engage questions of race and inequality by silencing race talk as 'not nice'. Castagno's interest is in institutional and ideological aspects of whiteness. That is, she explores both the ways in which 'white' normative behaviours become the required norms for others and how this works through institutional arrangements that are put in place and run by white people. The logic is as follows: nice people do not talk about race; talk about race is racist; no one should talk about race. This may work for people who can afford to ignore race, but it can damage those who cannot.

Drawing on the large scholarship on schools, Castagno is interested in patterned silencing, that is, teachers fairly consistently understanding some topics as off-limits and preventing students from talking about them, race being one of these. She suggests that, as a result, students are not given the vocabulary and tools to speak about their racialized experiences, and they come to learn that speaking about race is racist. For example, Castagno describes a conversation among a group of students at the poorer and more racially diverse of the two schools. A Pacific Islander student and some Latinx students are arguing about whether the label 'Tongano' always has negative connotations. A teacher intervenes, saying, 'stop talking about race and ethnicity because it's making you upset' (2008: 325). This kind of intervention actively prevents student-led resolutions around race terms and racialization. It also may generate a gap in students' hermeneutic resources for grappling with unsatisfactory situations or enabling epistemic justice.

In the richer and considerably whiter of the two schools studied, silence works in a different way. Castagno writes about two incidents of racist representations by students – of Japanese Second World War soldiers and a Native American group. No reprimands ensued, nor was the opportunity taken to teach about racism. On another occasion, a white student from an affluent family tells his classmates and teacher that he asked to go on a school trip organized for BILPOC students, to encourage interest in maths and science – fields in which they were under-represented – but that his request was refused. The student loudly says 'You know what bugs me about that – you have to be of ethnicality to go to that' (2008: 323). The teacher remains silent. Silence is also many teachers' response in the poorer school to a comment commonly made by non-white male students when disciplined: '[You are doing this] just because I'm Brown/Black'. Not explaining or challenging such comments reinforces students' ideas of unfair race-based treatment.

Castagno is careful to point out that teachers' practices of silence or silencing come partly from discomfort – they simply do not know how to handle race talk – and partly from their understanding that talking about race is racist, 'not nice' and might disturb students or not be in their best interests. However, ignoring race does not make it matter any less. Rather, because students bring it up and are ignored or silenced, it comes to matter more without their being given the resources to think about or work through the place of race/racism in their own lives.

Castagno emphasizes the need both for training that enables teachers to see their own colour muteness as a product of, and as reproducing, white privilege, and for support to help teachers engage with and enable race talk in pedagogically and socially productive ways.

How to know self, other and the world differently

Castagno, then, like others who attend to white privilege, argues that white ignorance needs to be dispelled. Although she does not spell it out in this way, her argument is that white people need to locate themselves as white in the racially unequal social worlds they inhabit and ask how being white privileges them. They need to recognize both how structures and systems favour them to the extent that they can afford to ignore race or avoid race talk and that such avoidance is harmful. Further, racialized groups also need to recognize that emotions such as frustration, fear, hopelessness and anger are subjective (one feels them) but not only so. They arise from unequal social structures and can be theorized as such.

This kind of recognition of the link between identity and experience can bring about change. Satya Mohanty (1997) argues, drawing from feminist epistemologies, that one can come to know one's experiences as resulting from one's social location, and thus gain a standpoint on social reality from a particular identity shared with others. Importantly, such knowledge is not just out there for the grasping. It is generated through careful collaborative explanatory accounts of stratification, the ways in which such stratification is reproduced and managed, and the particular social groups whose values and interests it serves to legitimate. Further, and importantly, the generation of such knowledge is continuous with and draws on oppositional struggles against distorted representations that benefit powerful groups and institutions. We can identify this as an activist theory of knowledge because such knowledge generation both attempts to construct explanations for problematic social phenomena *and* seeks transformation.

Whiteness studies, when it works as an activist theory of knowledge, produces anti-racist work. It does so by producing knowledge that dispels ignorance about where the real problem lies: in social structures and modes of knowing/not knowing that serve to reproduce dominance and oppression. Individuals from privileged groups are important in this story because they need to understand the forms and effects of their ignorance; so too are those from oppressed groups because they come to understand their problems not as unique to them but as shared with others like them. Each side is then empowered by knowing where the problem lies and can begin the work of self and world transformation (for ethnographic discussions of how this works in practice, see Hartigan 2010; Moreno Figueroa and Wade 2022). It goes without saying that the work of dismantling self-serving ignorance can be hard.

An important focus of whiteness studies is the phenomenon named 'white supremacy', which often refers to a conscious and knowing assertion of white or whiteness as best. This claim is usually based on a linkage between biology/nature and culture that assumes one kind of people is superior to others. In that sense, and contra Viveiros de Castro, when thinking about white privilege and white supremacy, the native can, indeed must, be deluded (or, in this language, ignorant) in order for the illusion of superiority to be maintained. This takes work; it requires the ongoing maintenance of the delusion and a wilful ignoring of the claims of non-white others to just and equitable treatment and consideration. It also requires the disciplining of bodies and the constant policing of boundaries, including the exclusion of those considered not 'properly' white and dangerous to 'proper' white folk (see Hartigan 2005) and also those considered race traitors (see Alcoff 2015). All of these others have to be constructed as guilty, deviant or otherwise lacking in order to shore up the assertions of white supremacy. In other words, a lot of effort goes into asserting and maintaining white supremacy. This can be studied ethnographically.

Let us put this all together. Ignorance is not simply the absence of knowledge; it can be an active modality of occupying the world, and it forms the basis for domination or, at the very least, the masking of privilege. White ignorance can be understood in this way and it requires attention. This kind of attention can be normative, that is, it seeks to dispel white ignorance, thus creating a more equitable world. It is not only white people who are susceptible to white ignorance; non-white people can be, too, because of relations of power and hegemony. Work is required to enable people to know how inequality is reproduced, managed and legitimated. Such knowledge is not out there; it has to be generated by empirical and theoretical work that connects individual experience and emotions to objective social structures and facts. Knowing in these new ways requires effort and demands the work of bringing about change. It can meet fierce resistance, as dominant groups struggle to retain their privileges, and indeed their ignorance, insofar as they can. Finally, although several Black scholars and activists have made these points in diverse ways, race, unlike gender, is only recently becoming an object of this kind of attention – its workings have been masked too well.

Keeping these points in mind, I now turn to a recent attempt to consolidate an anthropology of global white supremacy.

The anthropology of global white supremacy

White supremacy is the subject of a recent special section of *American Anthropologist*, edited by Aisha Beliso-De Jesús and Jemima Pierre. The editors argue the following:

An anthropology of white supremacy should:

(1) take the history of European expansion and the political, intellectual, cultural, and ideological sedimentation of presumed white superiority as given;
(2) understand that, whether or not it is acknowledged, this history informs the social practices of all the communities within which we work;

(3) shift from an overreliance on the deployment of white supremacy as identity (i.e., the 'white supremacist') to deal with the structural embeddedness of white supremacy in the world;
(4) situate the intersectional layers that understand white supremacy as constituent of patriarchy, heteronormativity, settler colonialism, mass incarceration, police violence, and other global and imperial violences in and between societies structured in racial dominance; and
(5) have a commitment to dismantling global structures of race and whiteness, structures within which the discipline of anthropology remains deeply implicated. (2020: 72)

The special section is strongest in its focus on the United States, in particular on institutions such as the police and the military. This is unsurprising, as much of the work discussed above originates in and speaks to the situation in the United States and, more broadly, the Americas. Thus, in an ethnographic paper in this edited collection, Beliso-De Jesús shows how diverse recruits in various US police training academies were reshaped into police who, however they looked on the outside (a Black man and a small Latina woman are paid specific attention), came to understand themselves in terms given by a certain kind of white masculinity (Beliso-De Jesús 2020). In a related vein, Jonathan Rosa and Vanessa Díaz describe the ways in which police and sections of the wider public see Black people, through what they call 'raciontologies', as always potential or actual criminals against whom pre-emptive defence and offence are justified (2020).

Throughout, the collection reveals that in places where white people dominate the polity, whether as majority groups or as powerful minorities, attending to forms and fantasies of white supremacy is crucial. It is important, however, to critically examine the second of the editors' aims for their project: to '[u]nderstand that, *whether or not it is acknowledged*, this history [of European expansion and white supremacy] informs the social practices *of all the communities within which we work*' (Beliso-De Jesús and Pierre 2020: 72, emphasis mine). This seems to argue that anthropologists already know, wherever they find themselves in the world, that the real issue informing social practices of all communities is white supremacy. While it is the case that the contemporary world is shaped by European colonialism and associated elevations of whiteness, such a strong statement belies the importance of research and the fresh insights it can offer outside of the researchers' a priori problematization. It also militates against the basic injunction to take ethnographic subjects' own understandings and theorizations about their worlds and lives seriously, as well as local histories and patterns, and to speak *from* them to issues rather than from an already decided understanding of the world.

Let us return to Nathanial Roberts's work (2016) discussed in the previous chapter. Yes, Dalit oppression did continue under British rule in India (Roberts 2016; Jangam 2021), but 'continue' is the key word here. Brahmanical and dominant-caste supremacy was already operational in oppressive ways. This oppression deploys the same linkage between ignorance and supremacy but, as Mills argues, there are other forms of ignorance based on group privilege. They do not all have to hinge on race. The work on white ignorance can give us ways to think about these, but it does not justify a focus on white supremacy per se. Indeed, some Dalit activists and scholars saw British rule (including changes in criminal law and the entry of the English language) as a way out of their imposed condition. Various things here should give us pause for thought with regard to Beliso-De Jesús and Pierre's second aim. It is possible to focus on how British rule in India, with its forms of white supremacy, contributed to the further oppression of Dalits. But this would miss crucial aspects of Dalit subjugation on the basis of caste-based logics and casted forms of ignorance. It is possible to talk about casteism as racism. Indeed, this argument has been made, mainly in international arenas, by Dalit and non-Dalit activists and equally hotly contested by other members of both constituencies. But even struggles against caste-based forms of oppression which name casteism as racism are not made with reference to whiteness. An anthropological question here is: what purchase does caste as race enable in transnational and national discussions of inequality beyond India? Most importantly, though, framing Anbu Nagar residents primarily through caste or race does violence to their own preferred ways of understanding their experiences and strivings. We do not learn why they want to ignore caste or how that kind of ignoring allows them to imagine a better world. A more activist theory would be oriented towards dispelling this ignorance, refusing its productive possibilities.

Let us also revisit Pilkington's work from the previous chapter. Here, it is easier to make an argument about white supremacy, even when discussing struggling white people. This is because several EDL activists are claiming that, *as* white native English people, their needs should be prioritized ahead of (usually non-white) immigrants' needs. EDL activists, it is clear from Pilkington's ethnography, both display and benefit from forms of white ignorance. Their claims of being second-class citizens and their demands to be prioritized, for instance, disregard the fact that Pakistani and Bangladeshi communities tend to be the most deprived in the United Kingdom and also that the greatest levels of ethnicity-based inequality were in the areas where they themselves lived (Pilkington 2016: 163). By contrast, they were very aware of class-based privilege and also their own status as unsavoury white people, who are routinely dismissed as racist. However, EDL activists consistently understand themselves as 'not racist' and separate their anti-Islam stance from an anti-Muslim position. They are not unique in their views: diverse opinion polls reveal that forms of Islamophobia are widespread through the British population (2016: 6), but are masked by class-based claims to liberal values. EDL activists thus comment on how higher-status whites and others who do not want to get their hands dirty use the EDL and similar groups in various ways for their own ends. Entanglements of religion, race and class, then, are complex.

Pilkington's work shows that any analysis of poor white people who make claims on the basis of their whiteness must go beyond analyses of white supremacy to explore their despair, their sometimes justified anger, the workings of class, religious tensions, the dismantling of the welfare state and the growth of free-market ideologies that have led to widespread suffering. In other words, an activist theory can be correct about the racialized workings of society; but a sympathetic ethnography that seeks not to unmask but to take seriously the simultaneous assertion of victimhood and entitlement by sections of the racial majority can ask different kinds of questions about the world and what needs to change beyond the dismantling of white supremacy.

Whiteness and white supremacy, it is clear, requires nuancing. Indeed, as EDL activists know, proper whiteness may never be fully achieved even by those who claim it because they also have to demonstrate values associated with whiteness in a given place. Similarly, John Hartigan Jr (2005) discusses how people characterized in the United States as 'white trash' have long been seen as threats to orderly social reproduction and to white moral superiority and norms. As such, they are subject to various forms of intervention, expulsion and distancing and even eugenic forms of control. Ghassan Hage, author of *White Nation*, which focuses on Australia, makes a related but somewhat different point: 'White has become the ideal of being the bearer of "Western" civilisation. As such, no one can be fully White, but people yearn to be so' (Hage 2000 [1998]: 58). In other words, white supremacy may be desired, but elusive – certainly for some kinds of white people. Indeed, ethnographies of race in the United States reveal the multifaceted and complex nature of whiteness beyond a focus on white supremacy (see Hartigan 2010 for a survey; and for philosophical and critical attention to race, see, e.g., Alcoff 2015).

It is important to think about what a framework of global white supremacy, as advocated by Aisha Beliso-De Jesús and Jemima Pierre and their co-authors, can do and what it might obscure. The collection is clearly a serious bid to get to grips with issues of prime import in the United States, within and beyond academia. It is a strong attempt to name race and engage it ethnographically and theoretically, including by moving away from a focus on identity when thinking about white supremacy and instead focusing on its embeddedness in larger structures. But I am particularly cautious about claims of a deeper insight into what underpins the social lives of all the communities in which anthropologists work, whether or not research participants acknowledge this themselves or whether or not these are the concerns in that particular place, with its specific histories and contemporary challenges (for a different kind of critique, see Haruyama 2024). This feels, and I am sure the authors do not intend it to at all, like a recentring of US anthropology's concerns in ways that look decolonizing but may colonize in new ways. I note that a more recent article by the two editors of and one of the contributors to this special collection does not reiterate the aims discussed above (Beliso-De Jesús, Pierre and Rana 2023).

The power of ignorance and ignoring

In this final section, I urge anthropological attention to how people hold on to ignorance and fight for its maintenance by exploring the controversy around the statue of Cecil Rhodes in an Oxford college.

The Rhodes Must Fall movement began in 2015 at the University of Cape Town, South Africa and, among other things, targeted a statue of Cecil Rhodes on campus, which was then removed. The campaign quickly moved to other universities and gained force as a mass movement for decolonization of universities across South Africa. It has received widespread attention, including from anthropologists, and I refer the reader to Nyamnjoh (2016) for a rich discussion of the campaign and related issues, including the place of whiteness, in South Africa.

The Rhodes Must Fall campaign, explicitly identified as decolonizing, was almost immediately taken up by several students at the University of Oxford, who have since, with allies, been pressing with ever-greater urgency for the removal from Oriel College of Cecil Rhodes's statue. Rhodes left a substantial legacy to the college, his alma mater.[5] The fact that he was a benefactor is not in doubt. But those who call for the removal cite Rhodes's English supremacist and imperial views. For instance, Rhodes stated, 'I contend that we are the first race in the world, and that the more of the world that we inhabit, the better it is for the human race' (in Stead 1902: 58), and '[w]e have got to treat natives, where they are in a state of barbarism, in a different way to ourselves. We are to be lords over them' (ibid.: 149). They point to his direct and indirect actions, which materially hurt and caused the deaths of many Black Africans in Southern Africa. They argue that his wealth came from the immiseration of Africans. Throughout the campaign, they have questioned his continuing valorization in educational institutions that lay claim to promoting justice through the furthering of knowledge. For a fuller account of the aims of the movement in Oxford, see Chantiluke and colleagues (2018).

Calls to remove the statue acquired new urgency in the wake of the 2020 brutal police killing of George Floyd in Minneapolis, United States, and the impetus of the subsequent Black Lives Matter protests. Oriel College, following the work and report of a specially appointed commission, decided initially to remove the statue, then decided against, citing 'costs and complex planning processes'.[6] Instead, it claimed to be 'determined to focus its time and resources on delivering the report's recommendations around the contextualisation of the college's relationship with Rhodes, as well as improving educational equality, diversity and inclusion with regard to its students and wider academic community'. The college website now has a page exploring Rhodes's legacy,[7] with a critical evaluation provided by William Beinart, Emeritus Professor of African History, and an appended response by Nigel Biggar, Regius Professor of Moral and Pastoral Theology. Biggar's response reveals the scale of ignoring and deflection this issue still commands.

The statue has divided opinion. While a large number of white and non-white people demanded that it be removed, there was also strong resistance from, sometimes, unexpected quarters. Classicist Mary Beard described the efforts to have the statue removed as 'a dangerous attempt to erase the past'.[8] British government ministers, too, have become involved, with then Education Minister Gavin Williamson tweeting against 'censoring the past'. It drew into alliance people from across different socio-economic classes. Activists, including from the EDL, began surrounding other statues on the grounds that British history and values needed their protection. A number of donors to Oriel College threatened to withdraw donations if the statue were removed, sparking allegations that the decision to retain it was financial. Conversely, ex-Oxford alumnus and tech entrepreneur Husayn Kassai 'pledged to make up for every penny any racist donors pull'.[9] One small college came to stand for the nation and one man for a cherished myth of a glorious past, national boundaries were redrawn and people's belonging questioned. The battle looks set to continue. And it is not simply a battle about one statue. It is about the place of the past in the present, questions of epistemic and epistemological justice, and the fight to maintain ignorance.

Defenders of the statue made three kinds of argument: first, that those who ask for a proper engagement with the past want to 'erase history'. Reappraisals of history and projects of epistemological and epistemic justice constitute neither erasure nor censorship. They push for proper, fuller knowledge and the end of ignorance and ignoring in ways that can pave the way for justice and proper flourishing.

Second, they argued that people such as Rhodes were 'of their time and that's what people did in those days'. This argument is, equally, based on wanting to ignore. Rhodes lived between 1853 and 1902. This was a time of significant growth of empire and also, as Gopal shows (2020), of metropolitan criticisms of empire and colonial practices as much as support for these. Historical sources, including those cited in Beinart's piece on the Oriel website, reveal that Rhodes was not universally celebrated by compatriots, even in his own time (see also Cohen 2020). Contemporary critics included writer Olive Schreiner (1855–1920), who knew Rhodes in South Africa and whose letters and novel *Trooper Peter Halket of Mashonaland* (1897) contain searing critiques of Rhodes's policies and the man himself.[10] Goldwin Smith, Regius Professor of History at Oxford from 1858 to 1866, wrote 'I cannot say that I saw with pleasure my old University made a pedestal for the statue of such a man as Rhodes' (cited in Gopal 2020: 454).

Third, the statue's defenders invoked the classic liberal values of whiteness: civility, tolerance and proportionality. These were placed against what were widely lampooned as 'facile', 'self-righteous' and 'anti-freedom' positions taken by 'mollycoddled' 'snowflakes' (all words in quotes were used). The mobilization of these values and the ad hominem attacks must be familiar to anyone seeking to change the status quo. They both shore up powerful forms of ignorance and enable ignoring, thus preventing just outcomes.

The statue remains in place.

What these and other arguments reveal is the powerful mobilization of ignorance and the right not to know. Similar arguments are made when defending other statues, monuments and practices. In that sense, they come up over and over again. Indeed, the fights over Rhodes's statue indicate the fruitfulness of anthropological attention to different forms of ignorance and what they do in arguments about the colonial past and the national present. Ethnographical and theoretical attention to ignorance and the mobilization of arguments and people to defend it might open up new ways of bringing about change. But this does require suppressing the activist desire to unmask or reveal the reality underneath the facade and instead explores why ignorance may be valued and sought by various kinds of people (domination is not the main focus here). I suggest that this kind of work on ignorance is similar to, and yet dissimilar from, activist work on ignorance which foregrounds domination and is committed to unmasking it to bring about social change. These two aims may not necessarily sit well together, and they do different kinds of work.

My argument is not that an anthropological focus on ignorance should replace activist theories of ignorance; but the issue with the latter is that people need to want to know in transformative ways, and some people (especially those who benefit from the status quo) may always resist. Nor do I argue that anthropologists must refrain from activism. Anthropological tools and methods that focus on resistance to knowing differently do not replace activism aimed at decolonization, but they may add important ways of understanding why activism fails.

Rouse asks what might be lost by predetermining what constitutes ethics and justice, and further suggests that quieting one's political beliefs can enable a better understanding of 'the moral majority' (2023: 362). I once met an EDL member at an event organized by the right-wing group among whom I was conducting research. When I introduced myself to him as an anthropologist, he immediately brought up Pilkington's work: 'She did not agree with us, but she listened, and she got something about where we are coming from.' This 'getting something' about those who profess 'distasteful views' might perhaps bear fruit in attempts to bring about positive change through other means than oppositional activism.

Conclusion

My argument in this chapter has been that although whiteness studies and critical understandings of white supremacy are invaluable, they could be usefully supplemented by ethnographic attention to not only what people know but also what they do not know and what they do not want to know. I have suggested that the growing anthropology of ignorance, as well as philosophical studies of ignorance and agnotology, can supplement the anthropological and ethnographic focus on knowledge in attempts to decolonize. But I add a cautionary note: such a focus on ignorance or forms of ignoring needs to hold back from exposing it to those identified as miscognizers. Rather, the object is to understand how ignorance does different things in different settings. It may be a valuable strategic tool to maintain and reproduce social and material interests. It may be mobilized in radical attempts to reshape the world and one's place in it. Equally, it may be time sensitive, allowing alliances across classes at times and reverting to mutual revulsion at others, as happened in the defence of the Rhodes statue. It may also be crucial in meaning-making projects of diverse kinds. Veena Das argues that the unethical and the ethical grow within the forms of life that people inhabit (2012). Opening up these forms of life to the anthropological gaze, including by focusing on the power of ignorance, may enable the cultivation of the kinds of sensibility required to repair the world.

The next chapter focuses on a site that is also identified with whiteness and forms an important target for calls to decolonize, about which we know both a lot and perhaps not enough (possibly even being deliberately ignorant of some things): the university.

–6–
Understanding and Transforming Universities: The Potential of Ethnography and Anthropology

The identification of the western university as a key site for the generation of colonial knowledge and the naturalization, production, institutionalization and consecration of colonialism is common (e.g., Bhambra, Gebrial and Nisancioglu 2018: 5). Indeed, some metropolitan universities are now making long-overdue acknowledgements of their roles in propagating and benefiting from colonialism (see Nash 2019 for a discussion of the United States; for the United Kingdom, see Ball 2022), albeit this often being too late and too little. Decolonizing in such cases includes the promotion of epistemological justice, with regard both to institutions' colonial entanglements and to research into the harms and benefits of colonialism in colonized and colonial centres respectively (see chapter 4). For others, however, the westernized university form, wherever it is found, can never shake off its colonial and colonizing characteristics. Thus, Ramón Grosfoguel argues that the knowledge structures of the westernized university are founded on racist and epistemic violence that stems from and is grounded in European expansion and conquests from the sixteenth century onwards (2013). The university itself, it is argued, needs radical reformation as a 'pluriversity', that is, as an institution that takes seriously diverse knowledge traditions and purposes without subordinating them to European-produced or Euro-centred understandings of what counts as knowledge proper (see Boidin, Cohen and Grosfoguel 2012).

Various ideas exist for how such a pluriversity could be instituted and the university decolonized (see the articles in Boidin, Cohen and Grosfoguel 2012). This chapter, however, takes as its point of departure Boaventura De Sousa Santos's recognition that strong questions about the future of the university in a post-colonial, globalizing and unequal world have hitherto received only weak answers in terms of organizational or other change (2012: 7–16). It thus inquires, in Laura Nader's words, about the 'fantastic resistance to change among those whose "options appear to be many"' (1972: 289). This includes the modern university. I argue that turning our anthropological gaze on the university as it is – whether the global form or particular institutions – and its imbrications with wider society can help further understandings of change and conservatism therein. This can reveal trajectories of calls for decolonization in particular institutions, including how and where they might succeed, how they are tamed or enclaved, how they intersect with diverse curricula and their effects on institutional culture at the macro and micro levels. It can also reveal changes to the *idea* of the university and instantiations and contestations thereof. I also draw on the lively 2022 debate in Manchester between Naisargi Davé, Kelly Gillespie, David Mills and Mwenda Ntarangwi (Venkatesan 2024) on whether the master's tools can dismantle the master's house to ask how anthropologists can attend to the task of reforming universities while preserving them as a space for thought and intellectual endeavours. This is, of course, a riff on Audre Lorde's famous statement that it cannot (1984).

As Stefan Collini (2012) and De Sousa Santos (2012) argue, the idea of the university – what it is and what it is for – has changed enormously in the years since the Second World War. Universities are increasingly subject to market logics, affected by globalization, and to demands for 'useful' knowledge, often tied to capitalist or semi-capitalist imperatives (e.g., Shumar 1997; Shore and Wright 1999; Strathern 2000; Posecznick 2017). Older ideas about the university continue, as do newer aspirations, including calls for more inclusive approaches to epistemology and the redressal of past and current harms. However, notwithstanding internal and external criticisms, the university remains a highly desirable institution for many. In that sense, the university may be understood as a kind of heterotopia, that is, a space in which to socially realize utopia, which is an 'imagined perfect place or state of things' (Foucault 1986), nonetheless connected to and affected by the wider world within which it is located.

I argue here that ethnographic and anthropological analysis can inform reform of and attempts to remake universities into more equitable institutions that promote rigorous and just scholarship. These things, I believe, are worth preserving. Thus, I favour reform not abolition, and furthermore I have a rather modest proposal: while anthropological tools may never be enough for full reform, we have them and we can use them to understand how modern westernized universities work and what might need to be done to promote racial and other forms of justice in the university.

On the whole, anthropological analyses and ethnographies in and of higher education institutions remain limited (see Pabian 2014; Anderson 2021), and scholars argue for more such studies in different university settings at the micro, macro and meso levels: respectively, a focus on subcultures of students, staff and academics in single university sites; a focus on structural transformations in higher education; and studies that centre institutional relations as objects of ethnographic inquiry. As Anderson writes:

> [e]thnography can be levered to explore how institutions are constituted in and through the dialectical relationship between actors' meaning-making and practices and the over-determining contexts in which they live and work. Ethnography's attention to culture and daily practices has the potential to explicate how

daily practices and institutional norms shape, redirect, and confound efforts to lead and transform colleges and universities. (Anderson 2021: 1810)

The changing (and not so different) university

Across the world, numbers of both universities and students are steadily increasing, with around five hundred universities opening every decade (Frank and Meyer 2020: 23–4). Something clearly remains attractive about the university, however flawed the model, including in its manifestation in different sites around the world, former colonial centres among these. Frank and Meyer remark that, while organizational structures vary, there is remarkable academic isomorphism, or what Jansen and Walters refer to as curriculum convergence (2022), across universities. By comparing professorships and degree programmes in different locations – Freiburg, Tokyo and Michigan in both 1895 and 2010 – Frank and Meyer show the high degree of similarity between the direct objects of university study in each site and suggest that this is perhaps unsurprising. They write:

> Of course, isomorphism is what one would expect from an institution that builds universalism into its name. But it is not what one would expect from an institution committed to preserving local cultural heritage, fueling local economic activity, or propping up local political structures. On the contrary, the isomorphism . . . reveals a striking decoupling between curricula and contexts . . . Place effects – tying local socioeconomic circumstances to university research and teaching – are conspicuously absent. (Frank and Meyer 2020: 35)

This place independence is one of the things targeted by calls to decolonize, which argue that place matters and so do the particularities of bodies and histories in knowledge generation and transmission. Place independence implies a view from nowhere, but such a view, of course, is always from somewhere, even if touted as universal. This is not to say that there is no such thing as universally applicable knowledge; rather, the point is to rigorously differentiate between what holds true across the board (HIV is not spread via unbroken skin-to-skin contact) and pseudo-universalisms (e.g., *homo economicus*). The latter serves someone, usually those in power. The conceit of place independence also does not problematize the mobilization of frameworks, concepts and theories produced in influential institutions or centres, deeming them generally illuminative and applicable. This has been extensively discussed with reference to decolonization, which insists on the importance of local, embodied or otherwise located knowledge.

For others, though, this isomorphism is precisely what is attractive; the fact that the degrees awarded by elite metropolitan institutions are legible across the world allows graduates to claim expertise in recognizable and evaluable knowledge. This enables mobility for either employment or further study. Indeed, large numbers of students from around the world join universities in Europe, the United States and Australia at huge economic and other costs. Collini cites figures showing that 25% or so of students at Australian universities are from overseas but argues that this number is easily exceeded by some individual universities in the United States and the United Kingdom. For instance, by 2010 some 60% of the student population of the London School of Economics and Political Science was said to be from overseas (Collini 2012: 16). Some of these students may remain, and some may return to their home countries. In the latter case, they expect the knowledge they have gained while at university to be recognized and applicable there, too. With too local a focus, the university may become less attractive to international students, who are massively important in terms of university income and are becoming more and more so, at least in places such as the United Kingdom where they pay far higher fees than home students. The university may also become less attractive to 'home' students, who might see it as a springboard to the world and to a different and better life, and as enabling upward mobility nationally or internationally. In the United Kingdom, for example, according to the Office for National Statistics, approximately one in three eighteen- to twenty-four-year-olds was in full-time education in 2016.[1] Although the proportions are not this high worldwide, they are rising rapidly.

Demographic changes also include massive growth in the numbers of female students worldwide, totalling 54% of all students according to a survey of 776 universities by UNESCO and Times Higher Education (2022).[2] This is similar to UK data that show that, in 2018–19, 57% of students in the United Kingdom were female.[3] Changes in ethnic compositions of students are also important. UK government data also show that among those entering UK universities to read for undergraduate degrees, the proportion of white British students decreased slightly between 2016 and 2021 (from 76% to 72.6%), while the proportion of ethnic minority groups rose from 24% to 27.4%, with the biggest increase seen in the numbers of British Asian entrants.[4] Significantly, the proportion of students at British universities who are from ethnic minorities is higher than in the United Kingdom's population itself, which in the 2021 Census was recorded at 18% for England and Wales.[5] However, ethnic minority students are less likely to be offered places in highly ranked, selective institutions, even if they have comparable qualifications to their white peers (Arday, Branchu and Boliver 2022). Barriers, then, still remain, even as change is in the air.

In the United States, too, the numbers are changing. According to the American Council on Education, in 2015–16 approximately 45% of undergraduate students identified as being a race or ethnicity other than white, compared with 29.6% in 1995–6. Much of this growth in the United States can be attributed to the increase in Hispanic or Latinx enrolment.[6]

In post-apartheid South Africa, where the 2015 student-led calls for decolonization of the university originated, although only 4.3% of Black eighteen- to twenty-four-year-olds attends university, these students, along with other non-white groups, make up the majority of university student populations. For instance, at the University of the Witwatersrand (Wits) in

Johannesburg, one of Africa's premier universities, around 66% of the 2022 student population was Black African and the total non-white population was around 83%, with white students making up the remaining 17%.[7] Although this still reflects the privilege of whites in South Africa, given that the white population comprised only 7.3% of the country's population in 2022,[8] it is worth comparing this with student numbers from 1937. In that year, of a total of approximately 2,000 Wits students, only ten were Black, of whom five were either 'Indian' or 'Coloured' (Odendaal 2019: 62; see also Murray 1990 for an account of arguments about the training of Black medical students at Wits in the interwar years).

The university, then, is not the same kind of thing as it was in the nineteenth and early twentieth centuries. Neither is the upper class, usually white, man, who made up the majority of the student body in the same period, the taken-for-granted model of the metropolitan university student today. When we consider these statistics, it is little wonder that different kinds of student are challenging various aspects of the metropolitan/westernized university and insisting that it fully and supportively acknowledge their presence and needs.

For our purposes, four observations are important about the metropolitan anglophone university, which, in line with my argument that we are best placed to speak from and attempt to transform the places where we live and work, is my main focus here, although I draw on work on universities elsewhere. First, colonial imperatives are no longer a driving force of the university in quite the same way as they were in the nineteenth and early twentieth centuries. However, there are continuities: universities remain key sites for the production of leaders, managers and administrators who are trained in certain universalist modes. Also, many universities – mostly elite ones – still benefit from financial legacies that originated in and remain entangled in diverse relations with rapacious corporations, some with continuities from the colonial era.[9]

Second, university demographics are changing, with large numbers of female and overseas students, as well as growing numbers of students from national minorities making their requirements known. These can, but do not only, focus on problematic colonial legacies or demand decolonization.

Third, and relatedly, neither the staff nor the student body as a whole may be committed to meaningful change that promotes social justice within and beyond the university. Indeed, the university may be understood by many students as a route into success in liberal capitalist terms. Some students may actively challenge progressive or critical agendas. One need only look at the pan-United States *Professor Watchlist* website, which features academics accused of undermining right-wing or conservative American values (https://www.professorwatchlist.org/).

Finally, and regretfully, although some people argue that universities should be about social justice, few universities fulfil this mandate satisfactorily. This is because the university is a site where many things are held together in uneasy alliances, for example, scholarship, personal ambition, prestige, the fulfilment of legal requirements, the satisfaction of standards laid down by professional bodies and financial considerations. Although universities in former colonial centres or settler colonies that are racially mixed proclaim commitments to diversity, some of this work can be more focused on optics and the production of proper documents that lay out desired action without their necessarily enacting or being able to enact it (Ahmed 2012).

All this is to say that universities can be rather conservative (with a small c) – resistant to change – partly because the university model has worked more or less well for various groups, individuals and sectors that value the status quo and want to maintain it. Universities are key sites for the acquisition and consolidation of different kinds of capital – social, cultural and economic, among others. As more or less selective institutions, universities can choose who they teach and thus can shape and reinforce extant hierarchies of class, race and gender. This is further compounded by the financial, opportunity and other costs of attending university. It is, then, an understandable, albeit possibly uncomfortable, fact that new kinds of entrant into universities may also be seeking similar acquisitions of capital. Within the university, this may look like what Gayatri Chakravorty Spivak refers to as demanding a greater share of the pie (in de Kock 1992: 45) but not a change of the recipe. Although discriminated-against minorities in university campuses legitimately claim advantages from which they are/feel barred, such demands, Spivak argues, often use the hegemonic discourse – they do not challenge it. A less harsh way of putting this is that diverse members of universities rightfully seek to be treated with dignity and be properly valued but do not necessarily pursue a complete change in the university form or its aims.

In sum, much is changing and yet some things remain the same. We need to understand these changes and continuities both globally and locally. Ethnography and anthropology offer one route to understanding the tension between what is offered and what is desired, and between structure and agency within the metropolitan anglophone university. We can think of this tension through a focus on the curriculum, to which the next section turns.

Curriculum

Much of the focus on decolonization of universities is on the curriculum. But what is the curriculum? How narrowly or broadly should it be understood? Is the educational curriculum (i.e., the content of what is taught) to be evaluated mainly in moral terms (i.e., the extent to which it promotes human liberation and flourishing) or instrumental terms (i.e., the transmission of useful and usable information that enables success in capitalist set-ups), or in some combination of the two? Why does it matter to think about the gap between what is taught and what is received? What is the relationship between content and context, or between teacher and taught? Is the university best thought of as 'plastic' – malleable, flexible and responsive – or as resistant, able to either wait out or tame – often through processes of bureaucratization or a focus on assessment and external validation – calls for radical change? What can a single decolonizing course do in the context of a broader curriculum?

These are big questions, and we do not really know the answers either in terms of decolonization or, indeed, in terms of the goals and actualities of the university experience. In this section, I draw inspiration from education and curriculum scholars, mainly from South Africa, who have thought carefully about these questions, both after the end of apartheid, when diverse curricula were redesigned, and in the wake of the 2015 student movements in that country (see Jansen 2019; and Jansen and Walters 2022). One thing seems clear: if transformation is to occur, we need to unpack big terms such as 'curriculum' and to understand the power-inflected relationships between teaching, learning, knowledge and context. Anthropologists can build on the work of education and curriculum scholars to design and undertake ethnographic studies to shed light on the questions raised above, both generally and in relation to specific institutions, disciplines and university constituents. This may not result in the kind of pluriversity for which scholars such as Grosfoguel (2013) call, but it may further some of the aims of decolonization by contributing to our understanding of how universities work and thus of what needs to be done to enable equitable flourishing.

Curriculum scholars often identify four coterminous types of curriculum, although exact nomenclature and even the number of types vary. The key points are that the curriculum is multiple rather than singular, and some types of curriculum are more resistant to change than others. Here, I discuss three types: the formal or explicit curriculum, the excluded curriculum and what I call the modelled curriculum, but which may also be called the institutional curriculum as opposed to the academic curriculum (Lange 2019: 86–7).

The **formal or explicit curriculum** is clearly specified, with teaching materials and methods aligned to learning objectives. It is on this curriculum that students are formally evaluated. Anyone with access to this curriculum can scrutinize it, which makes it particularly vulnerable to various kinds of challenge. It is important to note that the formal curriculum is not monolithic, and it is useful to make a distinction between the explicit curriculum, for example, the reading list and the forms and criteria of evaluation, on a given course and the programme curriculum, which is made up of many such courses with core and elective options. This is an obvious point, but one worth stating. Various courses are put together in a programme to comprise a particular qualification, but each course has its own intellectual agenda, aims and ability to participate in or open up conversations within and beyond the discipline. Individual academics may respond to initiatives to decolonize or to design radically transformative courses, even when the diverse types of curriculum at programme and university level remain resistant to change.

The **excluded curriculum** refers to those texts and other materials that are actively left out of the explicit curriculum, even when they are relevant or transformative. What is excluded may stem from a given knowledge regime and from what is authorized within a particular polity as official knowledge, rendering alternative or dissenting content illegitimate. It may, as Faye Harrison (2010 [1991]) argues, be based on ideas about what constitutes appropriate scholarship or who counts as a scholar within a particular discipline. Harrison's own focus is the exclusion in anthropology of Black scholars' work on Black issues, often on the grounds that it does not constitute a core contribution to the discipline but is somewhat niche and better located in other disciplines such as Black Studies. This can constitute a form of enclosure, as discussed earlier, and it requires the kinds of disenclosure that the 'decolonizing generation' (Allen and Jobson 2016) sought to bring about.

Paying attention to what has been excluded enables critical scrutiny of how particular ways of knowing are produced, including what counts as disciplinary knowledge. This, too, is an important aspect of calls for decolonization, as it promotes epistemological and epistemic justice.

Related to, but distinct from, the explicit and excluded curricula is what I call the **modelled curriculum**. This comprises the ways in which students and other university members are shown the values of the institution and who it perceives as its model or valued members, for example through architecture, spatial arrangements of rooms, rituals and choices of portraits, statues and marketing materials. The modelled curriculum also includes modelling of appropriate behaviours – who is allowed to speak and when, and what constitutes appropriate speech – in ways that can reproduce hierarchies and enable practices of ignoring and silencing.

The modelled curriculum can serve to train students experientially in the culture of the institution or of a particular teaching context, or even about their place in this social space. This curriculum, being infrastructural or just part of the fabric, may be hard to see or put together systematically but, once seen, is hard to ignore. This is why many challenges, including with regard to decolonization, are aimed at aspects of the modelled as much as of the explicit curriculum. We can see the Rhodes Must Fall movements in Cape Town and Oxford, discussed earlier, in this light.

Exploring curricular effects

The different types of curriculum often work together but not necessarily seamlessly. The tensions between different conceptions of what the university can and should do, and between the potentially very different and irresoluble views of different kinds of constituent, will be familiar to those who conduct institutional ethnographies. Meso-ethnographic research (Anderson 2021) can reveal the ways in which diverse aspirations and demands on the university from different stakeholders ('decolonizing' students and staff, 'status quo but better' students and staff, governments, accreditation bodies, employers, donors, administrators, university management, etc.) are managed and manifest, albeit perhaps always imperfectly, in the different types of curriculum. This can be important for understanding the trajectories of calls to decolonize.

Where the different kinds of curriculum collaborate to reproduce problematic hierarchies, they need addressing collectively. For example, I attended a conference panel where a student spoke of a lecturer at his university who was teaching a module on the Arab world. The lecturer, he told us, consistently dismissed Arab students' disagreements with particular analyses as 'typical Arab emotionalism'. It is hard to see how Arab students can find a voice in such a space and how non-Arab students can learn to take Arab students, or scholars, seriously.

The above seems to be a clear-cut case for investigation and disciplinary action. But it is also grounds for deeper questioning of the university, to understand how such an institutional culture is produced and tolerated. This could take the form of micro-level ethnographies that focus on staff cultures and student experiences of the university, as well as a meso-ethnographic focus on relations between different functionaries in the university to reveal pathways and blockages to equitable transformation in diversity policy and practice. Macro-level studies of the relationship between the university and the wider nation or region may show how the university participates in and reproduces biases against and marginalization of ethnic minorities or certain groups in wider society.

Attention should also be paid to the modelled curriculum, which covertly teaches acceptance of authority, that some ways of speaking are more acceptable than others, and that full belonging is restricted to certain kinds of body, which are taken more seriously and considered more fit for the kind of detached learning that universities are purported to promote. Do these set in place certain hierarchies of whose voice counts within the institution? Likewise, the course and broader programme reading lists also merit scrutiny. Do they feature orientalizing discourses uncritically, for example, and exclude critical voices – Arab or non-Arab?

The university in question above was a well-established European one. In other parts of the world, established universities in nations that have seen radical political transformations face other kinds of challenge. Thus, discussing post-apartheid South Africa, Jonathan Jansen (2009) details his attempts to transform the culture of the University of Pretoria (UP) when he took over as the first Black Dean of Education in 2000. Jansen describes UP as 'one of the key Apartheid institutions for higher learning and one that fulfilled its white nationalistic duty with considerable fervour' (2009: 3). How, he wondered, would UP students and staff respond to the changes that could not be stemmed – from the entry of Black students, to dual-language instruction, to changing compositions of staff – in a country that had decisively turned its back on apartheid and Afrikaner dominance? Jansen's attempts at reform were various, and included what might be best described as ethnographic explorations of the self-understandings of Afrikaner students and their families, and of key institutions that reproduced a certain self-understanding of Afrikaners and their place in South Africa. This is because he argues that it is important to understand how Afrikaner children raised in these ways grow up internalizing patriarchy, Afrikaner humiliation at the hands of the English, the heroic re-emergence of Afrikaners, white Afrikaner superiority, the importance of the Afrikaner language and the naturalization of apartheid logics. When they later encounter non-Afrikaner South Africans on terms of equality in university campuses or are forced to confront the horrors of apartheid, there is a powerful cognitive dissonance. This needs to be addressed, but in ways that do not undermine all prior understandings, only those that harm the equitable flourishing of all.

Under such circumstances, Jansen argues, a revamping of the curriculum and critical theory and a pedagogy of the oppressed are important but not sufficient. Liberation must be aimed at both oppressors and oppressed so that they can put in the work of living together and building something new that neither reproduces inequitable self and other understandings nor locks people into the roles of oppressor and oppressed. Jansen refers to this as a post-conflict pedagogy that focuses on 'the people there, the bodies in the classroom, who carry knowledge within themselves that must be engaged, interrupted and transformed' (2009: 259). This involves listening without agreeing, directly challenging in the interests of social justice, and interrupting incorporated knowledge through not only the explicit but also the modelled curricula. It is hard work, clearly, and perhaps not possible without a deep ethnographic understanding of what different kinds of student and staff know about themselves, their others and the world. Reading Jansen makes one think about the kinds of intervention that would be required to bring about a cultural shift in student attitudes towards Black academic staff in the US case discussed by Roxanna Harlow (2003). Harlow describes experiences of Black academics in a predominantly white university, especially when teaching. They face overt and covert questioning by students about their academic credentials, disciplinary knowledge and scholarly capacities. As Jansen argues, here the answer is not pedagogies of the oppressed, but rather post-conflict pedagogies that interrupt, challenge and transform. These require the full support of the university, including white colleagues.

Diversification

Harlow's and Jansen's work pushes us to think more carefully about an important component of calls to decolonize universities and curricula – diversification. Such calls are framed along the lines of 'Why do I have no Black professors?', or 'Why is my reading list so white?' As must be clear from the above, changing staff demographics through diversity practices must take into account properly supporting minority ethnic staff as they go about their work. For academics from under-represented groups, diversification in and of itself does not do much if they are consistently denied tenure, promotion or proper recognition for their work, or are not properly recognized as colleagues and scholars. This requires work from institutions, including the proper collection, publication and analysis of data on ethnicity gaps, patterns and outcomes of complaints and so on. It also requires broader support throughout the university body, including the courage to challenge student perceptions and evaluations where they affect particular kinds of member adversely.

When we turn to calls to change reading lists, although there is a strong case to be made for reading lists that reflect the demographic diversity of scholars and their contributions, it is worth exploring what reading lists actually do.

This includes asking questions such as: how and what do students read from a reading list? Does the fact of assessment instrumentally narrow reading choices? Does including a text on a reading list actually make a difference if it is not foregrounded in teaching? Do reading texts on course lists transform student understandings of the world or of themselves? Who feels emboldened about or committed to challenging the explicit curriculum, and who just wants readings that impart information in digestible ways? How seriously do we take claims that students from ethnic minorities in the metropole need to 'see' themselves in reading lists? What does 'seeing oneself' mean in this context? Does the South Asian student 'see herself' in the African-American author? How fine-grained does this need to be?

Curriculum scholars who have paid attention to these kinds of question (e.g., Stokes and Martin 2008; Piscioneri and Hlavac 2013; Schucan Bird and Pitman 2020) indicate the paucity of knowledge about student engagement with reading lists. Schucan Bird and Pitman, in particular, point to the lack of a robust theoretical framework to justify selection of readings on the basis of specific authorial characteristics, and they argue that such considerations seem lacking in the current moves to decolonize the curriculum through diversification of reading lists. Thus, they end with recommendations for further research – discipline-specific, local, sector-wide and global – including on methods for gathering data on diverse characteristics of students and staff, and qualitative work to understand what reading lists are meant to do and what they actually do or do not do as core educational tools. We might also want, when focusing on diversification of reading lists, to ask to what extent it is appropriate to divulge protected characteristics of authors (pertaining to ethnicity, sexuality, disability, etc.), unless they do so themselves and/or it is pertinent to the scholarly work in question. Making ourselves feel better cannot come at the cost of someone's privacy.

I am not for a second suggesting that explicit curricula do not need to change and that we should reproduce the same reading lists and modes of teaching. But curricular change has to be integrated into larger teaching goals. This might include identifying new disciplinary directions, as the 'decolonizing generation' in the United States did, on the basis of work by people who have been unjustifiably neglected or whose approaches challenge complacent liberalism.

When we put the above two together (diversification and the likelihood that newer entrants to the discipline/institution might be more likely to teach critical work) to think about transformative teaching, especially by scholars with protected characteristics or from minority groups, who are more likely to be challenged or undermined by students directly or through anonymous evaluations (Alexander and Arday 2015; Heffernan 2020), what support do academics receive? How might teacher–student or student–student relationships be affected when working with difficult or challenging texts on racism, whiteness, transsexuality and so on? For example, bell hooks argues from her experience that courses within women's studies programmes on Black feminism can sometimes cause unresolvable tensions, which can be difficult to manage (hooks 1994). Do academics, especially those with protected characteristics or from minority groups, eschew controversial topics out of worry? Do academics in general, especially from privileged groups, become defensive when asked to change ways of doing things, including what goes on reading lists (see Mogstad and Tse 2018)? Rigorously finding answers to these questions, including through ethnography, may inform how we think about decolonizing or otherwise transforming the curriculum.[10]

Differential awards

One area which might indicate some of the convergences and divergences between calls to decolonize and the experience of minority ethnic groups at universities is attainment gaps or, to use the newer and better terminology, awarding gaps. Here, I focus on the ethnicity awarding gap in the United Kingdom, that is the relationship between a student's race and ethnicity and their degree outcome, to explore where reform of the university might be required, albeit in ways other than those highlighted by calls to decolonize. Indeed, as I will discuss in the next section, assessment is rarely in the sights of calls to decolonize, but it should be.

A report commissioned by Universities UK and prepared in conjunction with the National Union of Students found that, in 2017–18, 80.9% of UK-domiciled white students left university with first or upper-second class degrees (i.e., 'good' degrees). Only 67.7% of UK-domiciled (i.e., non-overseas) Black, Asian and minority ethnic (BAME) students achieved this exit outcome (UUK-NUS 2019).[11] This gap is not new. Rather, it is persistent, appearing year on year. Worryingly, the report also tells us that at school BAME students attain at a higher level than white British pupils and are more likely to go to university (ibid: 6). Quite apart from systemic racial inequalities across the board in the United Kingdom (which the report discusses in some detail), something is clearly happening at university that is holding back these students as a group, even if not in every individual case. The report signals a growing awareness of this gap on the part of universities and the beginning of a concerted effort to understand its causes and address it with a view to eliminating it. However, progress seems slow, and it is not clear that the standard targets of calls to decolonize – diversification, introduction of critical pedagogies, challenging the basis of university-produced knowledge – are the answer, or the whole answer.

I argue in this section that anthropology has something to offer in its ability to provide nuanced and grounded understandings of the awarding gap through, particularly, micro- and meso-ethnographic research among students, faculty and administrators, as well as on organizational structures and relationships. This may not speak to radicals who demand a complete change of the university form, but it may do some important work in understanding why universities are systematically letting down certain kinds of student, and thence what might need to change.

Let us begin with a survey commissioned by and reproduced in the UUK-NUS report, specifically focusing on the awarding gap. This was completed by thirty-five institutions and sixty-nine students' unions, and gives us food for thought.

To the question 'Which of the following, if any, do you believe are relevant contributing factors to any ethnicity attainment gaps at your institution?', 78% of students' union respondents identified the lack of diverse senior leaders as the most significant. Institutional culture and leadership, students' socio-economic background and the lack of role models were clustered between 75% and 72%. Curriculum design and delivery came in quite low at 55% and 54% respectively (ibid.: 25).

Contrast this to what the thirty-nine institutions thought: lack of role models was quite high (much higher than in students' union responses) at 87%; curriculum design and delivery also came in much higher, at 82% and 78% respectively. Students' socio-economic groups ranked much lower than in the students' unions' understanding, coming in at 64% (ibid.: 22).

In other words, there are gaps in understanding between student bodies and institutions about causes of, and possible solutions to, the ethnicity awarding gap. These raise some questions. What does the low priority accorded to curriculum design and delivery by the student bodies say about frequent calls to diversify the curriculum? What might this tell us about the effects of, say, the modelled curriculum compared with the explicit curriculum? When we turn to the question of 'role models', ranked quite highly at 72% by students' unions and at 87% by institutions, other questions arise: who counts as a 'role model' for what kind of student? What kinds of emotional, performative and other labour might be expected from such a role model? In what ways is this labour recognized by and within the institution? This is not an argument against supporting diversity through employment practices where applicable but for more informed understandings of what is being highlighted as an issue and what support is offered to those identified as potential role models.

Surveys clearly have limited utility. Let us turn to some other studies specifically focused on the ethnicity awarding gap at universities. These include a report commissioned by Bristol Students' Union based on interviews, focus groups and visual diaries (Phillips, Rana-Deshmukh and Joseph 2017). All participants are from Black and minority ethnic groups, who form a definite minority in the institution and who experience this as a problem in various ways. But the proportion of BAME students at this university is actually higher than the national average, so we might need to know more about the non-university lives of these students as well as their university lives to explore expectations of homely belonging. Another study that focuses on the experiences of a similar demographic in an elite northern English university, this time with reference to retention, provides insights based on quantitative data over a five-year period and qualitative interview-based research, again only among students from ethnic minorities (Kauser et al. 2021). This is illuminating, especially because we can see patterns repeating over time.

However, although we learn some important things from the perspective of participating students, there is little to no participant observation in order to explore interactions on the ground in classes and other relevant spaces. There are also no discussions with academic staff about how they think about the experiences of minority groups in the classroom and their strategies for (or resistance to) enabling belonging or participation. There are no white participants in the study, so we cannot see how the university experience might be different for these students. Analyses of class are also absent. Importantly, none of these studies gets to the heart of quotidian interactions and encounters in teaching and other university or peri-university spaces that might be making a difference.

All of this indicates a need for micro-ethnographic research, particularly through participant observation in universities, including in lectures, seminars, student residences and other university and peri-university spaces. An example of this is Rebekah Nathan's ethnographic study (2005). Nathan writes that she joined as a freshman student at her own university because she found she simply did not understand many aspects of students' lives or concerns, or their approaches to university education and learning. Nathan's book, although raising ethical questions, contains insights that might inform further ethnographic work – about campus culture, race and what she calls the 'over-optioned university' that inhibits community. Work of this kind can contribute to a greater understanding of objective and subjective factors in student experiences of university. Ethnographic studies may also focus on university faculty, shedding light on the variety of ways in which academic staff individually and collectively encounter the university and its diverse members and also understand their own positionality, both as raced, classed and gendered individuals and as professionals trying to do a job with others who may have different priorities or interests. Such studies can shed light on the knowing and unknowing work of what has been described as whiteness, and its effects on experiences and outcomes.

Relatedly, meso- or institution-level ethnographic work can reveal how universities think about and work on the awarding gap, including a focus on discussions and negotiations between number crunchers, and on the kinds of data they have and what they do with them. This work would include admission teams, teaching and learning teams, academic staff, students' unions, equality and diversity teams, regulatory bodies, library staff and accommodation teams. Ethnographic work in meetings at or between different levels of the university can reveal much about intentions, compromises and optics. Such studies can shed light on formal and informal interactions and patterns of engagement in and over time.

I have focused on the United Kingdom here, but similar questions obtain in other university settings around the world where certain kinds of student may be consistently let down. While this may be laid at the door of colonialism, there may be other factors at play. We need to understand these and how they intersect or not with calls to decolonize or for radical transformation. My broader point, then, is that methods and tools from anthropology can help us understand universities with a view to repair and reform, especially with regard to racial and other forms of equity. Further, returning to a point I made on Roberts's work earlier, such studies may also reveal the possibility that different kinds of student, even if they share an ascribed identity as colonialism's others, may make different demands of the institution. Both the ethnicity awarding gap and calls to decolonize point to racial inequality, but the kinds of reform required to fix the former may militate against more radical transformations of the university form.

The fact of evaluation and the taming of radical ideas

Hoadley and Galant argue that student calls for decolonization rarely consider the role of evaluation or the assessment, via standardized criteria, of the merit of a student's work based on engagement with and demonstration of mastery over the explicit curriculum (2019). However, they write, drawing on education scholar Basil Bernstein's work, that:

> [e]valuative rules condense the process whereby knowledge becomes pedagogic communication in classrooms, lecture theatres and tutorials. These rules refer both to control over selection, pacing, criteria and the social relation between lecturer and student (framing), *as well as* to the knowledge transacted (classification). It would seem that much of the discourse around decolonising the curriculum focuses on framing and relations of control over the selection of what is to be taught, or its pacing or the social relation between teacher and taught. Less consideration is given to the evaluative rules (which concern classification as well). These evaluative rules distil the social-formative dimension of knowledge . . . and shape what counts in the end. 'What counts' goes beyond listing new topics in a curriculum. 'What counts' in this sense is not just what you know, but how you demonstrate what you know. Evaluative rules shape what questions get asked, as well as how questions are answered. (Hoadley and Galant 2019: 111, emphasis in original)

Most academics know from experience that a majority of students are concerned with doing well (i.e., obtaining good marks) and want teaching to enable that, including with learning objectives, clear marking criteria and answerable questions. The lament, especially when assessments come up, is familiar: 'It was all very interesting, but how do I get a good mark?' or, 'Which theories should I use?' or, even, 'How many references should I have to do well?' Here, we start to see some of the constraints on radical change or liberatory teaching.

Experiments are ongoing to change power relations around assessment. For example, US anthropologist Susan Blum is championing what she calls ungrading (2020). Similarly, Jesse Stommel (2020) writes about allowing students to grade themselves as experts in their own learning. This, he claims, can alleviate the unfairness baked into more standard forms of grading, which assume a level playing field, disadvantaging educationally under-served students. But this too raises questions. Do some students, white males for instance, tend to grade themselves more highly? Do students from under-served groups have higher expectations of the required standard and hence grade themselves more harshly? Even if these worries were allayed, the fact remains that successful navigation of evaluation is crucial to gaining a degree. We might also want to consider if experimental forms of assessment and pedagogy address the unsettling fact that those students who most need 'good degrees' for secure futures might see the least benefit in these, asking instead for more clarity, and for direction and instructions they can follow to produce work marked by their teachers according to published criteria.

For example, anthropologist Homa Hoodfar describes general dissatisfaction, expressed especially by first-generation university students at McGill and Concordia universities in Canada, with her attempt to introduce critical pedagogies, that is, pedagogies that encourage students to critically approach their own realities through a focus on power structures in the classroom and beyond with a view to enabling transformation. She writes about one mature student who 'said he was just a student, who, on top of his family responsibilities, wanted to graduate and perhaps to find a better job, and that he did not want to change the society nor did he believe such efforts could change the world' (Hoodfar 1992: 310). Indeed, this student believed more in the possibilities of the degree certificate he would get at the end of his studies than in the possibility that the world could be changed through education.

Even those who do believe in the latter might cave in when universities threaten to withhold degrees. Jansen and Walters (2022) observed, with reference to the decolonization movements in South Africa, that even the most radical activists ended up complying with institutional requirements and engaging with the content of the explicit curriculum so that they could take and pass exams and obtain their degrees. Universities, like other established institutions, are adept at sitting out demands for deep self-analysis and radical transformation; they can simply wait for things to peter out or for pragmatic considerations to kick in (ibid.). The fact that universities are the only institutions that can award degrees, and that degrees are important for most students, is under-recognized when considering the trajectories of calls for radical, or even equitable, change.

Indeed, universities may emphasize attainment in order to gloss over violent or exclusionary campus culture that marginalizes or threatens students seen as 'other'. With reference to his meso-ethnographic study of a US university, in which high-profile anti-Semitic, racist and anti-Native American acts by some students had led to widespread campus protests and demands for change from activists within and beyond the university, Anderson writes: '[The university president] was always quick to acknowledge that there were problems on campus but asserted that these problems were ubiquitous at colleges and universities across the country. When one considered the institution's impressive graduation and retention rates, he argued, it was clear that State University was a great place to be a student of color' (Anderson 2021: 10). Activists and concerned administrators did not share the president's sanguine assessment.

In sum, the importance of a degree to students, perhaps especially marginalized or non-traditional students, and the difference this might make to lives may allow institutions to carry on with business as usual, enclaving liberatory pedagogies or calls for radical change, so long as they do not affect assessments and thence graduation. The very fact of evaluation and the university's power to confer or withhold degrees, then, can contribute to de-radicalization or tame demands for radical transformation. This is something that both academics and students who want to bring about profound transformation via decolonization might want to consider in more detail, along with issues raised by awarding gaps that might be informed by colonial matrices, but not only. Micro and meso ethnographies around grading and accreditation, then, can open up the question of power differently, and also the balance between political and pragmatic action and desires for transformation versus the acceptance of the status quo, at least within the university.

Accidental effects

Even as we maintain our focus on what universities are getting wrong, and how they should be and do better, we might also want to ask what they do that is unforeseen, and how this might be built upon. For example, Swethaa Ballakrishnen's book *Accidental Feminism* (2021) shows how a concatenation of events, including the economic liberalization of India and the opening of elite law schools based on nationwide entrance exams, has led to an unlooked-for gender parity in corporate law firms in the country. Indeed, the number of women made partners in these firms is comparable to the figure for males. The 'accidental feminism' of these elite institutions and law firms, Ballakrishnen writes, poses food for thought. Gender equality is not achieved here through deliberate equality or diversity action. It does not challenge but rather benefits from the liberalization and globalization of India's economy, which has been a very mixed good. In that sense, it is neither liberatory nor solidary. And yet it offers unprecedented economic and social mobility to middle-class women, even from modest backgrounds. This, Ballakrishnen suggests, might have to lead to 'our slow but deliberate acknowledgment of more uncomfortable allies and framings. How we merge narratives with our unlikely allies might determine the course of our futures' (ibid.: 158).

What kinds of other unlooked-for effects might universities engender? In her book on Somali Muslim women in London, Giulia Liberatore describes how a group of friends, all devout young women, reject the Somali mosques their mothers attend, even as they strive to understand how to live as good Muslims. Instead, they 'mosque-hop' and also attend the increasingly popular English-medium independent Islamic organizations that 'employ an approach similar to that found in British higher education . . . [and] emphasize critical evaluation, self-directed learning, and topic-based teaching that utilizes a variety of different sources' (Liberatore 2017: 158). The young women also organize study groups, with participants taking it in turns to chair sessions and facilitate discussions of lectures and courses they have recently attended. In other words, being at university can inform expectations in other important areas of students' and graduates' lives that draw on the form, if not content, of university models of teaching and learning.

Likewise, university may radically change people's self-understandings and orientations. This somewhat shifts the assumption that teaching should speak to people's extant ways of being, supporting and nurturing these, especially those of people from minority groups. Marcy Knopf-Newman (2011) writes about how, having been schooled and socialized in certain ways as a child and a teenager, she arrived at university a Zionist American. She then encountered and became friends with Arab students. This led her to question her own ideas and political subjectivity and to actively learn about Palestine from both these new friends and her teachers. This in turn enabled her to interrogate the US settler state and its myths. She has subsequently developed resources to teach Americans, particularly young people, about Palestine.

Challenging long-held notions, unlearning and learning anew, and becoming politically active on the basis of new experiences and relations are all possibilities that universities can open up, sometimes despite, and sometimes because of, curricula. Students are not passive recipients of knowledge, nor do we know as much as we perhaps could about universities and university effects.

Conclusion

This chapter has focused on the deeply familiar, but nonetheless not fully known, space of the university to think both about how calls to decolonize play out in this kind of complex site with its changing demographic make-up and various agendas and expectations, all of which affect forms of and responses to calls for equity, reform, decolonization or transformation. These may not be one and the same thing. There are, as others discussed above have pointed out, too few ethnographies of universities – whether at the micro, macro or meso level – and of broader university effects. We need these if we are to understand what might become of calls to decolonize in the long run and also to inform attempts to reform and rectify persistent inequalities. It would be unfair to expect students, who often spearhead calls for decolonization, to know the ins and outs of universities. Even senior academics know only a part of these complex institutions and have a rather partial understanding of the many constituencies they serve. Things such as the curriculum, a word we all use loosely, turn out to be made up of many moving and immovable parts. Anthropological research, then, can offer new and perhaps startling perspectives.

As scholars of universities show (for example, Anderson 2021, Jansen and Walters 2022 and Ivancheva 2023), reform requires work and support, and seemingly endless negotiations through the slow work of meetings and committees with diverse stakeholders, in order to become practicable. 'Hacks' and runarounds may also be needed. Consensus might have to be built with those who prefer to maintain the status and battles carefully chosen. This is all precisely the stuff of anthropology. Studies of meetings, committees and negotiations are definitely boring compared with the open skies of ideas, hopes and aspirations, but they are necessary. Equally necessary are micro-ethnographies of the student experience to understand what the university is, does and affords from the perspectives of different kinds of university populations.

University anthropology requires a particular kind of courage; where we ourselves are actors involved in complex projects of transformation, collision, collusion and complicity, we have to turn our critical gaze onto our own practices, and their potentially harmful effects, or onto the compromises we make. We might have a lot to lose personally because these are also the sites of our own livelihood and evaluation. Anonymity may be impossible to maintain if we are working with publicly available marketing and other material from universities. Given this, universities may refuse permission for this kind of research (see Pabian 2014) or scholars may run into the kinds of issue faced by Rebekah Nathan (2005). And we still have to continue working with colleagues, however much we may differ in our views about education, evaluation and other aspects of pedagogical practice. Fighting for change is not easy, even in spaces that are committed to critical inquiry (see Mogstad and Tse 2018). Equally, and as I discussed in chapter 3, as anthropologists it might be necessary for us to hold our own desires for transformation or liberation in abeyance as we try to understand what the university might mean for other members who might want very different things from and for it. But if we want things to change, a deep understanding of the places in which we are embedded is necessary, including of pushes and pulls, tensions and unlooked-for alignments and effects. Anthropological tools and methods may provide these understandings.

Finally, critical awareness needs to be maintained about institutional forms of taming and capture. Many universities, including mine, have adopted a kind of box-ticking exercise around decolonization, for instance with the addition of the following question to course pro formas each year: 'Have you considered whether aspects of your course can be decolonized?' The next chapter, then, focuses on teaching and on responses from anthropology to general calls to decolonize.

–7–
On Courses and in Classes

In 2020, just as COVID was making itself felt across the globe, I embarked on a curricular experiment. With the intellectual input of paid student volunteers, I wanted to redesign my anthropology of religion course, which was compulsory for second-year anthropology undergraduates and open to second-year undergraduates in cognate disciplines. We would work with a course outline I had first put together in 2013 and explicitly try to engage with calls for decolonizing the curriculum. How might I do this, especially within a subfield – religion – that had been a mainstay of colonial and postcolonial anthropology? The experiment, as these things do, ended up doing some good things but, as I will discuss, it did not, at least to my mind, 'decolonize'. Indeed, it made me think much more systematically about the term 'decolonization' and the associated calls, in part leading me to take up the challenge of writing this book.

Calls to decolonize teaching are important because they invite us to think through choices we make as teachers: what we choose to put on reading lists, how we present the work of authors, including asking who is valorized and who is neglected, and how we make room for critical voices, whether from anthropology or beyond. Such calls push for the acknowledgement of scholars whose contributions have been overlooked in institutions that often reproduce white domination. They also encourage critical, careful examination of hidden and smuggled assumptions – many stemming from colonial, Christian or European understandings – that are universalized and do not do justice to diverse ways of knowing and being in the world. At the same time, some of the content of these calls poses issues. The tension between teaching how to think and what to think is something to consider carefully, especially where teachers hold strong moral or political positions. There is also a tension between teaching that is aimed at shaping the world and teaching that is aimed at studying the world.

I want to propose a more open-ended view of teaching as a moral experiment (following Mattingly 2014), that is, of teaching as involving making choices under specific constraints regarding outcomes that are not fully knowable, given the diversity and interests of participants in and beyond the teaching space. Sometimes these choices may be only good enough. The space itself has to be left open for learners to become teachers and vice versa, but there are also prior choices that are understood as choices – that is, they require defence or change where necessary. Although certain kinds of change are crucial to decolonizers, there might be a strong case for defending specific choices in disciplinary terms.

When we teach anthropology we are committed to teaching anthropology. This is our expertise and this is what students are there for. But what that anthropology looks like, how we engage it and what we *hope* anthropology will look like and enable people to do are open questions. Different people with different understandings of the discipline, and different hopes for a better, perhaps decolonized, world that the discipline may enable, will have their own ideas about the content and style of teaching and learning. For instance, how should we deal with the legacies of the past? Do we jettison problematic work or authors, do we retain them because some aspects remain productive while pointing out problems, do we juxtapose them with work that promotes epistemic and epistemological justice, or do we replace them with the latter? Teaching experiments that address these kinds of question are increasingly being published and are thus open to evaluation in terms both of calls to decolonize and in relation to the teaching of anthropology. These are not necessarily the easiest of bedfellows, as I will discuss. This chapter thus focuses on the teaching of anthropology in light of calls to decolonize, not necessarily the decolonization of anthropology. These are related but not identical.

My curricular experiment

To redevelop my second-year anthropology of religion course, I invited interested (undergraduate and postgraduate) students to a workshop to comment critically on my original course design, which I circulated in advance with marginal notes.[1] As I had designed the course, I could explain every choice and also had no compunction in ruthlessly deconstructing and rethinking it. My aim was twofold: to engage critically and constructively with student calls for decolonization by rethinking the presentation of canonical works; and to make explicit – to myself and to students – my choice of materials and themes and my course's 'story'. It is hard to say whether the fact of payment for intellectual labour influenced the demographic make-up of the group, but it certainly was diverse in terms of ethnicity and nationality.

We went through my original course outline with a fine-tooth comb. I found myself explaining every decision I had made. There was a lot of give and take, from my having to concede that sometimes I did not have very good reasons for a particular choice, to a student accepting that 'dead white men' did have some important, or at least interesting, things to say. We had an invigorating discussion on whether diversification constitutes decolonization. The answer: not necessarily, but that's not a reason to retain prevailing demographic patterns. We also explored the balance between 'theory' and 'ethnography' on the course. Following this, I came to the conclusion that one way to intellectually and rigorously interrogate the work of 'dead white men' who had shaped anthropological approaches to and early debates in the anthropology of religion was to ask whether it was still useful in light of religious people's own understandings and contemporary ethnographic work on religion.

The redeveloped 2020–21 Anthropology of Religion course thus required every student to read two ethnographic monographs in full, supported by guiding questions and weekly book workshops. Weekly lectures outlined key approaches in the subfield, beginning with influential definitions of religion (Tylor 2002 [1871]; Durkheim 1995 [1912]; Geertz 1966), and questions about both the utility and problems of such definition (Asad 1983). The aim was to interrogate anthropological approaches to religion *from* recent full-length ethnographic studies. We also critically examined the authors' own methods and their interactions with interlocutors.

Everyone read Tanya Luhrmann's *When God Talks Back* (2012), and each student then selected one from three choices: Giulia Liberatore's *Somali, Muslim, British* (2017), Ayala Fader's *Hidden Heretics* (2020) and Tulasi Srinivas's *The Cow in the Elevator* (2018). All four monographs are by female anthropologists, who are generally less cited than males (e.g., Lutz 1990; Dominguez, Gutmann and Lutz 2014; but see Chibnik 2014). I did not, however, manage to fully address Andrew Sanchez's criticism that 'despite decades of sustained critical attention to colonialism and its racialised structures of power, the anthropological conversation is still light on non-white voices' (2018: 3). But I was making choices on grounds other than racial diversity for specific reasons, including tailoring them to my own students.

For instance, Luhrmann's, Fader's and Liberatore's monographs are set in places that would be generally, if not intimately, familiar to my students: California, Chicago, London and New York. The focus on specific religious projects and people in these locations would, I hoped, estrange the familiar, and unsettle comfortable convictions about a 'secular, modern' West. It would also enable the multiplication of objections, as students would feel able to speak to the ethnographies from their own personal and located experiences of these or similar settings. Srinivas's monograph is located in Bengaluru city at the heart of India's booming IT sector. Her discussion of the rich, experimental nature of Hindu rituals in this place, and their ability to draw in highly educated and mobile professionals, further undermines the common opposition between religion and modernity.

All four monographs are very readable, foregrounding ethnographic voices. They are thoughtful, focusing on religious aspirations, practices, doubts and negotiations without reducing complexity or succumbing to a simplifying 'they think or do' narrative. The focus moves back and forth between individuals, the larger social groups within which they are embedded and the wider sociopolitical landscape, which inform and support, or render difficult, religious and other hopes and strivings. The monographs also reveal struggles within groups as people strive to convince others, wrestle with doubt and commitment, and cultivate belonging both within the group and in the larger social world. They reveal, in ways that shorter articles cannot, the tensions and richness of interactions in fieldwork. In three of the four cases, the anthropologist was an insider-outsider – a co-national but not religious in the same ways or not having the same religion as her interlocutors – and thus troubled the question of anthropology at home.

The monographs opened up stimulating and sometimes difficult conversations in my classes of 80–100 students each year, the majority of whom tend to be white British females, with smaller numbers of white male, Asian British, Black British and international students. One student, for instance, identifying himself as Christian, argued that the people in Luhrmann's monograph were not really Christian as he understood the term. This sparked heated discussions on recognition and acceptance and on anthropology's role in furthering or hindering these. It helped that we had set clear ground rules for civility in communication and disagreement.

I learned many things but, given that I had begun my exercise to try to respond to calls to decolonize the curriculum, a question remained. Had I managed that or was I simply, as Jonathan Jansen and Cyrill Walters argue is often the case, taking the calls for decolonization as an invitation to make my teaching better (2022)? We certainly did some good things: privileging the ethnographic monograph as a site from which to question theory; engaging closely and extensively with the work of female scholars; and focusing on religious people and their projects in experience-near places that students also recognized as their own but learned to think about differently. Importantly, and in line with calls for decolonization, I emphasized clearly throughout that explicit curricula are made not given, and that those who make them must be able to say why a given curriculum takes the form, and draws on the scholars or studies, that it does. But could I, should I, have been more radical on my course? And what was I trying to do, to decolonize anthropology via a focus on religion or to teach the anthropology of religion in decolonizing ways – its history, its problematics and problems, and its approaches to understanding religious belief, practice and doubt? These two aims are related but different, as are the kinds of reading and conversation they require.

In the following sections, I examine some common themes that appear in calls for decolonization and ask to what extent these can be rigorously implemented in teaching anthropology. What are their productive possibilities, and why might some aspects be problematic, even counterproductive? To do so, I draw both on my curricular experiment and on attempts by other scholars to decolonize or otherwise change the teaching of anthropology in light of calls to decolonize. I also draw on the content of such calls.

The problem of knowledge

The manifesto to decolonize the curriculum put forward by Keele University's Students' Union and its branch of the University and College Union of the United Kingdom, which is a fairly representative non-radical example of calls to decolonize, discusses the decolonization of knowledge as follows:

Decolonizing the curriculum means, first of all, acknowledging that knowledge is not owned by anyone. It is *a cumulative and shared resource that is available to all*. Knowledge (and culture) is collectively produced, and human beings of all races, ethnicities, classes, genders, sexual orientations, and disabilities have as much right as elite White men to understand what our roles and contributions have been in *shaping intellectual achievements and shifting culture and progress*. (Keele Manifesto 2018: 98)

Further, 'Decolonizing the curriculum means creating spaces and resources for a dialogue among all members of the university on *how to imagine and envision all cultures and knowledge systems in the curriculum*, and with respect to what is being taught and how it frames the world.' Also, 'Decolonization . . . will involve conscious, deliberate, nonhypocritical and diligent interest by both non-White and White members of the university *in all knowledge systems, cultures, peoples, and languages*' (Keele Manifesto 2018: 98; emphasis mine).

When certain ways of knowing and some epistemologies, including what counts as knowledge and therefore who is knowledgeable, come to be dominant, often through coercion but also via other means, they can, as has been well documented with regard to colonial projects, aid particular forms of governance, leading to appropriations, expropriations, enclosures and problematizations. This is what is commonly referred to as the colonization of knowledge and, more strongly, as epistemicide, that is, the destruction of ways of knowing and knowledges that do not correspond to the dominant epistemology. The modern western university and curricula, it is argued, have and continue to participate in such colonial projects of epistemicide and enclosure (Bhambra, Gebrial and Nisancioglu 2018). Some calls to decolonize attempt to recover lost or marginalized knowledges and recentre them. This may involve a turning away from colonial modes of knowing and thence of being. This is the kind of thing that Wangūi wa Kamonji, discussed in chapter

2, was doing in relation to African religions. For others, as in the manifesto discussed above and similar such manifestos, the point is not so much a turning away. Rather, they seek two things: first, the diversification of the curriculum; and, second, the incorporation of diverse ways of knowing into a more expanded understanding of what counts as knowledge. This aims to decentre European or privileged white male ways of knowing the world. Such a decentring may also involve exposing the conceit of certain claims to objective or disinterested knowledge and revealing its locatedness, thus provincializing it. This is the kind of work in which some anthropologists, historians, feminist scholars, queer studies scholars, political philosophers, Indigenous Studies scholars and activists, among others, have been engaged.

This type of work may originate in the university, but not only in the university. It is often done by people whose territories, bodies, stories, histories and life-worlds have been lost or ravaged by colonialism and racialized capitalism. However, it is increasingly finding its way into the university, and calls for decolonization insist that more of it do so, and affect how we think, and also how we engage in and with the world. It can and does offer different starting points for thought and action, as well as for epistemological and epistemic justice.

It is important to note some things at the outset, though. First, the idea of an *intellectual* contribution is a fairly niche one that mainly applies to scholarship. Within scholarship, yes, of course, hegemonic understandings of the figure of the scholar should be displaced and the field of legitimate knowers expanded, regardless of identitarian location, while maintaining criteria developed through participation in the disciplinary practice. This involves constructing and maintaining a respectfully listening, solidly reasoning, robustly debating 'we' of anthropology that is not restricted to certain kinds of bodies. This has to be a principled stance that is properly enacted, including by consistently subjecting academic knowledge to standards that are consonant with disciplinary practices, while accepting that these may be open to challenge and modification.

Let us turn to the more radical claim that university curricula treat all forms of knowledge in the same way. There is a fundamental problem with this. By its very definition, knowledge produced in universities is understood as contingent, falsifiable and subject to various forms of testing and critique. This is not the case for knowledges that are oriented towards other ends, including political. As we saw in the disagreements in Hawaii, subjecting some kinds of knowledge to the kinds of critique to which academic knowledge is standardly subjected can be bitterly resented. Equally, as I will show with a discussion of menstrual taboos, even cultural insiders may resist certain knowledges as harmful. A blanket statement about the value of all knowledges and cultures and calls to accord them equal status is not just unworkable, it may not even be emancipatory for people subject to these knowledges. It thus behoves anthropologists to pay attention to the ways of knowing, content and purposes of diverse knowledges. This means taking diverse knowledges seriously and thinking with them, without necessarily subscribing to them. In what follows, I ground some of the points made above, beginning with an ethnographic discussion.

In Tanya Luhrmann's *When God Talks Back*, a woman *knows* that God is teasing her when a bird shits on her at a moment when she is feeling particularly smug (2012: 96). Luhrmann the anthropologist knows, because of her ethnographic work among Vineyard Christians, how this woman and others like her have worked and learned, individually and collectively, to open themselves up to direct communications from God. Luhrmann's research interest is in the kinds of learning, discipline and collective practice, as well as the individual proclivities, that make God real to Vineyard members. She is clear that she cannot confirm or deny the reality of God; she can only reveal/describe what treating Him as real and interactive means for the collective and individual lives of church members and why they put the kind of work they do into bringing God into their lives. The intellectual (i.e., not applied directly to life) questions and contributions are Luhrmann's, not theirs; indeed, their own questions and even their work with her are much more practical and geared towards the emotional satisfaction of achieving and maintaining a loving and meaningful relationship with God. What counts as knowledge and why each kind of person wants to know something are different in each case.

This discussion allows us to think also about a common criticism of anthropology: that 'we' use 'their' knowledge and do things with it that they would not or that we 'take people's knowledge and transform it in ways that make little sense to the original knowers'. Such criticisms flatten complexities, and sometimes tend towards a 'thingifying' of knowledge, that is, treating it as a form of property over which ownership may be legitimately or illegitimately exercised, in the latter case alienating it from its original possessors. Writing of this trend, which he links to the growing emphasis on the 'knowledge economy', Dominic Boyer makes an analogy with the ways in which labour came to be conceptualized from the late nineteenth century onwards. He argues that knowledge is something that we increasingly speak of as produced, consumed, appropriated, uncompensated, alienated and so on (2005: 147). In this way of thinking, knowledge is valued as if it were a form of capital, and the sharing of knowledge as a zero-sum game: the more one person has, the less there is to go around.

Although it is important to call out moves to alienate and enclose commodifiable knowledge through legal devices such as patents, copyright or licences, learning from others and sharing what one knows is more complicated than this, as is clear from the brief discussion of Luhrmann's work. There is a dynamic poiesis that underpins human ways of knowing, and of sharing what they know and making sense of it in terms of their own priorities and concerns. Much of what we think about as anthropological knowledge derives from specific interactions between anthropologists and their interlocutors. It is neither fixed nor out there to be found, but emergent. These interactions are, of course, inflected by diverse inequalities in power but not necessarily in straightforward ways. Nor is it the case that different parties in these interactions are doing, knowing or learning for the same kinds of reason. Teaching with anthropological knowledge that is based on equitable research relations, even if the anthropologist's and research participants' motivations and purposes are different, can expose students to better ways of doing anthropology. This kind of work can enable us to think through knowledge, intellectual or otherwise, in richer ways.

We might ask, as some of my students did, whether Luhrmann was wrong to ignore the politics of Evangelical Christianity in the United States, including the suppression of reproductive, sexual and gender rights and the links with white supremacy. But in taking some of their purposes seriously and learning from them, she neither has to make her purposes their own nor agree with other causes they espouse. This turns us to anthropological questions: the knowledge that is generated by the specific questions different anthropologists ask, what they hope to understand, to what debates they hope to contribute, and what gets left out or ignored in the course of answering these questions. Luhrmann's work, of course, does not preclude other questions being asked about Evangelical Christianity in the United States or elsewhere, or about the imbrications of religion and politics. Indeed, a PhD student of mine, Thomas Long, is doing precisely that. In that sense, anthropological knowledge is open-ended. Each set of questions and the answers to these generate more questions, which sometimes seek to build on original questions and sometimes repudiate them altogether as self-serving or otherwise problematic. This too is an intellectual task and not necessarily of wider interest. But it is crucial in the classroom and in research.

Knowledge gaps and limits

There are always limits to, and gaps in, knowledge, anthropological or otherwise. Teaching must discuss such limits and gaps. This is because these may signal a 'no-go' area for research participants, which in itself is interesting, or they may indicate new lines of research or lead to discussions about the ethics of knowledge generation and about limitations in what one can or wants to know.

In the Tamil Hindu India in which I grew up, proper female fertility is a major concern and menarche is celebrated. Equally, a female on her period is known to be polluting and is often barred from various activities and from spaces such as the kitchen. These two knowledges – periods as good and periods as bad – can and do sit uneasily with each other. Fighting against period taboos has occupied some of my friends and me since our early teenage years. We have rarely succeeded, though, because women in our families, older women in particular, have not been able to let go of their knowledge that periods are polluting. My grandmother, for instance, would be apologetic whenever I cried, argued and tried to tell her that periods were natural, but she struggled to enact the changes I demanded. In some sense, she held both knowledges – that she was wrong and she was right, and also that I was wrong and I was right – bodily, emotionally and in her relations with me and with human and non-human others to whom she felt answerable. This also raises questions about epistemic disobedience, as advocated by Walter Mignolo among others. To what extent is it possible to unknow certain things that are corporeal and deeply felt or that underpin relational and social norms? These things may arise from colonization or, as in this case, do not, but epistemic disobedience is still hard and may be studied anthropologically.

Ideas about periods and about what women can and cannot do persisted throughout my doctoral and post-doctoral fieldwork in two different Tamil villages, although I did not argue with anyone there. By then, I had read Louis Dumont, McKim Marriott and Valentine Daniel and was willing to explore the premise of substance transfer as a systematic explanation for what I still considered utterly wrong. I could also, as other scholars (and activists) have, show how this kind of knowledge has real social effects: cultural elaborations of periods as polluting can have the effect of barring women, including through self-exclusion, from certain roles or activities even when not on their period. This advantages men who bear no such pollution and who do not 'have to step out' for a few days every month. It also means that women who are not on their period may be expected to forgo other responsibilities (work or school, for instance) in order to remain at home to do chores that women on their period cannot. That is, particular ways of knowing may shape social life in ways that do not fit comfortably within a positivist notion of 'contributions' or, indeed, of 'progress'. In that sense, knowledge does not lay down a road that one can traverse in some linear way. This has implications for anthropological description and analyses. For example, when studying development initiatives on period poverty and practices, as Manchester PhD student Jennifer Moore is, it is important to be critical about problematic aspects of said interventions without valorizing period-based marginalizations when they occur. Many research situations do not present clear-cut either/or stances.

Further, even as some ways of knowing/knowledges are inaccessible to others (even cultural insiders; see High, Kelly and Mair 2012) and some things are not possible to unknow, refusal, too, may play a part. As discussed in chapter 5, ignorance and ignoring can be powerful strategies. I do not want to share my grandmother's incorporated understanding of periods as polluting, notwithstanding our close relationship of over forty years, as it might derail other projects I privilege (see also Chua 2009 for a discussion of interlocutors' avoidance of certain knowledges).

Other anthropologists, too, have been concerned with what has been termed 'ethnographic refusal' in the generation and transmission of knowledge. Such a refusal might take two forms. The first, as Audra Simpson describes it, is the research participants' 'not wanting to go there' or 'enough now' stance, which anthropologists must respect, even though they can productively and analytically engage the fact and nuances of refusal (2007). The second form is anthropologists' refusal to share thick ethnographic details that might be utilized against research participants. Deniz Yonucu discusses this form of refusal in her work on policing in Istanbul and on security forces' use of anthropological work in diverse ways, including to gain information on certain neighbourhoods and use it in counter-insurgency activity (2022). Yonucu argues that the anthropological urge for thick description and the texture of places and people's lives must, in some cases, be avoided. These discussions militate against a straightforward understanding of knowledge as 'out there' and accessible or transmissible, or indeed as helpfully contributing to progress.

Knowledge, then, really is a complex beast. Diverse knowledges do not make up a whole cloth that we can think of as the sum of human knowledge. Knowledges often exist in complex configurations and push back or settle down in relation to one another in ways that defy simple assumptions of displacement of one kind of knowledge by another, or the positing of additive understandings of knowledge. Knowledge can equate to power, but it does not have to. Although the diverse sources of intellectual contribution and progress should be properly acknowledged as the Keele and similar manifestos demand (albeit with due consideration for privacy), as anthropologists, we might want to think about knowledge more expansively and also more rigorously. Given that anthropology as a discipline has always been concerned with knowledge (Crick 1982), one way to develop and enrich decolonizing approaches to knowing is through critical engagement with diverse anthropological modes of knowing.

Anthropological modes of knowing

In this regard, Dominic Boyer's indicative summary is useful, and I list various anthropological modes of knowing below with brief explanations (2005: 143–4):

- Empirical: knowledge based on experience and observation
- Ideational: relating to the formation of ideas and concepts that guide knowing
- Praxiological: a focus on human activity, particularly on making and doing, and knowledge of objective and subjective agencies

- Poetic: self-awareness in tension with creative, imaginative capacities
- Semiological: involving the use of symbols, mainly but not restricted to language in its broadest sense
- Psychoanalytic: involving and thus entailing a focus on the unconscious mind, especially with regard to desires
- Historicist: a focus on the processes by which particular phenomena or practices come to take the forms they do
- Critical: foregrounding a focus on the wider issues affecting a particular object of focus as well as an in-depth engagement with the object itself. This questions both the possibility and grounds of knowing fully by embodied and embedded persons, while simultaneously pushing towards some possibility of perfection.

These different modes and methods of knowing are not mutually exclusive. They are open to critical examination and challenge. Thus, we ask, and encourage students to ask: whether a given approach or framework is the most productive; what is foregrounded and what neglected (for example, a focus on holism might neglect dissent); and whether a different framework or set of methods might generate different kinds of knowledge, including destabilizing taken-for-granted anthropological concepts and understandings.

Decolonizing scholars tend to employ historicist and critical approaches, and they may sometimes criticize other approaches as being insufficiently political or not oriented towards positive change. This may lead to the kinds of charge some of my students levelled against Luhrmann's *When God Talks Back* – of neglecting the politics of US Christian Evangelism, including white supremacist ideologies, and of producing a 'redemptive' narrative that takes Evangelicals' aspirations and struggles seriously rather than their effects on various kinds of marginalized group and in political, social and economic life. There are various answers to such charges, including emphasizing the value of research among 'repugnant others', but the key point is that the lecturer should be able to explain, and where necessary defend, a choice. My own answer was threefold. First, Luhrmann's book teases out Evangelicals' struggles with doubt and belief in a pluralistic, albeit mainly Christian, national space. It thus turns the gaze to religion 'at home' and opens the categories of 'Christian' and 'the West' up to critical anthropological scrutiny. Second, it follows a growing move to destabilize and complicate the notion of belief, which has been a central concept in the anthropology of religion since colonial times, mainly because of Christian influences. Third, the book's focus on how committed people learn through individual practice and social support to know themselves, the world and its workings and hence build new relations might offer lessons in bringing about radical change that could apply beyond the Evangelical context. One student raised Luhrmann's middle-class whiteness as a problem. This feels objectionable when asked of an individual who cannot help their personal characteristics and is producing fine work, but can it be legitimately raised with regard to the anthropology canon?

The canon and the problem of the dead (or alive) white man

Several years ago, an undergraduate student challenged me about the presence of Louis Dumont's *Homo Hierarchicus* (1980 [1966]) on my anthropology of Hinduism reading list, asking 'Why should I care about what a dead white man says?' I explained both how Dumont's work attempted to synthesize the complexity of the caste system by analysing it as a hierarchy based on the Hindu contrast between pure and impure, and how it was at once extremely elegant and deeply problematic, spawning critical engagements, including from Indian scholars, ever since publication. These engagements have opened up the study of caste in diverse ways. They have also spawned strong critiques of the seductions of holism. In that sense, Dumont's work is canonical within and beyond the anthropology of Hinduism. In my own course, I had placed Dumont's book in critical comparison with

Viramma: Life of an Untouchable, authored by Viramma with Josianne and Jean-Luc Racine (1997). The point was to show that caste on the ground was much more complicated than Dumont's holistic and synthesizing analysis admitted, notwithstanding the continuing importance of the purity/pollution framework. Dumont was necessary to the course as I had conceived it.

In curriculum terms, a canon is an assembly of texts deemed important and worthy of continued critical attention within an academic field. The canon shapes a particular field of study and tends to define what should be discussed. It also forms the basis for critique and innovation. Many critics, including students, argue that the dominance of male and (what we would today identify as) white scholars in the early anthropology canon reflects and reproduces colonial-era patterns. Efforts to decolonize the anthropology canon include the production of alternative reading lists, which are demographically diverse by design, for example, in the alternative curriculum assembled by students of the Graduate Social Theory Class in the Applied Anthropology Program at Oregon State University (Buell et al. 2018) and the Alternative Reading List Project.[2]

Some of the mostly male, white scholars of the standard canon problematized in these alternative curriculum projects are read by almost every anglophone undergraduate, usually in introductory or theory courses. In the United Kingdom, they include Edward Burnett Tylor (usually on culture or religion), Emile Durkheim (religion, society and social facts; also division of labour), Marcel Mauss (usually the gift and also perhaps the body), Max Weber (often capitalism, but also ideal-types, disenchantment, and the organization of modern life), Franz Boas and Bronisław Malinowski (both on methods, but also on substantive work), Alfred Radcliffe-Brown (social structure), Max Gluckman (the extended case study and the tension between functionalism and social change), Lévi Strauss (structuralism), Edmund Leach (structuralism; also kinship and social structure and cultural change), E. E. Evans-Pritchard (rationality, anthropology and history; also stateless societies), Margaret Mead (sex and gender) and Ruth Benedict (cultural patterns). These authors are usually mobilized to tell a linear story of early anthropology – its subject matter, its often quite fierce debates, and the changes in its foci and approaches over time.

In the United States, too, as Alex Golub shows in his analyses of the contents of two anthologies used in teaching (2014), certain authors and their key contributions appear in more or less the same order to cover the period from 1850 to 1950. After 1950, there are divergences, and after 1974 agreement rapidly decreases. Between 1950 and 2014, works by only ten authors are anthologized in both books.

Golub's comparative exercise reveals that the story told about anthropology as a discipline to undergraduate anglophone learners, focusing on some key early authors and texts, is reasonably unified only up to a point, after which the field becomes much more fragmented (ibid.). Should these early authors be there at all? Different people have different answers. My own view is that where an author has spawned a debate or a series of debates that continue to shape and direct disciplinary conversations, then yes. Durkheim, for instance, placed the opposition between a focus on society (good) and the individual (not so good) squarely within anthropological thought. This opposition and attempts to resolve it to understand human action continue to drive much anthropological work. Similarly, Franz Boas made culture a central anthropological concept, with some anthropologists denouncing it and others rejuvenating it, albeit in altered forms. Both Durkheim and Boas are firmly in the anglophone anthropological canon, but this does not mean uncritical acceptance in teaching of either their work or the context in and means by which it was produced. Nor does it mean that every work by a famous dead white male anthropologist makes it into the canon. There is, for example, a rather prurient and (to my mind) pointless article by Evans-Pritchard on Zande sex that should never have been published, but it was, and in *American Anthropologist* no less, as late as 1973. It has since sunk into well-deserved oblivion, unlike *Witchcraft, Oracles and Magic among the Azande* (Evans-Pritchard

1937), which anthropologists continue to read, teach, build on and challenge.

The crucial points are that not every article by a prominent author survives the test of time and that a canonical text is not beyond question – rather, it is the kind of text that is most subject to questioning, challenge and critique. Also, those who include a particular text should expect to be asked to justify its inclusion. Where particular premises have proved limiting or harmful or have advanced causes inimical to research participants or relevant others, this should be made clear to students in order to inform and guide future work in more equitable and thoughtful ways. Work exhibiting these latter qualities should be introduced and placed in critical conversation with problematic aspects of standard or canonical work. None of the above is new; various anthropologists have been experimenting with different ways of teaching and engaging canonical works or of bringing alternative works into the canon, increasingly under the decolonizing rubric. More and more of these experiments are being published. I discuss two below.

Experiments and critical inclusions

In a 2022 paper on designing an anthropology theory course, Joshua Liashenko discusses his pairing of a podcast outlining Boas's contributions and his critiques of biological reductionism with Lee Baker's 2021 article, 'The Racist Anti-Racism of American Anthropology'. Baker's article, among other things, critically discusses Boas's theory of assimilation, which he argues took on a eugenic form. The point Baker is making, and Liashenko also, is that some anti-racist positions and work may reproduce or privilege race, and even be racist, in ways that bear scrutiny (see also Bashkow 2023). Similar points are made by John Hartigan Jr in his discussions of ethnographies of anti-racist work in the United States (2005: 232–56), by Ghassan Hage in his discussion of good white nationalists who welcome non-white Australians (2000 [1998]: 78–104) and by Shalini

Shankar in her focus on 'diversity' as a way of making white people feel better about themselves (Shankar 2020). This kind of work can be used to initiate classroom discussions about liberal positions that mask assumptions about who belongs and how they manage the entry of others into 'white' spaces including, where applicable, the university.

Liashenko is not sanguine about the decolonization of anthropology for reasons he explains in his article. But another anthropologist, Mariam Durrani, also in the United States, is more hopeful (2019). Calling for an approach to the canon based on the Greek notion of *kairos*, or the seizing of a critical or opportune moment, Durrani argues that although we cannot evade our discipline's colonial past, we do not have to reproduce it in our teaching. The moment is ripe, she argues, for finding other ways and other texts with which to teach. This could begin, she suggests, with two questions that directly address troubling social issues: 'What have anthropologists already done in terms of these issues?' and 'Why have these attempts not gained broader traction?' In other words, what is anthropology doing wrong and how can it do better?

Durrani suggests turning to radical anthropological texts and learning from these as well as from recent scholarship about how to think about and critically intervene in the world. Thus, she describes how she begins her senior thesis class with Zora Neale Hurston's *Barracoon: The Story of the Last 'Black Cargo'*, completed in 1931 but not fully published until 2018. *Barracoon*, Durrani writes, is an exemplary account of ethical and respectful fieldwork that charts the complex, intricate relationship between researcher and participant – one from which students beginning an independent research project can and should learn.

Barracoon foregrounds the self-narrations of an elderly man, Kossula, who was kidnapped from what is now Benin in West Africa by a neighbouring group – the Dahomey – sold into slavery at the age of nineteen and transported to the United States, remaining enslaved for five years before his emancipation in 1865. Based on interviews and deep hanging out over three months in 1927 at a pace set by Kossula, the book is heavy with the weight of Black enslavement and post-emancipation struggle in the United States. Reading it made me cry. It also raises more abstract questions. Hurston refused the publishers' demand to rewrite the text in standard US English; this delayed publication by more than half a century. How is a balance to be found? Further, how do we engage the resistance shown by some African Americans to *Barracoon*'s publication, based on discomfort with Kossula's initial kidnap by members of another African group who then sold him on? How do we work with and think through this first-hand account of Black involvement in the slave trade? Alice Walker writes in the foreword to the book:

> Reading *Barracoon*, one understands immediately the problem many black people, years ago, especially black intellectuals and political leaders, had with it. It resolutely records the atrocities African peoples inflicted on each other, long before shackled Africans, traumatized, ill, disoriented, starved, arrived on ships as 'black cargo' in the hellish West. Who could face this vision of the violently cruel behavior of the 'brethren' and the 'sistren' who first captured our ancestors? Who would want to know, via a blow-by-blow account, how African chiefs deliberately set out to capture Africans from neighboring tribes, to provoke wars of conquest in order to capture for the slave trade people – men, women, children – who belonged to Africa? And to do this in so hideous a fashion that reading about it two hundred years later brings waves of horror and distress. This is, make no mistake, a harrowing read'. (Walker 2018)

Achille Mbembe raises similar unsettling questions in *Out of the Dark Night* (2021).

Zora Neale Hurston's is an extremely important voice, and *Barracoon* raises important and complex issues that deserve thought; it is also a good way to introduce the ethics, practicalities and emotional aspects of fieldwork. The book has been widely reviewed. Although almost entirely positive about the book, scholars and reviewers ask some searching questions both about the conditions under which the book was produced (e.g., see Ryan 2018) and Hurston's own politics.[3]

In other words, work that appears in the canon or new work that is brought into reading lists and actively taught is subject to diverse kinds of testing over time: Are its claims well founded? What were the conditions of its production? Are the points made generalizable? What does it enable and what does it miss? What kinds of consideration, including biographical, might underpin decisions to keep a particular piece of work in place, remove it from a curriculum or retain it while also unsettling it? Those of us who are free to make such choices should exercise them to the benefit of our disciplinary practice and our students.[4] We might call this decolonizing or we might not, but the calls for decolonization certainly encourage this kind of scrutiny of the canon and of authors, leading teachers to think about what they might want to work with instead of, or in addition to, established texts.

Perhaps another fruitful way to think about reading lists is that they can expose us to a variety of approaches and content. Although not precluding adding new texts or replacing 'classics' in line with a course's pedagogical or decolonizing aims, engaging with the wealth of critical engagements with canonical texts can sharpen the ability to critique, which can then be extended to any text or view we might encounter. There will always be nasty or problematic texts (e.g., Gilley 2017), and it is important to teach students explicitly to challenge them. Thus, I follow Edward Said in his argument that 'learning is a kind of travel, a willingness to go into different worlds, use different idioms and understand a variety of disguises, masks, and rhetorics' (cited in Leonardo 2018: 16). We do not have to stay in these worlds, but entering them allows us to see how they are organized and why we might want to build other kinds of world for ourselves. They may also offer hitherto unlooked-for insights into how we might build these other worlds.

A focus on questions

Focusing on questions that generate a given body of knowledge offers a different way of approaching disciplinary knowledge, the canon and specific works. Here, rather than treating the published work as authoritative, we ask questions of it to explore how said knowledge was generated in the encounter between anthropologist and research participants, between anthropologists away from the field and between anthropologists and diverse stakeholders. Such an approach reveals the limits, possibilities and problems of anthropological knowledge projects:

- Does the body of the anthropologist – raced, classed, aged, gendered, casted or otherwise classified – make a difference to interaction in and beyond the field and to the knowledge so generated? How is the anthropologist's body produced in the research site?
- What was the anthropologist seeking to discover? This question includes the underpinning research questions and the frameworks within which the anthropologist is working, either in terms of contributing to them or challenging them.
- How was the knowledge generated? To whom was the anthropologist talking, and what were the methods and underpinning methodologies? What did the anthropologist concretely do?
- What/who was left out of the research?
- Why was the anthropologist interested in these questions?
- Who is meant to be the beneficiary of this research, the group among whom the research is conducted, the anthropologist's origin society or the corpus of anthropological knowledge? It may be all of these, of course, and this raises further questions of how exactly and to what extent.
- What assumptions underlie the research and what assumptions does it challenge? How does it engage with extant anthropological and other work and ideas in the public domain to do so?

- Are we judging the work or the author? Can we or should we separate the two?

Finally, following Audra Simpson, we might ask what anthropological analysis would look like in situations where the goals and aspirations of research participants informed the methods and the shape of the anthropologist's research, theorizing and analysis (2007: 68). Also following Simpson, does the text in question reveal the limits of inquiry in any given case? (ibid.: 73).

These are not all the questions to ask, of course, but they will do to start with. They can underpin teaching and enrich it because they encourage students to ask similar questions of any text they encounter within and beyond reading lists.

The question of theory in decolonization

We might also want to make a distinction between the decolonization of anthropology and decolonization as a framework for wider diagnoses and transformation. Among wider decolonization frameworks today, two are dominant: modernity/coloniality/decoloniality and whiteness/white supremacy. Both offer powerful ways of diagnosing the ills of the world, along with some solutions. Although originating in specific locations, both have had a long reach and have acquired massive explanatory force, influencing anthropological, other disciplinary and activist thinking. As anthropologists, how should we teach these frameworks?

The obvious first step is to show what the frameworks do in explaining and problematizing the world, how they do so and from where. The MCD framework, for instance, describes the world shaped by a modernity that is a product of the colonial matrix of power, and asks how that world can be undone. The second step is to approach the frameworks critically. Does the uncompromising stance adopted by prominent MCD theorists (and I can write only of those translated into English) close off the asking of anthropological and ethnographic questions that try to understand diverse post-colonial desires and aspirations, including in relation to modernity/modernities or capitalism? Do the kinds of diagnosis this framework proffers travel well to other locations with other histories of colonialism? How does the framework interact with or challenge different kinds of post-colonial project of understanding and change?

Similarly, with regard to whiteness/white supremacy, although its significance is undoubted in places with a dominant white presence, does it plausibly explain contemporary anti-Blackness or anti-darkness in places where white people are not numerically significant, for example in Arab North Africa, Japan or India? Even in racially mixed places with white majorities, is anthropologist John Hartigan Jr's criticism apposite? He writes: 'by asserting the "fact" of whiteness – the durability of its dominance and the pernicious nature of its effects – [whiteness studies] may have the unintended consequence of undermining the concept of "race" as constructed' (2005: 191). How might ethnography complicate the picture? In the United States in particular, in addition to work highlighted by and also produced by Harrison and others of the 'decolonizing generation', I am thinking, for example, about Hartigan's work on race and class relations in Detroit (1999), his survey of diverse ethnographies of race on the ground (2005) and his thoughts about a post-racial United States (2010); John L. Jackson's work on race and class, and sincerity and authenticity (2001, 2005); Angelina Castagno's work on teachers' silencing of students' race talk, discussed earlier (2008); and Heath Pearson's work in a small town in Indiana where displays of white supremacy as well as white forms of ignoring and ignorance affect both Black belonging and white allyship (2015). These ethnographies reveal the many contradictions, uncertainties and intersectional aspects of race relations on the ground, and both complement and complicate ethnographic studies of (e.g., Beliso-De Jesús 2020; Rosa and Díaz 2020) and more programmatic work on the (re)production of white supremacy (e.g., Beliso-De Jesús and Pierre 2020; Beliso-De Jesús, Pierre and Rana 2023). Yet other ethnographies go beyond the Black/white dichotomy in US race relations, focusing on what might be called the racial middle, people who identify as neither white nor Black and whose relationship to whiteness and Blackness may be differently constituted and theorized.

The point is not to do away with theory. Indeed, I agree with bell hooks (1994) about the debilitating anti-intellectual division commonly found in certain circles, including among some activists, between theory and practice, thinking and feeling, and understanding and doing. Rather, the point is to approach theories critically, asking both what they afford and also how Theories (with a capital T) may capture ways of thinking in ways that do not necessarily make space for nuance, difference and change. These three elements are the strength of ethnographically informed anthropological theorization and analysis. Indeed, it might be worth emphasizing the usefulness of what Satya Mohanty calls 'small theories' (1997; see also Alcoff 2015: 45–7; Mafeje 1998a), which have explanatory force but do not claim a universal scope. They may not be as exciting, but excitement is not everything.

There is a further issue with some decolonization/decoloniality frameworks, and that is generalized hostility towards science and various academic disciplines based on identifying these with colonization, whiteness, Europe or the global North. For example, take this assertion made in a 2018 report produced by the University of Cape Town's Curriculum Change Working Group in response to calls to decolonize: 'Being a great musician or a great doctor is tantamount to being a colonial subject who aspires to white supremacist patriarchal and western (classical) ways of being rather than a reflection of local influence and ways of being' (cited in Jansen and Walters 2022: 30).

Such an attitude, in the name of decolonization, denies the work, contributions and achievements of racialized people in fields uncompromisingly identified as colonial and western, thereby erasing or refusing them along essentialist lines. The point is not to be unconditionally celebratory but to be critical and aware of both the reproduction of hierarchies and status in scientific and academic fields, and of attempts to enclose and dispossess, including along racialized or essentializing lines. Anthropology and ethnography can bring such critical awareness, as well as take seriously the efforts of people who are cultivating expertise in, and contributing to, adapting, domesticating or otherwise shaping, areas once identified as European or western. This may not decolonize according to some understandings of the term, but such understandings should perhaps themselves be objects of study.

Other approaches that are not strictly ethnographic can also inform anthropological teaching, both generally and in specific subfields. For example, Kim TallBear's critical polyamory (2020) takes note of colonial and other legacies in the reproduction of heteronormativity and sexual exclusivity while advocating for multi-relational ways of being in the world. Such a critical polyamory may also be extended to think about anthropology's relationships with other disciplines or ways of knowing. TallBear's work, whether with regard to critical polyamory or to genomics research (2013), sparks ways of thinking beyond identity and property and with a focus on relationality, which can inform decolonizing projects. This kind of work is simultaneously deeply located and critical, with strong ethical moorings from which it reaches out into fresh ways of thinking, doing and being. It merits critical appraisal, of course, but it also enables new questions and destabilizes settled understandings.

Conclusion

Calls to decolonize teaching encourage reflection and stimulate more careful consideration of what goes on reading lists, how and what we teach, how to approach knowledge and so on. They push academics to think through course design and teaching anew. They have also spurred experimentation in teaching practice. The growing publication of the details of such experiments enables widespread awareness and may prompt further experimentation. This may result in radical courses or courses that push students and teachers in important ways, even if broader curricula remain resistant (sometimes, although not always, with good reason). Even if academics continue to teach what they do, the calls to decolonize require them to justify their choices, and that is a good thing.

However, I also suggest that it is important to adopt a sympathetic attitude of reticence and dissidence to such calls (Gerber, discussed in chapter 2). This is partly because many calls to decolonize teaching are general and not specifically applicable to anthropology, which has its own discipline-specific challenges and responses. Further, if we think of decolonization as a process and not as a clearly articulated destination, we can learn from diverse articulations of what it means to decolonize while bringing tools from anthropology and ethnography to bear on and shape this process. This might mean challenging some decolonizing/decoloniality agendas while remaining fully alive to anthropology's own colonial past and current inequities, and attempting to be and do better as anthropologists. Finally, even as some forms of decolonization might seek the 'dismantling of the master's house', it is important to recognize that students who seek to study anthropology want more than a sustained critical scrutiny of the discipline and its colonial legacies, important though these are. They also want to learn how to ask anthropological questions, how the particular questions that we recognize as anthropological have come to take the forms they have, and what they themselves can do with anthropology to understand about, participate in and shape the world. In that sense, we have to be committed to teaching anthropology, both how it has come to be what it is and what it can be. This does not mean brushing under the carpet colonial legacies or current inequities. But it does mean showing what anthropology can and does (or cannot and does not) do in the world today, and how it can shed light on diverse forms of human meaning-making projects and the world in which these projects come to take the forms they do. After all, there is a reason why we continue to call ourselves anthropologists, dissatisfied though we might be with aspects of it and thus striving to make anthropology do and be better.

–8–
Conclusion

Olúfẹ́mi O. Táíwò (2022) argues that we need to think about two things when trying to make things better. The first concerns what is going on in the room that needs to change. How do people enter the room? Who has captured the room, and how might such capture be undone? The second is the relation between the room and the outside. How do people in the room inform what is outside, how do they understand what is going on outside, and what should or can they do about it? I find this a very useful way to think about both the internal make-up of anthropology as an academic discipline and anthropology's relationship to the world. It is these two questions that the book has tried to address.

Let us begin by focusing on what is inside the room, with some slight modifications. First, rather than being a room, anthropology is more like a house with many rooms. Within this house some rooms may be big and some small, some more open to the outside and some more closed in. Different rooms are devoted to different purposes and have gatekeepers. Calls to decolonize offer a way of redrawing the relationship between the rooms. They focus on the walls that close the house and divide it into rooms. They ask who is allowed into the biggest and grandest rooms, and who perforce remains in smaller, less well-connected ones. They also ask about the relationship between the rooms, and about which have money, resources and opportunities pouring in and which do not. How does this affect who is heard and who goes unheard? How do race and location pattern these things? To what extent are these colonial legacies?

It is these last two questions that bring the above into the purview of decolonization. The argument is that these patterns are a continuation of the European colonization of large tracts of the world from the fifteenth century onwards, and the elevation of Europe and whiteness in practically every subsequent endeavour. If this is to change, decolonizers argue, colonial patterns and legacies need to be undone. The house needs to be re-imagined and rebuilt. And the tools for this work need to be chosen selectively and judiciously from not only anthropology but also other relevant scholarship. These tools can build the house in a more just way. They include, but are not restricted to, Indigenous studies, Black studies, feminist scholarship, gender studies, queer studies and other critical/radical disciplines that interrogate diverse inequities, exclusions and unjust arrangements and seek to change the status quo. They also need to draw from those not identified as scholars but who can teach, through their own experiences and knowledges, what anthropology could be and do for them. Thus, those who focus on the decolonization of anthropology argue that ethnography, the main anthropological method, also needs to be reshaped as an ethically motivated enterprise that serves to benefit the people among whom the anthropologist conducts research, rather than only the anthropologist and anthropology. This includes both ethnographic research and writing.

Decolonizers also call for other changes within anthropology, among them reappraisals of the discipline's development to date. These include the foregrounding of scholars who, they argue, have been unjustly pushed to anthropology's margins because their bodies and scholarship challenge the comfortable whiteness of the discipline. How might anthropology have developed, they ask, if anthropologists had paid attention to African-American scholars in early twentieth-century United States and, later, to their analyses of race, which include the ignorance obscuring the vision of those who claim the privileged centre, leaving them to both be and set the norm? Would the discipline have spent so long on concepts that circle around race (such as culture) rather than confronting it head-on as a set of categories systematized to maintain and further white dominance? Would anthropology have been a more effective ally in attempts to obtain racial and other forms of justice? What can redressing these past exclusions and neglects teach contemporary anthropologists about what they and anthropology can do not only to rectify various wrongs in the discipline's own practice but also in attempts to build more just presents and futures, both locally and more generally? Decolonization thus extends outwards, from a focus on the house to a focus on the world. And, because the term is everywhere right now, its usages have become diverse and somewhat unwieldy.

Accordingly, I began this book with the term 'decolonization' and its polysemous nature. Too much seems to be packed into this word, some of it contradictory. Consequently, I have argued that it is imperative to figure out what we mean when we use it. I thus surveyed diverse uses of the term, and of the related but qualitatively different term 'decoloniality'. This survey reveals a number of things. First, the term 'decolonization' needs to be qualified in ways that recognize the multiplicity of colonial forms and their effects in different parts of the world, including the metropole, which I also understand (following Nandy 1998 [1983]) as post-colonial and profoundly shaped by colonization. Decolonization work will perforce look different in different places. India, for instance, does not have the same histories of slavery as the Americas, but Indian indentured labourers throughout the British Empire nevertheless faced harsh, brutal conditions (see, for example, Bahadur 2013). Race, then, is not a dominant focus *in* post-colonial India, unlike, for instance, in the Americas. Nor do Indigenous struggles play out there in the same ways as they do in settler states. These differences matter in preventing scholarship from ending up with forms of recolonization produced by powerful decolonization moves from the centres of anthropological production – in the anglophone world, mainly the United States.

There are, however, some common themes that cut across diverse settings. Many of these may be identified as based on the *logic of the colonizer*, that is, the definition of a centre and the subordination to its purposes of all that is not understood as the centre. I have addressed these themes by building on vocabularies and conceptual frameworks other than, although inspired by the larger term of, decolonization. These include Achille Mbembe's term 'disenclosure' (2021) as developed by Schalk Hendrik Gerber (2018).[1] Disenclosure refers to the dismantling of the logic of the colonizer by the removal of ways of thinking, knowing and being that divide people from one another, pushing some to the margins and reproducing the interests of those in the centre. The point, Gerber argues, is not to construct a new centre but rather to keep the space of the centre open, difficult though this may be. This means that ways need to be found of being *with* others in the world in ways that promote equity and justice without eliminating difference. To think through what this could look like, I drew on Silvia Rivera Cusicanqui's conceptualization of the motley (2020). This is a generous and rigorous concept. It offers a way to think about how to build something new from and with difference, rather than collapsing or papering away differences. It keeps open the possibility of conflict (it is hard to live with some fundamental differences) and also that of domestication, that is, it eschews the temptation to radicalize difference, asking how things become other than they were. This kind of approach prevents re-enclosure through insistence on authenticity or essentialisms, a point I also draw from Olúfẹ́mi Táíwò (2022). The post-colonial world is a motley kind of world, and it is important to appreciate and work with it. This does not mean eschewing universalist ideals of equity or justice or aims of liberation, but it does mean recognizing their provisional nature and remaining attentive to and making room for new forms in the process of articulation and struggle. The question throughout is what to do with colonial legacies. Might it be useful to treat them, as Benoît de L'Estoile argues (2008), not as testaments but as arrangements and as somewhat poisoned gifts to be engaged, discarded or reshaped?

These concepts, I suggest, work well in rethinking and rebuilding the house of anthropology, including the relations within and between its rooms. Some of this may not happen; resources are too concentrated in certain places, and so too is the power to shape the discipline and the potential to abuse that power. This distorts the practice of anthropology. These issues, as others have indicated, need sorting out, although it is hard to know how in some global way. What primarily needs to be done, though, is changing harmful cultures internal to the practice of anthropology, including, but not restricted to, racism and other forms of privilege-based inequities.

I refer to anthropology as a practice following Alasdair MacIntyre. MacIntyre defines a practice as a complex, coherent form of socially established activity, the internal rewards of which are only achievable through participation in that activity. As people engage in the practice, it is extended (1981: 30). What this means is that the practice has no clear end point and, so long as it maintains its core coherence, it can morph in different ways. One thing about a practice in this sense is that it is worth doing for its own sake. What is it that each of us finds worthwhile about participating in the practice of anthropology, and how can we best enable these different forms of disciplinary participation? I follow Marilyn Strathern's definition of a discipline as 'a body of data, a set of methods, a field of problematics; it is also a bundle of yardsticks, that is, criteria for evaluating products and maintaining standards' (2006: 199). That is, participation in the discipline is subject to these criteria, but this does not mean that they cannot change or be challenged. This is key. Disciplines, Strathern argues, renew themselves through disagreement. Such a renewal may take the form of refusing to name a centre, and keeping alive a much more motley practice through intra- and interdisciplinary conversations that refresh and extend it.

The above definition of a discipline is why, when encountering work to be begun or carried on under the aegis of anthropology, we ask: Is this anthropological? What is the contribution to anthropology? Reasoned answers to these questions can show how they speak to anthropological data and concerns and shape new directions for the discipline, based on, and refining, existing tools and methods. This extends the practice and, like all disciplinary work, invites engagement and critique. But these questions and critique need to begin from the basic assumption that all practitioners of anthropology are accorded equitable belonging and deserve to be taken seriously as members of a community of critics. This cannot happen if conditions of epistemological, epistemic or other forms of injustice prevail.

Indeed, the commitment to epistemic and epistemological justice must mark all scholarship. This includes rigorously examining the underlying assumptions and methods of scholarly knowledge production, giving credit where credit is due, remaining accountable for the selection and treatment of sources, claims and arguments, and addressing objections and disagreements, including from research participants and fellow practitioners. Where these conditions are not fulfilled, we can assert that injustice has been committed. I argued in chapter 4 that the corpus of scholarship naming and redressing injustices of this kind is growing, especially with regard to the colonial period and in thrall to colonial logics. Some of this corpus names itself as 'decolonizing' while other scholarship does not. However, their aims are similar: to promote justice and produce work that is not oriented towards furthering the interests of privilege-based groups.

In anthropology, in addition to the above, the promotion of justice has increasingly taken the form of calls for work that are explicitly oriented towards furthering the aims of research participants. Where research participants articulate clear aims for the research, with which the anthropologist agrees and also has the necessary competencies to support, this can work well while also extending the practice of anthropology and generating anthropological knowledge. However, not all research is conducted with people who need such support (that among elites, for example), and disagreements may also exist between research participants' and the anthropologist's own political or other convictions. Such work is no less necessary, nor does it demand lower standards of epistemic or epistemological justice. It may even reveal epistemic standpoints that complicate straightforward divisions between oppressors and oppressed. It may shift discussions away from divisions based on geopolitical terms (global North/global South) to more nuanced discussions of the one-third and the two-thirds, distributed around the world in diverse and unstable ways (Mohanty 2003). Intellectual goals – goals aimed at understanding something for its own sake or for advancing disciplinary thinking – are also no less important. Tying disciplinary work too narrowly to impacts can, in the long run, impoverish the discipline. Indeed, even in conflictual or unsatisfactory situations, understanding, and communicating this understanding, might, as Ghassan Hage argues, be the best contribution an academic can make *as an academic* (2000 [1998]: 21).

One area in which such a contribution can be made is that of ignorance, a topic of growing interest in various fields including anthropology. White ignorance has been theorized by Mills (2017) as playing an important role in masking the workings of privilege, in particular (although not only) from the privileged themselves. Mills argues, therefore, that it is important to take ignorance and its effects as seriously as knowledge and its effects. His reason is normative; he seeks to understand, unmask and thence dispel false knowledge based on ignorance. This kind of approach to ignorance has informed anti-racist work, including within anthropology. Equally, as High, Kelly and Mair (2012) propose, we might want more nuanced approaches to ignorance, not only in terms of self-protective ignorers, but as something actively sought or manufactured, even as constitutive of personhood. Anthropological methods and tools lend themselves well to studying ignorance and ignoring and can reveal, among other things, why projects of decolonization can meet fierce resistance from those who wish to reproduce the status quo or to tame demands for change. Equally, it may reveal other kinds of stresses, strains and desires that escape the decolonization lens but might be significant. This type of scholarship can make the kind of academic contribution that Hage argues is important in informing activist attempts to promote justice.

The final two chapters turn to the university and to teaching anthropology. Universities, of course, have been a prime focus of calls to decolonize, although some scholars are not sure this is possible. Kehinde Andrews, Professor of Black Studies at Birmingham City University in the United Kingdom, argues that 'It's uncomfortable to think that our role essentially helps to maintain racial oppression, because that's what the university does. But if we think about it differently, that role allows us to do things that can really be liberatory' (cited in Hill 2002).

While I do not go as far as Andrews in my understanding of universities, it is in line with the university pessimism that many decolonizing scholars evince. My own argument is somewhat different: there is definitely a need to reform universities and make them more equitable. But we have to understand their diverse workings first. Accordingly, chapter 6 argued for the deployment of critical approaches, tools and methods developed in anthropology to study universities – both particular universities and the global university form. Where data exist, we should mine them and we should flesh out these data through ethnographic and other means to try and enable a positive difference, especially with regard to racial and other inequities. Such a difference may or may not fall within the broader rubric of decolonization as currently and variously conceived, and it may also reveal fractures in approaches to universities evinced by different kinds of people identifiable as colonialism's others. Indeed, the term may be co-opted and tamed by institutions, especially around questions of assessment and attainment, and require critical appraisal. Chapter 7, then, turned to calls to decolonize and to the responses from anthropology, especially with regard to teaching.

I argued that students come to anthropology to learn how to think with it and do things with it, and we have to be committed to teaching them the potential of the discipline, alongside pointing out its blind spots. Statistically speaking, a very small number of undergraduates will become academic anthropologists, but whatever they do may remain informed by anthropology – its critical approaches, research methods and conceptual tools. Teaching, then, can extend the tools and methods of anthropology into the world alongside research and publication. It can make a difference in unexpected ways. A former student, Charlotte Antilogus, who was part of this book's workshops, is now employed in a community union as a fieldworker. The aim of the union is to encourage renters on housing estates to push collectively for better conditions for renters as well as build up other shared competencies and resources.[2] Charlotte tells of how she has to engage with some people's understanding that it is immigration that causes problems with housing in order to build common cause about the predicaments of renting that are faced by everyone in these low-income areas. Having studied anthropology and being able to think about this work as partly ethnographic and partly applied helps, she says. This kind of work reveals the importance of holding back on identifying all knowledge (e.g., of immigrants as the source of problems) as valid, while paying attention to how and why people know certain things, and then working with them to generate new knowledge that shapes a different and more equitable world. This is the promise of applied anthropology outside the university.

Olúfẹ́mi O. Táíwò (2022) argues that sometimes people in the room can get too caught up with what is wrong with the room and with their attempts to fix it. They expend so much energy on fixing the room that they forget that, really, the room mirrors the problems in the world, and what they are trying to do is rebuild the world or a part of it that concerns them. The point is to not stop trying to fix the room; however, this may not happen completely satisfactorily, and we have to understand why. Likewise, scholarship and teaching on their own cannot change deep structural and systemic inequalities and injustices, but they can get people thinking together about them in ways that open up the possibilities of challenge and change. And scholars can take what they have learned out into the world.

Thus, Kehinde Andrews argues that the real work of Black emancipation and education happens outside the university, albeit drawing on work that is produced within. He talks about the centrality of 'community activism, community work, and especially community education' in Black Studies (in Hill 2002). Aditya Chakraborty (2018) describes community economics courses organized by the charity Economy (now People's Economy),[3] wherein university-trained (sometimes academic) economists present formal economics models to be discussed (torn apart, even) by interested lay participants who try to understand the relationship between these models and their lives. The aim is to build other models that work for them and to see whether they can be enacted. A PhD student at Manchester, Elsayed Abdelhamid, studies the work of Al Sharq Academia based in Istanbul, which commissions academics from different universities to produce and teach free online courses relevant to the Middle East and North Africa region to students, activists and others from that region.[4] In other words, academic knowledge produced in universities can inform teaching outside universities – we can take the university outside the university and render its forms of knowledge useful, usable and vulnerable.

Even as we try to rebuild the house of anthropology, conduct research or teach in more equitable, even liberatory, ways, it is also worth asking how anthropologists can engage, not as teachers, but as co-participants in a motley world outside these practices. As anthropologists, we are trained in ethnographic methods, to suspend belief or disbelief and to listen and understand, to do things with people and to see what that doing does. We are exposed to a huge number of ways of knowing the world and being in it. We are trained to engage these critically and to try to analyse how things work, which things work, why and why not, and what else happens that is not intended. We are also trained to put things together that do not, at first glance, seem to fit together and to place things occurring at different scales in conversation with each other. These are skills we can put to good use in interactions with others – not only students or research participants – to build a shared, if not always harmonious, world.

A colleague, Michelle Obeid, used to run a book club in Manchester's Central Library whose members – anyone who was interested – read novels written by Middle Eastern writers. The idea was to explore the world as understood and written about by people from a different part of it. I am a regular (and am now conducting research) at a local community philosophy group, which gathers weekly to discuss topics chosen in advance by members, for example, 'Is anti-whiteness destroying British society?' and 'What is reason?' The group, mainly comprising white men, tries to think through these kinds of question from different perspectives. Some of the topics are supercharged. Everyone has a say. There is no deference, only attention and sometimes engagement. I sometimes speak as an anthropologist, sometimes as a female, sometimes as a local resident, sometimes as someone who grew up in India . . . And, all the time, like everyone else in the space, I am struggling to figure something out by taking other people's points of view into consideration. I take this as the ethos of friendship (Davé 2015): a commitment to making something more of ourselves *with* others.

The point I want to make is that we can take the stuff we have learned as professional scholars and put it out there in the world for people to do with what they will. This is not as experts who teach or publish (although these things are crucial) but as participants in conversations. When we fixate on 'the discipline' as a thing with clear boundaries that is located in one place – the university – and takes from another – the field – with definite raced hierarchies and presumptions of authority, we miss these other ways of doing anthropology. These things are true, the problems are real, but they are not all there is. As Naisargi Davé argued in the 2022 Manchester debate on decolonization (Davé 2024), life goes on outside of the particular concerns that absorb us, and we can participate in this life with our anthropological (as well as other) sensibilities.

None of this amounts to saying that all that is needed is more public engagement. Rather, the research, scholarship, publication and teaching that anthropologists do are crucial to the practice of the discipline. These need to be rigorously scrutinized, with justice, courage and honesty, and problems addressed not only within the house of anthropology but in relation to everyone who contributes in diverse ways to the making of anthropological knowledge. If anthropology wants to remain a lively and relevant discipline in and beyond the space of the university, it needs to keep asking questions of itself and responding to these. Equally, it is important to hold on to the fact that we (whoever 'we' are) chose to be anthropologists and, if the reasons for that choice continue to hold, it is worth fighting to shape a better practice both for ourselves as participants in the practice and as students of and actors in the world. This must mean, among other things, resisting the reproduction of the logic of the colonizer, but it also involves naming and addressing a host of inequities and exclusions. We may want to call this decolonization, or we may, like Tuck and Yang (2012), want to resist metaphorical usages of the term. The point is that building a better world and a better anthropology will always be an ongoing and unfinished task. Even as some form of emancipatory closure is achieved, new challenges will emerge. We need to be open to understanding and engaging these, as well as remaining open to how we understand older and enduring challenges. That self-critical openness is at the very heart of scholarship.

Stefan Collini argues that '[t]he default condition of the scholar is one of intellectual dissatisfaction . . . one can never (and perhaps should never) entirely banish the sense that the current state of one's work can only ever have the status of an interim report, always vulnerable to being challenged, corrected or simply bypassed' (2012: 66).

I have learned a lot from writing this book. I have read, benefited from discussions and struggled to overcome my own preconceptions as I have tried to think through the decolonization of anthropology carefully and well. I am not yet fully there in my thinking and knowing, but that is always the way. I now leave it open to engagement and critique.

Notes

Chapter 1 Introduction: Decolonizing Anthropology and a Decolonizing Anthropology
1. https://www.cusas.socanth.cam.ac.uk/decolonising-anthropology/

Chapter 2 What is Decolonization?
1. https://www.historians.org/publications-and-directories/perspectives-on-history/october-2015/a-typology-of-colonialism
2. https://www.theelephant.info/reflections/2019/02/08/decolonising-my-soul-my-journey-to-reclaim-african-spirituality/
3. https://wangui.org/bio/
4. For a detailed annotated bibliography of engagement with questions around coloniality and decoloniality, see the Oxford bibliographic entry on the topics: https://www.oxfordbibliographies.com/display/document/obo-9780199766581/obo-9780199766581-0017.xml#obo-9780199766581-0017-bibItem-0026
5. I have not read the book since and imagine that I would respond to it rather differently now.
6. https://www.youtube.com/watch?v=jKI0IJY5jp8
7. Neither Ngũgĩ nor wa Thiong'o is his 'last name' in the western sense. He returned to the traditional Gikuyi form of his name, which roughly means 'Ngũgĩ son of Thiong'o'. He is referred to on his own website as Ngũgĩ: https://ngugiwathiongo.com/
8. Macaulay's Minute on Education is worth reading in full and can be found at http://www.columbia.edu/itc/mealac/pritchett/00generallinks/macaulay/txt_minute_education_1835.html

9 I thank Molly Geidel, Rivera Cusicanqui's translator (2020) for confirming my understanding of her vision.
10 Ferguson argues that those on the receiving end of these migrations may well have seen them as a 'white plague' (2004: 54).
11 Somewhat confusingly, there are two scholars with very similar names: Olúfẹ́mi Táíwò and Olúfẹ́mi O. Táíwò. I engage work by both in this book.

Chapter 3 Colonialism–Anthropology

1 However, see the recent AHRC project on early Indian anthropologists: https://www.ed.ac.uk/history-classics-archaeology/research/about/research-projects/other-from-within-indian-anthropologists
2 Similar moves have been made in sociology, based on the work of W. E. B. Du Bois, now increasingly hailed as the father of American sociology and founder of the Atlanta School of Sociology. Du Bois's works on the plight of African Americans, whiteness and urban sociology are now fully acknowledged as key contributions to the discipline and as pivotal in its decolonization. See Burawoy (2021); also Meghji (2021).
3 Summarized in Aidid's article, available at: https://africasacountry.com/2015/03/can-the-somali-speak-cadaanstudies
4 Tobin capitalizes 'Native' throughout and I maintain this style when writing about Hawaiians.

Chapter 4 Epistemological and Epistemic Justice

1 The title is clearly a riff on Niall Ferguson's controversial book *Empire: How Britain Made the Modern World* (2004).
2 Nuno Palma, an economist of early modern Europe (e.g., Palma 2016) to whom I took these figures, cautioned me that they seemed a bit exaggerated. But even if the numbers are halved, the colonies were still making a significant contribution to British economic growth. I also thank Juan Manuel del Nido, who helped me parse unfamiliar economic terms in Mukherjee's paper.
3 Sanghera attributes this statement to Ambalavaner Sivanandan, the Sri Lankan Tamil and British writer who was director of the Institute of Race Relations (London) and editor of the journal *Race* (later *Race and Class*). Sanghera also refers to the remark by British-Nigerian historian David Olusoga: 'If you don't want Nigerians in the UK all you need to do is go back to the nineteenth century and persuade the Victorians not to invade Nigeria' (Sanghera 2021: 69).

4 Sanghera cites historian David Starkey who, addressing a teachers' conference in 2011, said that 'Britain is a white monoculture and schools should focus on our own history' (Sanghera 2021: 78).
5 For just a small sample, see Herbert S. Lewis (2021), Charles Menzies (2021), Ira Bashkow (2023) and David Stoll (2023).

Chapter 5 Ignorance and Ignoring

1 https://www.dailymail.co.uk/news/article-7910667/Laurence-Fox-slams-Oscar-winning-director-Sam-Mendes-incongruous-Sikh-soldier-1917.html
2 https://www.spectator.co.uk/article/laurence-fox-s-clumsy-criticism-of-1917-is-good-for-british-sikhs
3 https://metro.co.uk/2020/01/21/laurence-fox-claims-sikh-soldier-sam-mendes-war-eProdcpic-1917-forcing-diversity-viewers-12093965/
4 https://www.ukip.org/
5 Rhodes's will is reproduced in Stead (1902). The volume also contains chapters on his political and religious ideas, partly based on his speeches and correspondence, both collated and written by Stead, an ardent Rhodes admirer.
6 https://www.bbc.co.uk/news/uk-england-oxfordshire-57175057
7 https://www.oriel.ox.ac.uk/about/the-rhodes-legacy/
8 https://www.independent.co.uk/news/education/education-news/mary-beard-says-drive-to-remove-cecil-rhodes-statue-from-oxford-university-is-a-dangerous-attempt-to-erase-the-past-a6783306.html
9 https://www.theguardian.com/world/2020/jun/18/rhodes-statue-tech-boss-pledges-to-cover-funds-pulled-by-racist-donors
10 The letters are available at https://www.oliveschreiner.org/vre?page=295

Chapter 6 Understanding and Transforming Universities: The Potential of Ethnography and Anthropology

1 https://www.ons.gov.uk/peoplepopulationandcommunity/birthsdeathsandmarriages/livebirths/articles/howhasthestudentpopulationchanged/2016-09-20
2 https://www.timeshighereducation.com/press-releases/global-universities-address-gender-equality-gaps-remain-be-closed
3 https://www.hesa.ac.uk/news/16-01-2020/sb255-higher-education-student-statistics/numbers

4 https://www.ethnicity-facts-figures.service.gov.uk/education-skills-and-training/higher-education/first-year-entrants-onto-undergraduate-degrees/latest
5 https://www.ethnicity-facts-figures.service.gov.uk/
6 https://www.equityinhighered.org/indicators/enrollment-in-undergraduate-education/race-and-ethnicity-of-u-s-undergraduates/. Although, see Hartigan (2005) on issues with self-identification in the United States, particularly in the census.
7 https://www.wits.ac.za/about-wits/quick-stats/
8 https://www.gov.za/about-sa/south-africas-people#people
9 For example, Eugene Richardson describes a donation made by John A. Paulson, the single largest shareholder of AngloGold Ashanti. Of the more than US$1.5 billion-worth of gold mined by the company in Tanzania between 2000 and 2007, only 9% remained in the country as royalties and taxes. Paulson's gift of US$400 million to Harvard University's John A. Paulson School of Engineering and Applied Sciences was the largest in the university's history (Richardson 2020: 99–100). This kind of donation is not restricted to Harvard, of course.
10 Not all challenges are aimed at raising consciousness, broadening the curriculum or opening it up to include hitherto neglected fields, scholars or perspectives. Authoritarian, majoritarian or nativist impulses may actively seek to narrow the curriculum and force exclusions of further specific ideologies. See, for example, Nandini Sundar and Gowhar Fazili's 2020 status report on academic freedom in India.
11 https://www.universitiesuk.ac.uk/sites/default/files/field/downloads/2021-07/bame-student-attainment.pdf

Chapter 7 On Courses and in Classes
1 The students were Tom Boyd, Oluwatamilore (Tammie) Clinton, Nancy Corgnale, Jared Davis, Samantha Diefenbacher, Claudia Eggart, Alyssa Erspamer, Lucy Evans, Andrea Lopez Garza, Celie Hanson, Rebecca Higginbottom, Regina Ho, Jade Isaacs, Esther Jones, Ananya Kaul, Rebecca Langella, Michaella Lawrence, Thomas Long, Tashinga Matewe, Annabel McCosker, Carola Ludovica Giannotti Mura, Maria Obrebska, Julia Perczel, Nanditha Plakazhi, Niya Pozharlieva, Angela Cardenas Sanchez, Emily Storey, Isabel Sturges, Samuel Tettner, Judy Thorne, Matilda Trevitt, Toby Walkland, Cassandra Watson and Sorrel Wilson.

2 https://thealternativereadinglistproject.wordpress.com/anthropology/
3 I myself came to Zora Neale Hurston because of my work on English libertarians and also via following up on Rose Wilder Lane, who was a silent co-author of her mother Laura Ingalls Wilder's widely loved but deeply problematic books, retrospectively written about her childhood as a pioneer's daughter, including *Little House on the Prairie* (1935). In that sense, I knew her first as a founding libertarian. See also Bieto and Bieto (2008).
4 We should not take this privilege to change or even radically re-haul our readings lists lightly. As noted earlier, governments can and do try to override academic decisions about what goes on such lists. I have also met anthropologists from different parts of the world who are told they are to teach from set textbooks, with little or no scope for deviation.

Chapter 8 Conclusion
1 The dates are explained by the fact that Gerber draws on Mbembe's earlier work on disenclosure, including in French. I have drawn on work translated later into English.
2 https://www.acorntheunion.org.uk/
3 https://peopleseconomyuk.org/what-were-building/
4 https://academia.sharqforum.org/en/about-us

References

Achebe, Chinua. 1997 [1965]. English and the African Writer. *Transition* 75/76: 342–9.
Agnihotri, Rama Kant. 2015. Constituent Assembly Debates on Language. *Economic and Political Weekly* 50(8): 47–56.
Ahmed, Sara. 2012. *On Being Included: Racism and Diversity in Institutional Life*. Durham: Duke University Press.
Alcoff, Linda Martin. 2015. *The Future of Whiteness*. Cambridge: Polity.
Alexander, Claire and Arday, Jason (eds). 2015. *Aiming Higher: Race, Inequality and Diversity in the Academy*. London: Runnymede Trust.
Allen, Jafari Sinclaire and Jobson, Ryan Cecil. 2016. The Decolonizing Generation: (Race and) Theory in Anthropology since the Eighties. *Current Anthropology* 57(2): 129–48.
Alonso Bejarano, Carolina, Mijangos García, Mirian A., López Juárez, Lucia and Goldstein, Daniel. 2019. *Decolonizing Ethnography: Undocumented Migrants and New Directions in Social Science*. Durham: Duke University Press.
Anderson, Kirk R. 2021. Ethnography and the University: Current Trends and Future Directions. *International Journal of Qualitative Studies in Education* 36(9): 1809–24.
Appadurai, Arjun. 2021. Beyond Domination: The Future and Past of Decolonization. *The Nation*, 9 March. https://www.thenation.com/article/world/achille-mbembe-walter-mignolo-catherine-walsh-decolonization/

Appiah, Kwame Anthony. 2021. Digging for Utopia. *New York Review*, 16 December. https://www.nybooks.com/articles/2021/12/16/david-graeber-digging-for-utopia/?lp_txn_id=1519747

Arday, Jason, Branchu, Charlotte and Boliver, Vikki. 2022. What Do We Know About Black and Minority Ethnic (BAME) Participation in UK Higher Education? *Social Policy and Society* 21(1): 12–25.

Asad, Talal. 1973. *Anthropology and the Colonial Encounter*. Amherst: Humanity Books.

Asad, Talal. 1983. Anthropological Conceptions of Religion: Reflections on Geertz. *Man*. New Series 18(2): 237–59.

Asher, Kiran. 2013. Latin American Decolonial Thought, or Making the Subaltern Speak. *Geography Compass* 7(12): 832–42.

BAAS (British Association for the Advancement of Science). 1874. *Notes and Queries on Anthropology*. London: Edward Stanford.

Bahadur, Gaiutra. 2013. *Coolie Woman: The Odyssey of Indenture*. London: C. Hurst and Co.

Baker, Lee D. 2021. The Racist Anti-Racism of American Anthropology. *Transforming Anthropology* 29(2): 127–42.

Baldwin, James and Mead, Margaret. 1972. *A Rap on Race*. London: Corgi Books. Excerpt available on YouTube: https://www.youtube.com/watch?v=3WNO6f7rjE0

Ball, Philip. 2022. Imperialism's Long Shadow: The UK Universities Grappling with a Colonial Past. *Nature*, 19 October. https://www.nature.com/articles/d41586-022-03253-y

Ballakrishnen, Swethaa S. 2021. *Accidental Feminism: Gender Parity and Selective Mobility among India's Professional Elite*. Princeton: Princeton University Press.

Barth, Fredrik. 2005. Britain and the Commonwealth, in Fredrik Barth, Andre Gingrich, Robert Parkin and Sydel Silverman, *One Discipline, Four Ways: British, German, French, and American Anthropology. The Halle Lectures*. Chicago: University of Chicago Press, 3–57.

Bashkow, Ira. 2023. There's More to Anthropology's Past than Most of Us Know. *American Anthropologist* 125(1): 177–80.

Baviskar, Amita. 2023. Decolonizing a Discipline in Distress. *American Ethnologist* 50(3): 387–95. Forum: Decolonizing Anthropology: Global Perspectives: 1–9. https://doi.org/10.1111/amet.13197

Beliso-De Jesús, Aisha. 2020. The Jungle Academy: Molding White Supremacy in American Police Recruits. *American Anthropologist* (Special Section: Anthropology and White Supremacy) 122(1): 143–56.

Beliso-De Jesús, Aisha and Pierre, Jemima (eds). 2020. *American Anthropologist* (Special Section: Anthropology and White Supremacy) 122(1): 65–162.

Beliso-De Jesús, Aisha, Pierre, Jemima and Rana, Junaid. 2023. White Supremacy and the Making of Anthropology. *Annual Review of Anthropology* 52: 417–35.

Betts, Raymond F. 2012. Decolonization: A Brief History of the Word, in Els Bogaerts and Remco Raben (eds), *Beyond Empire and Nation: The Decolonization of African and Asian Societies, 1930s–1970s*. Leiden and Oxford: Brill, 24–39.

Bhambra, Gurminder K. 2021. Decolonising Critical Theory? Epistemological Justice, Progress, Reparations. *Critical Times* 4(1): 73–89.

Bhambra, Gurminder K. 2022. Relations of Extraction, Relations of Redistribution: Empire, Nation and the Construction of the British Welfare State. *British Journal of Sociology* 73: 4–15.

Bhambra, Gurminder K., Gebrial, Dalia and Nisancioglu, Kerem. 2018. *Decolonising the University*. London: Pluto Press.

Bieto, David T. and Bieto, Linda Royster. 2008. Isabel Paterson, Rose Wilder Lane and Zora Neale Hurston on War, Race, the State and Liberty. *Independent Review* 12(4): 553–73.

Blum, Susan D. (ed.). 2020. *Ungrading: Why Rating Students Undermines Learning (and What to Do Instead)*. Morgantown: West Virginia University Press.

Boidin, Capucine, Cohen, James and Grosfoguel, Ramón. 2012. Introduction: From University to Plurality: A Decolonial Approach to the Present Crisis of Western Universities. *Human Architecture: Journal of the Sociology of Self Knowledge* X(1) Article 2: 1–10.

Boyer, Dominic. 2005. Visiting Knowledge in Anthropology: An Introduction. *Ethnos* 70(2): 141–8.

Brown, Richard. 1973. Godfrey Wilson and the RLI, in Talal Asad (ed.), *Anthropology and the Colonial Encounter*. Amherst: Humanity Books, 173–98.

Buell, Rebecca Renee, Burns, Samuel Raymond, Chen, Zhuo et al. 2018. Decanonizing Anthropology: Reworking the History of Social Theory for 21st Century Anthropology: A Syllabus Project. https://footnotesblogcom.wordpress.com/2019/02/15/decanonizing-anthropology/

Burawoy, Michael. 2016. Sociology as a Vocation. *American Sociological Association* 45(4): 379–93.

Burawoy, Michael. 2021. Decolonizing Sociology: The Significance of W. E. B. Du Bois. *Critical Sociology* 47(4–5): 545–54.

Campbell, Emahunn Raheem Ali. 2012. A Critique of the Occupy Movement from a Black Occupier. *Black Scholar* 41(4): 42–51.

Carey, Grace A. 2019. Anthropology's 'Repugnant Others'. *American Ethnologist*, 23 April. http://americanethnologist.org/features/reflections/anthropologys-repugnant-others

Castagno, Angela. 2008. 'I Don't Want to Hear That!' Legitimating Whiteness through Silence in Schools. *Anthropology and Education Quarterly* 39(3): 314–33.

Chakrabarty, Dipesh. 2000. *Provincializing Europe: Postcolonial Thought and Historical Difference*. Princeton: Princeton University Press.

Chakraborty, Aditya. 2018. What Happens When Ordinary People Learn Economics? *Guardian*, 20 June. https://www.theguardian.com/commentisfree/2018/jun/20/ordinary-people-learn-economics-manchester-classes

Chakravarti, Ananya. 2019. Caste Wasn't a British Construct – and Anyone Who Studies History Should Know That. *The Wire*, 30 June. https://thewire.in/caste/caste-history-postcolonial-studies

Chantiluke, Roseanne, Kwoba, Brian and Nkopo, Athinangamso (eds). 2018. *Rhodes Must Fall: The Struggle to Decolonise the Racist Heart of Empire*. London: Zed Books.

Chibnik, Michael. 2014. From the Editor: Gender and Citations in 'American Anthropologist'. *American Anthropologist* 116(3): 493–96.

Chua, Liana. 2009. To Know or Not to Know? Practices of Knowledge and Ignorance among Bidayuhs in an 'Impurely' Christian World. *Journal of the Royal Anthropological Institute* 15(2): 332–48.

Chua, Liana and Mathur, Nayanika (eds). 2018. *Who Are 'We'? Reimagining Alterity and Affinity in Anthropology*. Oxford: Berghahn.

Clammer, John. 1973. Colonialism and the Perception of Tradition in Fiji, in Talal Asad (ed.), *Anthropology and the Colonial Encounter*. Amherst: Humanity Books, 199–222.

Clifford, James and Marcus, George E. 1986. *Writing Culture: The Poetics and Politics of Ethnography*. Berkeley: University of California Press.

Cohen, Robin. 2020. Falling Statues and Morality. Oxford and Colonialism Project, University of Oxford. https://oxfordandcolonialism.web.ox.ac.uk/article/falling-statues-and-morality-cecil-rhodes-cant-be-rescued-history

Cohn, Bernard S. 1987. The Census, Social Structure and Objectification in South Asia. In *An Anthropologist among the Historians and Other Essays*. New Delhi: Oxford University Press, 224–54.

Collini, Stefan. 2012. *What are Universities For?* London: Penguin.

Comaroff, Jean and Comaroff, John L. 1991 and 1997. *Of Revelation and Revolution*. Vol. 1 (1991), *Christianity, Colonialism and Consciousness in South Africa*; and Vol. 2 (1997), *The Dialectics of Modernity on a South African? Frontier*. Chicago: University of Chicago Press.

Comaroff, Jean and Comaroff, John L. 2012. *Theory from the South: Or, How Euro-America is Evolving towards Africa*. New York: Routledge.

Crick, Malcolm. 1982. Anthropology of Knowledge. *Annual Review of Anthropology* 11: 287–313.

D'Andrade, Roy. 1995. Moral Models in Anthropology. *Current Anthropology* 36(3): 399–408.

Das, Veena. 2012. Ordinary Ethics, in Didier Fassin (ed.), *A Companion to Moral Anthropology*. Oxford: Wiley Blackwell, 133–49.

Daswani, Girish. 2021. The (Im)possibility of Decolonizing Anthropology. *Everyday Orientalism.* https://everydayorientalism.wordpress.com/2021/11/18/the-impossibility-of-decolonizing-anthropology/

Davé, Naisargi N. 2012. *Queer Activism in India: A Story in the Anthropology of Ethics.* Durham: Duke University Press.

Davé, Naisargi N. 2015. Love and Other Injustices: On Indifference to Difference. *Humanities Futures.* Franklin Humanities Institute Inter-departmental seminar, 25 March. https://humanitiesfutures.org/papers/love-and-other-injustices/

Davé, Naisargi. 2024. On the Tools of the House and Dwelling Otherwise, in Soumhya Venkatesan (ed.), A Decolonial Anthropology: You Can Dismantle the Master's House with the Master's Tools. The 2022 meeting of the Group for Debates in Anthropological Theory. *Critique of Anthropology* 44(2): 118–22.

de Kock, Leon. 1992. Interview with Gayatri Chakravorty Spivak: New Nation Writers Conference in South Africa. *ARIEL: A Review of International English Literature* 23(3): 30–47.

de L'Estoile, Benoît. 2008. Introduction: The Past as It Lives Now: An Anthropology of Colonial Legacies. *Social Anthropology* 16(3): 267–79.

De Sousa Santos, Boaventura. 2012. The University at a Crossroads. *Human Architecture: Journal of the Sociology of Self Knowledge* X(1): 7–16.

Dilley, Roy. 2010. Reflections on Knowledge Practices and the Problem of Ignorance. *Journal of the Royal Anthropological Institute* 16(1): S176–S192.

Dirks, Nicholas. 2001. *Castes of the Mind: Colonialism and the Making of Modern India.* Princeton: Princeton University Press.

Dominguez, Virginia R., Gutmann, Matthew and Lutz, Catherine. 2014. Problem of Gender and Citations Raised Again in New Study. *Anthropology News* 55(3–4): 29–30.

Donner, Henrike. 2006. Committed Mothers and Well-Adjusted Children: Privatisation, Early-Years Education and Motherhood in Calcutta Middle-class Families. *Modern Asian Studies* 40(2): 339–64.

Drake, St Clair. 1980. Anthropology and the Black Experience. *Black Scholar* 11(7): 2–31.

Dumont, Louis. 1980 [French original 1966]. *Homo Hierarchicus: The Caste System and its Implications*, trans. Mark Sainsbury, Louis Dumont and Basia Gulati. Chicago: University of Chicago Press.

Duranti, Alessandro. 2006. The Social Ontology of Intentions. *Discourse Studies* 8(1): 31–40.

Durkheim, Emile. 1995 [1912]. *The Elementary Forms of Religious Life*, trans. Karen Fields. New York: The Free Press.

Durrani, Mariam. 2019. Upsetting the Canon. *Anthropology News*, 8 April. DOI: 10.1111/AN.1134

Elbourne, Elizabeth. 2003. Word Made Flesh: Christianity, Modernity and Cultural Colonialism in the Work of Jean and John Comaroff. *American Historical Review* 108(2): 435–59.

Evans-Pritchard, E. E. 1937. *Witchcraft, Oracles and Magic among the Azande*. Oxford: Clarendon Press.

Evans-Pritchard, E. E. 1973. Some Notes on Zande Sex Habits. *American Anthropologist* (New Series) 75(1): 171–5.

Fabian, Johannes. 2014 [1983]. *Time and the Other*. New York: Columbia University Press.

Fader, Ayala. 2020. *Hidden Heretics: Jewish Doubt in the Digital Age*. Princeton: Princeton University Press.

Fanon, Frantz. 1963 [1961]. *The Wretched of the Earth*, trans. Constance Farrington. New York: Grove Press.

Farmer, Paul. 1996. On Suffering and Structural Violence: A View from Below. *Daedalus* 125(1): 261–83.

Ferguson, Niall. 2004. *Empire: How Britain Made the Modern World*. London: Penguin.

Fluehr-Lobban, Carolyn. 2005. Anténor Firmin and Haiti's Contribution to Anthropology. *Gradhiva* 1: 95–108. https://journals.openedition.org/gradhiva/302

Foucault, Michel. 1986. Of Other Spaces, trans. Jay Miskowiec. *Diacritics* 16(1): 22–7.

Frank, David John and Meyer, John W. 2020. *The University and the Global Knowledge Society*. Princeton: Princeton University Press.

Fricker, Miranda. 2007. *Epistemic Injustice: Power and the Ethics of Knowing*. Oxford: Oxford University Press.

Fuller, Chris. 2014. Classifying India: A Review of Peter Gottschalk's *Religion and Empire: Classifying Hinduism and Islam in British India*. Anthropology of This Century 10.

Fuller, C. J. 2017. Ethnographic Inquiry in Colonial India: Herbert Risley, William Crooke, and the Study of Tribes and Castes. *Journal of the Royal Anthropological Institute* 23(3): 603–21.

Gago, Veronica. 2020. Introduction: The Silvia Rivera Cusicanqui Principle: The Rebellion of Thought, in Silvia Rivera Cusicanqui, *Ch'ixinakax utxiwa: On Practices and Discourses of Decolonization*. Cambridge: Polity Press, vii–xxxiii.

Geertz, Clifford. 1966. Religion as a Cultural System, in *The Interpretation of Cultures: Selected Essays*. New York: Basic Books, 87–125.

Gell, Alfred. 1998. *Art and Agency: An Anthropological Theory*. Oxford: Clarendon Press.

Gerber, Schalk Hendrik. 2018. From Dis-Enclosure to Decolonisation: In Dialogue with Nancy and Mbembe on Self-Determination and the Other. *Religions* 9(4): 128. Not paginated in original, although page 3 of 18 in downloaded online version: https://www.mdpi.com/2077-1444/9/4/128

Gershon, Ilana and Raj, Dhooleka Sarhadi. 2000. Introduction: The Symbolic Capital of Ignorance. *Social Analysis* 44(2): 3–13.

Ghosh, Amitav and Chakrabarty, Dipesh. 2002. A Correspondence on Provincializing Europe. *Radical History Review* 83 (Spring): 146–72.

Gilley, Bruce. 2017. The Case for Colonialism. *Third World Quarterly*. DOI 10.1080/01436597.2017.1369037. (The article has since been withdrawn by the journal's editors following widespread complaints and protests.)

Golub, Alex. 2014. Is There an Anthropological Canon? Evidence from Theory Anthologies. *Savage Minds*. https://savageminds.org/2014/04/06/is-there-an-anthropological-canon-evidence-from-theory-anthologies/

Gopal, Priyamvada. 2020. *Insurgent Empire: Anticolonial Resistance and British Dissent*. London: Verso.

Gopal, Priyamvada. 2021. On Decolonisation and the University. *Textual Practice* 35(6): 873–99.

Gott, Richard. 2007. Latin America as a White Settler Society. *Bulletin of Latin American Research* 26(2): 269–89.

Gough, Kathleen. 1968. New Proposals for Anthropologists. *Current Anthropology* 9(5): 403–35.

Graeber, David and Wengrow, David. 2021. *The Dawn of Everything: A New History of Humanity*. London: Allen Lane.

Green, Sarah. 1997a. *Urban Amazons: Lesbian Feminism and Beyond in the Gender, Sexuality and Identity Battles of London*. London: Macmillan.

Green, Sarah. 1997b. Urban Amazons. *Trouble and Strife* 35. http://www.troubleandstrife.org/articles/issue-35/urban-amazons/

Grosfoguel, Ramón. 2013. The Structure of Knowledge in Westernized Universities: Epistemic Racism/Sexism and the Four Genocides/Epistemicides of the Long 16th Century. *Human Architecture: Journal of the Sociology of Self-Knowledge* XI(1): 73–90.

Guha, Ramachandra. 1999 (September). *Seminar*. https://www.india-seminar.com/1999/481.htm

Gupta, Akhil and Stoolman, Jessie. 2022. Decolonizing US Anthropology. *American Anthropologist* 124(4): 647–925.

Hage, Ghassan. 2000 [1998]. *White Nation: Fantasies of White Supremacy in a Multicultural Society*. New York: Routledge.

Hall, Stuart. 2017. *Familiar Stranger: A Life between Two Islands*. Durham: Duke University Press.

Harding, Susan. 1991. Representing Fundamentalism: The Problem of the Repugnant Cultural Other. *Social Research* 58(2): 373–93.

Harlow, Roxanna. 2003. 'Race Doesn't Matter, But . . .': The Effect of Race on Professors' Experience and Emotion Management in the Undergraduate College Classroom. *Social Psychology Quarterly* 66(4): 348–63.

Harrison, Faye V. 2008. *Outsider Within: Reworking Anthropology in the Global Age*. Urbana: University of Chicago Press.

Harrison, Faye (ed.). 2010 [1991]. *Decolonizing Anthropology: Moving Further Toward an Anthropology for Liberation*. Arlington: American Anthropological Association.

Harrison, Ira E. and Harrison, Faye V. (eds). 1999. *African*

American Pioneers in Anthropology. Urbana and Chicago: University of Illinois Press.

Hartigan, John Jr. 1999. *Racial Situations: Class Predicaments of Whiteness in Detroit*. Princeton: Princeton University Press.

Hartigan, John Jr. 2005. *Odd Tribes: Towards a Cultural Analysis of White People*. Durham: Duke University Press.

Hartigan, John Jr. 2010. *Race in the 21st Century: Ethnographic Approaches*, 2nd edn. New York: Oxford University Press.

Haruyama, Justin Lee. 2024. Anti-Blackness and Moral Repair: The Curse of Ham, Biblical Kinship and the Limits of Liberalism. *Cultural Anthropology* 39(1): 118–45.

Heffernan, Troy. 2020. Sexism, Racism, Prejudice, and Bias: A Literature Review and Synthesis of Research Surrounding Student Evaluations of Courses and Teaching. *Assessment and Evaluation in Higher Education* 47(1): 144–54.

High, Casey, Kelly, Ann H. and Mair, Jonathan (eds). 2012. *The Anthropology of Ignorance: An Ethnographic Approach*. New York: Palgrave Macmillan.

Hill, Karlos K. 2002. The University Cannot Be Decolonized. *The Nation*, 16 March. https://www.thenation.com/article/society/kehinde-andrews-interview/

Hoadley, Ursula and Galant, Jaamia. 2019. What Counts and Who Belongs? Current Debates in Decolonising the Curriculum, in Jonathan Jansen (ed.), *Decolonisation in Universities: The Politics of Knowledge*. Johannesburg: Wits University Press, 100–14.

Hobart, Mark. 1993. *An Anthropological Critique of Development: The Growth of Ignorance*. London: Routledge.

Hoodfar, Homa. 1992. Feminist Anthropology and Critical Pedagogy: Anthropology of Classrooms' Excluded Voices. *Canadian Journal of Education* 17(3): 303–20.

hooks, bell. 1994. *Teaching to Transgress: Education as the Practice of Freedom*. New York: Routledge.

Hurston, Zora Neale. 2018 [1931]. *Barracoon: The Story of the Last 'Black Cargo'*. New York: Harper Collins.

Hymes, Dell (ed.). 1972. *Reinventing Anthropology*. New York: Random House.

Ivancheva, Mariya. 2023. *The Alternative University: Lessons from Bolivarian Venezuela*. Stanford: Stanford University Press.

Jackson, John L. 2001. *Harlemworld: Doing Race and Class in Contemporary Black America*. Chicago: University of Chicago Press.

Jackson, John L. 2005. *Real Black: Adventures in Racial Sincerity*. Chicago: University of Chicago Press.

James, C. L. R. 2013 [1963]. *Beyond a Boundary*. Durham: Duke University Press.

Jangam, Chinnaiah. 2021. Decolonizing Caste and Rethinking Social Inequality in South Asia. A virtual CASI seminar, University of Pennsylvania, 8 April. https://casi.sas.upenn.edu/events/chinnaiahjangam

Jansen, Jan C. and Osterhammel, Jurgen. 2017. *Decolonization: A Short History*, trans. Jeremiah Riemer. Princeton: Princeton University Press.

Jansen, Jonathan. 2009. *Knowledge in the Blood: Confronting Race and the Apartheid Past*. Stanford and Cape Town: Stanford University Press and University of Cape Town Press.

Jansen, Jonathan (ed.). 2019. *Decolonisation in Universities: The Politics of Knowledge*. Johannesburg: Wits University Press.

Jansen, Jonathan and Walters, Cyrill. 2022. *The Decolonization of Knowledge: Radical Ideas and the Shaping of Institutions in South Africa and Beyond*. Cambridge: Cambridge University Press.

Jenkins, Dudley Laura. 2003. Another 'People of India' Project: Colonial and National Anthropology. *Journal of Asian Studies* 63(4): 1143–70.

Kauser, Sophia, Yaqoob, S., Cook, A., O'Hara, M., Mantzios, M. and Egan, H. 2021. Learning from the Experiences of Black, Asian and Minority Ethnic (BAME) University Students Who Withdraw from their Undergraduate Degree. *SN Social Sciences* 1: Article no. 121.

Keele Manifesto for Decolonizing the Curriculum. 2018. *Journal of Global Faultlines* 5(1–2): 97–9.

Kelly, John D. 1995. Threats to Difference in Colonial Fiji. *Cultural Anthropology* 10(1): 64–84.

Knopf-Newman, Marcy Jane. 2011. *The Politics of Teaching*

Palestine to Americans: Addressing Pedagogical Strategies. New York: Palgrave Macmillan.

Kothari, Rita. 2013. Caste in a Caste-less Language: English as a Language of 'Dalit' Expression. *Economic and Political Weekly* 48(39): 60–8.

LaDousa, Chaise. 2014. *Hindi Is Our Ground, English Is Our Sky: Education, Language, and Social Class in Contemporary India.* New York: Berghahn Books.

Laidlaw, James. 2002. For an Anthropology of Ethics and Freedom. *Journal of the Royal Anthropological Institute* 8(2): 311–32.

Lange, Lis. 2019. The Institutional Curriculum: Pedagogy and the Decolonisation of the South African University, in Jonathan Jansen (ed.), *Decolonisation in Universities: The Politics of Knowledge.* Johannesburg: Wits University Press, 79–99.

Lawson, Stephanie. 2010. The 'Pacific Way' as Postcolonial Discourse: Towards a Reassessment. *Journal of Pacific History* 45(3): 297–314.

Lehmann, David. 2022. *After the Decolonial: Ethnicity, Gender and Social Justice in Latin America.* Cambridge: Polity Press.

Leonard, Patrick. 2019. Land and Belonging in an Indo-Fijian Rural Settlement. PhD diss. in Anthropology, University of Manchester.

Leonardo, Zeus. 2018. Dis-orienting Western Knowledge: Coloniality, Curriculum and Crisis. *Cambridge Journal of Social Anthropology* (Canon Fire: Decolonizing the Curriculum) 36(2): 7–20.

Lewis, Herbert S. 2014. *In Defence of Anthropology: An Investigation of the Critique of Anthropology.* New Brunswick: Transaction.

Lewis, Herbert S. 2021. On the Counterfactual History of Anthropology. https://easaonline.org/downloads/networks/hoan/HOAN_Newsletter_21j-202112_Lewis_Open_Letter_AAA.pdf

Lewis, Jovan Scott. 2018. Releasing a Tradition: Diasporic Epistemology and the Decolonized Curriculum. *Cambridge Journal of Social Anthropology* (Canon Fire: Decolonizing the Curriculum) 36(2): 21–33.

Liashenko, Joshua. 2022. Teaching Anthropological Theory: Reflections on Course Design and Pedagogy. Teaching Tools, *Fieldsights*, 15 November.

Liberatore, Giulia. 2017. *Somali, Muslim, British: Striving in Securitized Britain*. London: Bloomsbury.

Lorde, Audre. 1984. *Sister Outsider: Essays and Speeches*. Berkeley: Crossing Press.

Luhrmann, Tanya. 2012. *When God Talks Back: Understanding the American Evangelical Relationship with God*. New York: Alfred Knopf.

Lutz, Catherine. 1990. The Erasure of Women's Writing in Sociocultural Anthropology. *American Ethnologist* 17(4): 611–27.

MacIntyre, Alasdair. 1981. The Nature of the Virtues. *The Hastings Centre Report* 11(2): 27–34.

Mafeje, Archie. 1998a. Anthropology and Independent Africans: Suicide or End of an Era? *African Sociological Review/Revue Africaine de Sociologie* 2(1): 1–43.

Mafeje, Archie. 1998b. Conversations and Confrontations with My Reviewers. *African Sociological Review/Revue Africaine de Sociologie* 2(2): 95–107.

Magubane, Bernard M. and Faris, James C. 1985. On the Political Relevance of Anthropology. *Dialectical Anthropology* 9: 91–104.

Mahmood, Saba. 2011. *Politics of Piety: The Islamic Revival and the Feminist Subject*. Princeton: Princeton University Press.

Mair, Jonathan, Kelly, Ann H. and High, Casey. 2012. Introduction: Making Ignorance an Ethnographic Object. In Casey High, Ann H. Kelly and Jonathan Mair (eds), *The Anthropology of Ignorance: An Ethnographic Approach*. New York: Palgrave Macmillan, 1–32.

Maldonado-Torres, Nelson. 2007. On the Coloniality of Being. *Cultural Studies* 21(2–3): 240–70.

Mamdani, Mahmood. 1996. *Citizen and Subject: Contemporary Africa and the Legacy of Late Colonialism*. Princeton: Princeton University Press.

Mark, Jan. 1991. *Man in Motion*. London: Puffin.

Mattingly, Cheryl. 2014. *Moral Laboratories: Family Peril and the Struggle for a Good Life*. Oakland: University of California Press.

Mbembe, Achille. 2021. *Out of the Dark Night: Essays on Decolonization.* New York: Columbia University Press.

McCarthy, Cameron and Sealey-Ruiz, Yolanda. 2010. Teaching Difficult History: Eric Williams' *Capitalism and Slavery* and the Challenge of Critical Pedagogy in the Contemporary Classroom. *Power and Education* 2(1): 75–84.

McGranahan, Carole and Rizvi, Uzma Z. (eds). 2016. Decolonizing Anthropology. *Savage Minds.* https://savageminds.org/2016/04/19/decolonizing-anthropology/

Meghji, Ali. 2021. *Decolonizing Sociology: An Introduction.* Cambridge: Polity Press.

Memmi, Albert. 2003 [1957]. *The Colonizer and the Colonized*, trans. Howard Greenfield. London: Earthscan.

Menzies, Charles. 2021. American Anthropology, Apologies and Apologetics. https://charlesmenzies.blogspot.com/2021/12/american-anthropology-apologies-and.html

Meyer, Birgit. 2020. Religion as Mediation. *Entangled Religions* 11(3). https://er.ceres.rub.de/index.php/ER/article/view/8444/8019

Mignolo, Walter D. 2009. Epistemic Disobedience, Independent Thought and Decolonial Freedom. *Theory, Culture and Society* 26(7–8): 159–81.

Mignolo, Walter D. and Walsh, Katherine E. 2018. *On Decoloniality: Concepts, Analytics, Praxis.* Durham: Duke University Press.

Mills, Charles W. 2017. White Ignorance, in *Black Rights/White Wrongs: The Critique of Racial Liberalism*. New York: Oxford University Press, 49–71.

Mogstad, Heidi and Tse, Lee-Shan. 2018. Decolonizing Anthropology: Reflections from Cambridge. *Cambridge Journal of Social Anthropology* (Canon Fire: Decolonizing the Curriculum) 36(2): 53–72.

Mohanty, Chandra Talpade. 2003. 'Under Western Eyes' Revisited: Feminist Solidarity through Anticapitalist Struggles. *Signs* 28(2): 499–535.

Mohanty, Satya P. 1997. *Literacy Theory and the Claims of History.* Ithaca, New York: Cornell University Press.

Moosavi, Leon. 2020. The Decolonial Bandwagon and the Dangers of Intellectual Decolonisation. *International Review of Sociology* 30(2): 332–54.

Montaigne, Michel De. 2003. On the Cannibals, in *Michel De Montaigne: The Complete Essays*, trans. M. A. Screech. London: Penguin, 228–41.

Moreno Figueroa, Mónica G. and Wade, Peter. 2022. *Against Racism: Organizing for Social Change in Latin America*. Pittsburgh: University of Pittsburgh Press.

Mosse, David. 2006. Anti-Social Anthropology? Objectivity, Objection, and the Ethnography of Public Policy and Professional Communities. *Journal of the Royal Anthropological Institute* 12(4): 935–56.

Mukherjee, Aditya. 2010. Empire: How Colonial India Made Modern Britain. *Economic and Political Weekly* 45(50): 73–82.

Murray, B. K. 1990. Wits as an 'Open' University 1939–1959: Black Admissions to the University of the Witwatersrand. *Journal of Southern African Studies* 16(4): 649–76.

Nader, Laura. 1972. Up the Anthropologist: Perspectives Gained from 'Studying Up', in Dell Hymes (ed.), *Reinventing Anthropology*. New York: Random House, 284–311.

Nandy, Ashis. 1998 [1983]. *The Intimate Enemy: Loss and Recovery of Self under Colonialism*. New Delhi: Oxford India Paperbacks.

Narayan, Kirin. 1993. How Native is a 'Native' Anthropologist? *American Anthropologist* NS 95(3): 671–86.

Nash, M. 2019. Entangled Pasts: Land Grant Colleges and American Indian Dispossession. *History of Education Quarterly* 59(4): 437–67.

Nathan, Rebekah. 2005. *My Freshman Year: What a Professor Learned by Becoming a Student*. Ithaca: Cornell University Press.

Ngũgĩ wa Thiong'o. 1987 [1981]. *Decolonising the Mind: The Politics of Language in African Literature*. Harare: Zimbabwe Publishing House.

Ntarangwi, Mwenda. 2010. *Reversed Gaze: An African Ethnography of American Anthropology*. Urbana: University of Illinois Press.

Nyamnjoh, Anye-Nkwenti. 2022. Decolonisation, Africanisation and Epistemic Citizenship. PhD thesis in Politics and International Studies, University of Cambridge.

Nyamnjoh, Francis B. 2016. *#RhodesMust Fall: Nibbling at

Resilient Colonialism in South Africa. Bamenda: Langaa Research and Publishing Common Initiative Group.

Nyamnjoh, Francis B. 2017 [2015]. Incompleteness: Frontier Africa and the Currency of Conviviality. *Journal of Asian and African Studies* 52(3): 253–70.

Odendaal, Rehana Thembeka. 2019. Wits Imagined: An Investigation into Wits University's Public Roles and Responsibilities, 1922–1994. Master of Arts diss. in Historical Studies, Faculty of the Humanities, University of Cape Town.

Ortner, Sherry B. 2009. *Studying Sideways: Ethnographic Access in Hollywood*. New York: Routledge.

Ortner, Sherry B. 2010. Access: Reflections on Studying Up in Hollywood. *Ethnography* 11(2): 211–33.

Pabian, Petr. 2014. Ethnographies of Higher Education: Introduction to the Special Issue. *European Journal of Higher Education* 4(1): 6–17.

Palma, Nuno. 2016. Sailing Away from Malthus: Intercontinental Trade and European Economic Growth, 1500–1800. *Cliometrica* 10: 129–49.

Pearson, Heath. 2015. The Prickly Skin of White Supremacy: Race in the 'Real America'. *Transforming Anthropology* 43(1): 43–58.

Pels, Peter. 1997. The Anthropology of Colonialism: Culture, History and the Emergence of Western Governmentality. *Annual Review of Anthropology* 26: 163–83.

Pete, Shauneen. 2018. Meschachakanis, a Coyote Narrative: Decolonising Higher Education, in Gurminder K. Bhambra, Dalia Gebrial and Kerem Nisancioglu (eds), *Decolonising the University*. London: Pluto Press, 173–89.

Phillips, Alice, Rana-Deshmukh, Aisha and Joseph, Chante. 2017. *BME Attainment Gap Report*. Bristol Students' Union. https://www.bristol.ac.uk/media-library/sites/sraa/Website%20bme-attainment-gap-report.pdf

Pilkington, Hilary. 2016. *Loud and Proud: Passion and Politics in the English Defence League*. Manchester: Manchester University Press.

Piscioneri, Matthew and Hlavac, Jim. 2013. The Minimalist Reading Model: Rethinking Reading Lists in Arts and

Education Subjects. *Arts and Humanities in Higher Education* 12(4): 424–45.

Poets, Desiree. 2020. Settler Colonialism and/in (Urban) Brazil: Black and Indigenous Resistances to the Logic of Elimination. *Settler Colonial Studies* 11(3): 271–91.

Posecznick, Alex. 2017. *Selling Hope and College: Merit, Markets and Recruitment in an Unranked School*. New York: Cornell University Press.

Prasad, Chandra Bhan. 2007. The Vilification of Lord Macaulay: Will Capitalism Suffer the Same Fate? *India in Transition*, 18 November. https://casi.sas.upenn.edu/iit/prasad

Prasad, Leela. 2007. *Poetics of Conduct: Oral Narrative and Moral Being in a South Indian Town*. New York: Columbia University Press.

Proctor, Robert N. 2008. Agnotology: A Missing Term to Describe the Cultural Production of Ignorance (and Its Study), in Robert N. Proctor and Londa Scheibinger (eds), *Agnotology: The Making and Unmaking of Ignorance*. Stanford: Stanford University Press, 1–36.

Proctor, Robert N. and Scheibinger, Londa (eds). 2008. *Agnotology: The Making and Unmaking of Ignorance*. Stanford: Stanford University Press.

Quijano, Anibal. 2000. Coloniality of Power, Eurocentrism, and Latin America, trans. Michael Ennis. *Nepantia: Views from South* 1(3): 533–80.

Raj, Kapil. 2000. Colonial Encounters and the Forging of New Knowledge and National Identities: Great Britain and India, 1760–1850. *Osiris* 15: Nature and Empire: Science and the Colonial Enterprise: 119–34.

Richardson, Eugene T. 2020. *Epidemic Illusions: On the Coloniality of Global Public Health*. Cambridge, MA: MIT Press.

Risley, Herbert. 1908. *The People of India*. Calcutta: Thacker, Spink and Co.

Rivera Cusicanqui, Silvia. 2020. *Ch'ixinakax utxiwa: On Practices and Discourses of Decolonization*, trans. Molly Geidel (chs 1 and 2); Brenda Baletti (ch. 3). Cambridge: Polity Press.

Roberts, Nathaniel. 2016. *To Be Cared For: The Power of*

Conversion and Foreignness of Belonging in an Indian Slum. Oakland: University of California Press.

Rosa, Jonathan and Díaz, Vanessa. 2020. Raciontologies: Rethinking Anthropological Accounts of Institutional Racism and Enactments of White Supremacy in the United States. *American Anthropologist*, Special Section: Anthropology and White Supremacy 122(1): 120–32.

Rouse, Carolyn. 2023. An Anti-Genealogical Take on US Anthropology and Disciplinary Reform: From Antiracism to Decolonization. *American Ethnologist* 50(3): 356–67.

Ryan, Laura. 2018. Something to Feel About: Zora Neale Hurston's *Barracoon*: The Story of the Last Slave. *U.S. Studies Online*, 12 November. https://usso.uk/2018/11/something-to-feel-about-zora-neale-hurstons-barracoon-the-story-of-the-last-slave/

Said, Edward. 1978. *Orientalism*. New York: Pantheon.

Sanchez, Andrew. 2018. Canon Fire: Decolonizing the Curriculum. *Cambridge Journal of Social Anthropology* 36(2): 1–6.

Sanghera, Satnam. 2021. *Empireland: How Imperialism Has Shaped Modern Britain*. London: Viking.

Saxena, Akshya. 2022. *Vernacular English: Reading the Anglophone in Postcolonial India*. Princeton: Princeton University Press.

Scheper-Hughes, Nancy. 1995. The Primacy of the Ethical: Propositions for a Militant Anthropology. *Current Anthropology* 36(3): 409–40.

Schreiner, Olive. 1897. *Trooper Peter Halket of Mashonaland*. Digitized by Project Gutenberg. Release Date: 15 September 2008 [EBook #1431]. http://www.gutenberg.org/files/1431/1431-h/1431-h.htm

Schucan Bird, K. and Pitman, Leslie. 2020. How Diverse Is Your Reading List? Exploring Issues of Representation and Decolonisation in the UK. *Higher Education* 79: 903–20.

Shah, Alpa. 2017. Ethnography? Participant Observation, a Potentially Revolutionary Praxis. *Hau: Journal of Ethnographic Theory* 7(1): 45–59.

Shankar, Shalini. 2020. Nothing Sells Like Whiteness: Race, Ontology and American Advertising. *American Anthropologist* 122(1): 112–19.

Shoemaker, Nancy. 2015. A Typology of Colonialism. *Perspectives on History*. https://www.historians.org/publications-and-directories/perspectives-on-history/october-2015/a-typology-of-colonialism

Shore, Chris and Wright, Susan. 1999. Audit Culture and Anthropology: Neo-liberalism in British Higher Education. *Journal of the Royal Anthropological Institute* 5(4): 557–75.

Shumar, Wesley. 1997. *College for Sale: A Critique of the Commodification of Higher Education*. New York: Routledge.

Silverman, Sydel. 2005. The United States, in Fredrik Barth, Andre Gingrich, Robert Parkin and Sydel Silverman, *One Discipline, Four Ways: British, German, French, and American Anthropology. The Halle Lectures*. Chicago: University of Chicago Press, 257–328.

Simpson, Audra. 2007. On Ethnographic Refusal: Indigeneity, 'Voice' and Colonial Citizenship. *Junctures* 9: 67–80.

Smith, Katherine Leigh. 2011. Whatever Happened to Dominant Discourse? *Anthropology in Action* 18(2): 19–32.

Srinivas, Tulasi. 2018. *The Cow in the Elevator: An Anthropology of Wonder*. Durham: Duke University Press.

Stead, W. T. (ed.). 1902. *The Last Will and Testament of Cecil Rhodes with Elucidatory Notes to which are added some chapters describing the Political and Religious Ideas of the Testator*. London: Review of Reviews Office. Digitized in full by the Internet Archive in 2007. https://www.surfdome.com/en-SG/?gclid=EAIaIQobChMIyJ-Z9f3M6gIVB7LtCh0ZSgIkEAAYASAAEgKJUPD_BwE

Stokes, Peter and Martin, Lindsey. 2008. Reading Lists: A Study of Tutor and Student Perceptions, Expectations and Realities. *Studies in Higher Education* 33(2): 113–25.

Stoll, David. 2023. Decolonizing Anthropology – or Racializing it? How Narrow Political Orthodoxies Took Over the Field. *Chronicle of Higher Education*, 7 November. https://www.chronicle.com/article/decolonizing-anthropology-or-racializing-it

Stommel, Jesse. 2020. Ungrading: An FAQ. *Jesse Stommel*, 6 February. https://www.jessestommel.com/ungrading-an-faq/

Strathern, Marilyn. 1987. The Limits of Auto-Anthropology, in

Anthony Jackson (ed.), *Anthropology at Home*. Abingdon: Routledge, 59–67.

Strathern, Marilyn. 2000. *Audit Cultures: Anthropological Studies in Accountability, Ethics and the Academy*. New York: Routledge.

Strathern, Marilyn. 2006. A Community of Critics? Thoughts on New Knowledge. *Journal of the Royal Anthropological Institute* 12(1): 191–209.

Sundar, Nandini and Fazili, Gowhar. 2020. Academic Freedom in India: A Status Report, 2020. *India Forum*, 27 August. https://www.theindiaforum.in/article/academic-freedom-india

Táíwò, Olúfẹ́mi. 2022. *Against Decolonisation: Taking African Agency Seriously*. London: Hurst.

Táíwò, Olúfẹ́mi O. 2021. Being-in-the-Room Privilege: Elite Capture and Epistemic Deference. *The Philosopher* 104(8). https://www.thephilosopher1923.org/post/being-in-the-room-privilege-elite-capture-and-epistemic-deference

Táíwò, Olúfẹ́mi O. 2022. *Elite Capture: How the Powerful Took Over Identity Politics (and Everything Else)*. London: Pluto Press.

TallBear, Kim. 2013. *Native American DNA: Tribal Belonging and the False Promise of Genetic Science*. Minneapolis: University of Minnesota Press.

TallBear, Kim. 2020. Identity is a Poor Substitute for Relating, in Brendan Hokowhitu, Aileen Moreton-Robinson, Linda Tuhiwai-Smith, Chris Andersen and Steve Larkin (eds), *Routledge Handbook of Critical Indigenous Studies*. London: Routledge, 467–78.

Te Punga Somerville, Alice. 2021. OMG Settler Colonial Studies: Response to Lorenzo Veracini: 'Is Settler Colonial Studies Even Useful?'. *Postcolonial Studies* 24(2): 278–82.

Tobin, Jeffrey. 1994. Cultural Construction and Native Nationalism: Report from the Hawaiian Front. *boundary 2* 21(1): 111–33.

Todd, Zoe. 2016. An Indigenous Feminist's Take on the Ontological Turn: Ontology is Just Another Word for Colonialism. *Journal of Historical Sociology* 29(1): 4–22.

Trembath, Sarah. 2018. Decoloniality. *Antiracist Praxis*. https://subjectguides.library.american.edu/c.php?g=1025915&p=7715527

Trouillot, Michel-Rolph. 1995. *Silencing the Past: Power and the Production of History*. Boston: Beacon Press.

Tuck, Eve and Yang, Wayne K. 2012. Decolonization is Not a Metaphor. *Decolonization: Indigeneity, Education & Society* 1(1): 1–40.

Tuhiwai Smith, Linda. 2012 [1999]. *Decolonizing Methodologies: Research and Indigenous Peoples*. London: Zed Books.

Tyler, Katherine. 2009. Whiteness Studies and Laypeople's Engagements with Race and Genetics. *New Genetics and Society* 28(1): 37–50.

Tylor, Edward B. 2002 [1871]. Religion in Primitive Culture, in Michael Lambek (ed.), *A Reader in the Anthropology of Religion*. Oxford: Blackwell, 21–33.

Uperesa, Lisa. 2016. A Decolonial Turn in Anthropology? A View from the Pacific, in Carole McGranahan and Uzma Z. Rizvi (eds), *Savage Minds: Decolonizing Anthropology*. https://savageminds.org/2016/06/07/a-decolonial-turn-in-anthropology-a-view-from-the-pacific/

UUK-NUS (Universities UK and National Union of Students). 2019. Black, Asian and Minority Ethnic Student Attainment at UK Universities: #Closing the Gap. https://www.universitiesuk.ac.uk/sites/default/files/field/downloads/2021-07/bame-student-attainment.pdf

Veerapandiya Kattabomman. 1959. Prod. and dir. B. R. Panthulu. Padmini Pictures.

Venkatesan, Soumhya. 2009. *Craft Matters: Artisans, 'Development' and the Indian Nation*. Delhi: Orient Blackswan.

Venkatesan, Soumhya. 2010. Learning to Weave: Weaving to Learn What? *Journal of the Royal Anthropological Institute* 16(S1): S158–S175.

Venkatesan, Soumhya. 2012. Sometimes Similar, Sometimes Dangerously Different: Exploring Resonance, Laminations and Subject-Formation in South India. *Ethnos* 77(3): 400–24.

Venkatesan, Soumhya (ed.). 2019. Violence and Violation are at the Heart of Racism: The 2017 Debate of the Group for Debates in Anthropological Theory, Manchester. *Critique of Anthropology* 39(1): 12–51.

Venkatesan, Soumhya. 2020. Object, Subject, Thing: Tamil Hindu Priests' Material Practices and Practical Theories of Animation and Accommodation. *American Ethnologist* 47(4): 447–60.

Venkatesan, Soumhya. 2021. The Wedding of Two Trees: Connections, Equivalences and Subjunctivity in a Tamil Ritual. *Journal of the Royal Anthropological Institute* 27(3): 478–95.

Venkatesan, Soumhya (ed.). 2024. A Decolonial Anthropology: You Can Dismantle the Master's House with the Master's Tools. The 2022 Meeting of the Group for Debates in Anthropological Theory. *Critique of Anthropology* 44(2): 99–140.

Venkatesan, Soumhya and Yarrow, Thomas. 2012. *Differentiating Development: Beyond an Anthropology of Critique*. Oxford and New York: Berghahn.

Veracini, Lorenzo. 2008. 'Emphatically Not a White Man's Colony': Settler Colonialism and the Construction of Colonial Fiji. *Journal of Pacific History* 43(2): 189–205.

Viramma, Racine, Josianne and Racine, Jean-Luc. 1997. *Viramma: Life of an Untouchable*, trans. Will Hobson. London: Verso.

Viveiros de Castro, Eduardo. 2003. *And: After-Dinner Speech given at* Anthropology and Science, *The 5th Decennial Conference of the Association of Social Anthropologists of the UK and Commonwealth, 2003*. Manchester Papers in Social Anthropology No. 7. Manchester: University of Manchester.

Wade, Peter. 2015. *Race: An Introduction*. Cambridge: Cambridge University Press.

Walker, Alice. 2018. Those Who Love Us Never Leave Us Alone with Our Grief: Reading *Barracoon: The Story of the Last 'Black Cargo'*. Foreword to Hurston 2018 [1931]. *Barracoon: The Story of the Last 'Black Cargo'*. New York: HarperCollins.

Wangūi wa Kamonji. 2019. Decolonising My Soul: My Journey to Reclaim African Spirituality. *The Elephant*, 8 February. https://www.theelephant.info/reflections/2019/02/08/decolonising-my-soul-my-journey-to-reclaim-african-spirituality/

Weber, Max. 1946 [1919]. Politics as a Vocation; Science as a Vocation, in *Max Weber: Essays in Sociology*, trans., ed., and with an introduction by H. H. Gerth and C. Wright Mills. New York: Oxford University Press, 77–156.

Werbner, Richard. 2020. *Anthropology after Gluckman: The Manchester School, Colonial and Post-Colonial Transformations*. Manchester: Manchester University Press.

Wilder, Laura Ingalls. 1935. *Little House on the Prairie*. Harmondsworth: Penguin.

Williams, Eric. 1994. *Capitalism and Slavery*. Chapel Hill: University of North Carolina Press.

Wiredu, Kwasi. 1998. Towards Decolonizing African Philosophy and Religion. *African Studies Quarterly* 1(4): 17–46.

Yonucu, Deniz. 2022. *Police, Provocation, Politics: Counterinsurgency in Istanbul*. Ithaca, NY: Cornell University Press.

Index

Abdelhamid, Elsayed 212
Achebe, Chinua 51, 54
activism
  anthropology and 3–4
  community activism 212
  drivers 113
  ignorance and 143–4
  knowledge and 128
agnotology 25, 127–8
Aidid, Safia 80–1
Algeria 33
Allen, Jafari 77, 78, 156
Alonso Bejarano, Carolina 79–80, 87
alterity
  colonialism's other 210
  ethnographic other 63
  fascination with 74
  repugnant other 92–4, 144
American Anthropological Association 81
American Council on Education 151
Anderson, Kirk 148–9, 169
Andrews, Kehinde 210, 212
anthropology
  British colonial case studies 65–73
  colonial legacies 8–13
  colonialism 24, 62–95
  disagreements 85–8, 95, 98, 118–21, 209
  dissolution 16
  gaze 16
  inappropriate engagement 88–92
  liberation 3, 24, 81–5, 91, 92, 94, 159–60
  personal journey 16–22, 44–5, 87
  practice 13–16, 207
  problems 76
  radical questioning 104–7
  rethinking 73–92
  teaching. *See* anthropology teaching; universities
anthropology teaching
  canon 190–6
  curricula 154–60
  diversification 160–2, 177
  excluded 156
  experiment 175, 177–9
  explicit 155–6
  modelled 155, 156–7, 158–9
  dead white men and 190–2

anthropology teaching (*cont.*)
  decolonization 26, 175–202
    theory 198–201
    experiments 175, 177–9, 193–6
    focus on questions 197–8
    knowledge problem 180–8
      gaps and limits 185–8
    purpose 210–11
    reading lists 160–1, 190–6
    universities 146–74
anticoloniality 71
Antilogus, Charlotte 211
Appadurai, Arjun 43
Appiah, Kwame Anthony 105
Argentina 40
Asad, Tal 65, 70
Asher, Kiran 43
Australia 32, 139, 193

Baker, Lee 193
Baldwin, James 60
Ballakrishnan, Swetha 170–1
Barth, Fredrik 69, 73
Baviskar, Amita 115, 121
Beard, Mary 141–2
Beinart, William 141, 142
Beliso-De Jesús, Aisha 135–7, 139
Benedict, Ruth 192
Berstein, Basil 167
Betts, Raymond 34–5, 58
Bhambra, Gurminder 97
Biggar, Nigel 141
Black Lives Matter 141
Blum, Susan 168
Boas, Franz 11, 191, 192
Bolivia 117
Boyer, Dominic 184, 188–9
Brazil 40
Brexit 92–3
Britain *See* United Kingdom
British Association for the Advancement of Science 67

Cambridge Decolonise Social Anthropology Society 19–20
Canada, universities 168–9
canon 190–6
Carey, Grace 93
Castagno, Angelina 131–3, 199
caste 48–9, 68, 110–12, 137–8, 190–1
Chakrabarty, Dipesh 9, 51, 52, 60
Chakraborty, Aditya 212
Char, René 7
China, Opium War 32
Christianity 35–6, 72, 92, 104, 111, 183, 185, 189–90
Chua, Liana 10, 73–4
Clammer, John 70
Clifford, James 63
Cohn, Bernard 68
Cold War 62
Collini, Stefan 147, 150, 214
colonialism
  anthropological legacies 8–13
  anthropology 24, 62–95
  British anthropological case studies 65–73
  demography 58
  extractive colonialism 31
  imperial power colonialism 32
  legacies 5–13, 207
  legal colonialism 33
  liberation 81–5, 91, 94
  logic 206
  meaning 2
  missionary colonialism 33
  not-in-my backyard colonialism 32–3

planter colonialism 31
postcolonial colonialism 34
rogue colonialism 33
romantic colonialism 34
settler colonialism 31, 37–40, 58, 72, 136, 171
trade colonialism 31–2
transport colonialism 32
types 30–5
universities and 146–7
violence 136
coloniality 40–4, 198–9
Comaroff, Jean and John 21, 71–2
community activism 212
COVID 175
cricket 49, 50
critical knowledge 189

Dalits 48–9, 52, 110–12, 137–8
D'Andrade, Roy 64
Daniel, Valentine 186
Das, Veena 18, 84, 145
Daswani, Girish 1, 13
Daunton, Martin 103
Davé, Naisargi 82–3, 91, 119, 147, 213
decoloniality 40–4, 198–9, 205
decolonization
  aims 1–2, 9, 28–9
  decolonizing the mind 44–8, 52
  focus 4–5
  meaning 2–4, 28–61, 205–6
  questioning 52–60, 61
  reverse migration 58–9
  theory and 198–201
  See also specific aspects
decolonization max 37–40
Díaz, Vanessa 136
Dirks, Nicholas 66

disagreements 85–6, 95, 98, 118–21, 209
disenclosure 24, 54–60, 77–80, 100, 108–9, 115, 156, 206
domestication 44, 47, 49, 50–2, 53, 66, 71–2, 201, 206
Donner, Henrike 47, 51
Du Bois, W.E.B. 216n2
Dumont, Louis 186, 190–1
Duranti, Alessandro 20
Durkheim, Émile 11, 191, 192
Durrani, Mariam 194
Dyer, Reginald 125

East India Company 45
economics 102–3, 212
Elbourne, Elizabeth 72
empirical knowledge 188
engagement, inappropriate engagement 88–92
English Defence League (EDL) 112–13, 138–9, 142, 144
epistemic justice
  academic projects 100–4
  belonging 107–9, 115
  epistemic privilege 109–14
  epistemological and epistemic 98–100
  imperial amnesia 107–9
  insiders/outsiders 97, 112
  knowledge and 95, 95–122
  natural resources and 101–4
  possibilities 114–18
  radical questioning 104–7
  requirements 208
  social inequality 104
  space for critique 118–21
  teaching 116
  See also ignorance; knowledge; social justice

epistemic privilege 109–14
Epstein, A.L. 69
ethnicity *See* race/ethnicity
Evans-Pritchard, E.E. 65, 191, 192–3
extractive colonialism 31

Fabian, Johannes 63
Fader, Ayala 178
Fanon, Frantz 7, 23, 34–5, 96–7, 100, 101
Faris, James 16
Farmer, Paul 84–5
feminism 83, 133, 162, 170–1
Ferguson, Niall 58
Figueroa, Moreno 44
Fiji 34, 70–1, 90
Firmin, Anténor 77–8
Floyd, George 141
Foucault, Michel 148
Fox, Laurence 124
France
 1789 Revolution 50
 colonial migration 59
 colonialism 32, 33
 social inequality question 104, 105
Frank, David John 149
Fricker, Miranda 98–9, 100, 113, 128
Fuller, Chris 66

Galant, Jaamia 167
Gaugin, Paul 34
Geddes, W.R. 70
Gell, Alfred 18
gender *See* feminism; women
Gerber, Schalk Hendrik 55–6, 57, 61, 202, 206
Gershon, Ilana 124
Ghosh, Amitav 60
Gillespie, Kelly 147
globalization 72, 147–8, 170

Gluckman, Max 65, 68, 69, 191
Goldstein, Daniel 79
Golub, Alex 192
Gopal, Priyamvada 6–7, 8–9, 59–60, 106, 142
Gough, Kathleen 62
Graeber, David 104–5
Great Britain *See* United Kingdom
Green, Sarah 83–4, 91
Grosfoguel, Ramón 9, 146, 155
Guha, Ramachandra 49, 87
Gupta, Aktil 81, 87, 97, 115, 116, 117, 118–19, 122, 131

Hage, Ghassan 139, 193, 209, 210
Haiti 50, 85, 106, 125
Hall, Stuart 50
Harding, Susan 92, 93
Harlow, Roxanna 160
Harrison, Faye 2, 3, 11, 12, 24, 58, 63–4, 73–7, 80, 81, 90, 94, 97, 156
Hartigan, John 139, 193, 199
Hawaii 88–91, 183
Herskovits, Melville 12
heteronormativity 82, 83, 136, 201
heterotopia 148
Heyerdahl, Thor 34
High, Casey 125–7, 209
Hindu Arya Samaj 71
Hinduism 18, 20, 29, 48, 49, 68, 179, 186, 190–1
historicism 189
Hoadley, Ursula 167
holism 189, 190–1
homosexuality 29, 82
Hoodfar, Homa 168–9
hooks, bell 162, 200
Hurston, Zora Neale 194–6

Ibbetson, Denzil 67
ideational knowledge 188
ignorance
  activism and 143–4
  agnotology 25, 127–8
  anthropology and 125–8
  dispelling 133–5
  effects 209–10
  forms 125
  group privilege and 137
  moral ignorance 129
  national ignorance 123
  power 140–4
  race and 123–5, 128–9
  role 123–45
  silencing race talk 131–3, 199
  strategy 125, 144, 187
  white ignorance 128–9, 135
  wilful ignorance 99, 134
imperial power colonialism 32
India
  1857 rebellion 106
  anthropological disagreements 85–6
  anthropology 121
  British colonial anthropology 66–8
  British Indian Army 124
  caste 48–9, 67, 68, 110–12, 137–8, 190–1
  colonial labour 205
  Dalits 48–9, 52, 110–12, 137–8
  gender and 93
  globalization 170
  Hinduism 18, 20, 29, 48, 49, 68, 179, 186, 190–1
  homosexuality 29, 82
  Jallianwala Bagh massacre (1919) 125
  language 46–51
  lesbianism 82–3
  natural resources 102–4
  Penal Code 49
  period taboos 186–7
  Industrial Revolution 102
  Islamophobia 138

Jackson, John L. 199
Jain, Jyotindra 17
Jamaica, Morant Bay rebellion (1865) 106
James, C.L.R. 50
Jansen, Jonathan 1–2, 43, 158–60, 169, 179–80
Japan 32
Jehovah's Witnesses 71
Jobson, Ryan 77, 78, 156
justice *See* epistemic justice; social justice

Kassai, Husayn 142
Kattabomman 45
Keele manifesto 180–1, 188
Kelly, Ann 125–7, 209
Kelly, John 70
King, Martin Luther 45
Knoof-Newman, Marcy 171
knowledge
  gaps and limits 185–8
  holistic knowledge 126
  modes 188–90
  problem 180–8
  property rights over 184
  value 126, 127
  See also epistemic justice; ignorance
Kothari, Rita 48, 49

LaDousa, Chaise 47, 51
Laidlaw, James 19
language 45–52
Lawson, Stephanie 71, 90
Leach, Edmund 191
legacies
  anthropological legacies of colonialism 8–13

legacies (*cont.*)
  colonialism 5–13
  West problem 9–10
legal colonialism 33
Lehmann, David 42–3
Leonard, Patrick 71
lesbianism 82–3
L'Estoile, Benoît de 5–6, 7, 207
Lévi-Strauss, Claude 11, 191
Lewis, Herbert 62
Liashenko, Joshua 193, 194
liberation 3, 24, 81–5, 91, 92, 94, 159–60
Liberatore, Giulia 80–1, 171, 178
Linnekin, Jocelyn 88–90
London School of Economics 150
Long, Thomas 185
López Juárez, Lucia 79–80
Lorde, Audre 147
Luhrmann, Tanya 178, 179, 183, 184, 185, 189–90

Macaulay, Thomas Babington 48, 49, 52
McGranahan, Carole 77, 78
MacIntyre, Alasdair 13–14, 15, 207
Mafeje, Archie 63
Magubane, Bernard 16
Mahmood, Saba 84
Maine. Henry 67
Mair, Jonathan 125–7, 209
Maldonado-Torres, Nelson 40–1
Malinowski, Bronislaw 65, 191
Mamdani, Mahmood 30
Marcus, George 63
Mark, Jan 123
Marquesas 34
Marriott, McKim 186
Marshall Islands 33
Mathur, Nayanika 10, 73–4
Mattingly, Cheryl 18, 176
Mauss, Marcel 191
Mbembe, Achille 56, 57, 59–60, 77, 109, 195, 206
MCD 40–4, 198–9
Mead, Margaret 60, 191–2
Memmi, Albert 8
Mendes, Sam 124
methodology 22–4
Meyer, John 149
Mignolo, Walter 42, 43, 121, 186
Mijangos García, Mirian 79–80
Mills, Charles 128–9, 137, 209
Mills, David 147
missionaries 71, 72, 104–5
missionary colonialism 33
modernity/coloniality/decoloniality (MCD) 40–4, 198–9
Mohanty, Chandra 21–2
Mohanty, Satya 133, 200
Montaigne, Michel de 105
Moore, Jennifer 187
Moosavi, Leon 28
moral ignorance 129
Mosse, David 85–6, 87
motley 24, 57, 59–60, 80, 85, 115, 121, 206
Mukherjee, Aditya 102
Muslims 18, 20

Nader, Laura 147
Nancy, Jean-Luc 56
Nandy, Ashis 59–60, 205
Narayan, Kirin 84
Nathan, Rebekah 165–6, 173
Nation+ 101, 109
national ignorance 123
National Union of Students 163–4

Nesfield, John 67
Netherlands 59
New Zealand 33, 75
Ngũgĩ wa Thiong'o 45-6, 48, 50, 51, 52
Nigeria 53, 54
not-in-my backyard colonialism 32-3
Ntarangwi, Mwenda 16, 17, 147
Nyamnjoh, Anye-Nkwenti 29, 140

Obeid, Michelle 213
objectivity 12, 86, 168, 182
Occupy movement 38, 39, 40
Orientalism 12, 49, 108
other *See* alterity

Panama Canal 32
Papua New Guinea 69
parochialism 26-7, 116
Patel, Neerav 48, 51
patriarchy 82, 83, 136, 159, 200
Pattamadai 17-18, 19
Paulson, John 218n9
Pels, Peter 65
People's Economy 212
period taboos 186-7
Perry, Matthew 32
personal journey 16-22, 44-5, 87
Pete, Shauneen 123
Pierre, Jemima 135-7, 139
Pilkington, Hilary 112-13, 138-9, 144
Pitman, Leslie 161
planter colonialism 31
pluriversalism 56-7, 77, 147, 155
poetic knowledge 189
polyamory 201
populism 19, 47, 93, 112-13

postcolonial colonialism 34
Prasad, Chandra Bhan 49, 51
Prasad, Leela 19
praxiological knowledge 188
Proctor, Robert 125
psychoanalytic knowledge 189

Quijano, Anibal 41-2, 117

race/ethnicity
  anthropology and 76, 77-8
  critical theory 128
  dead white men 190-2
  ignorance and 123-5, 128-31
  justice and 100
  problem 10-11
  scholarship and 178
  silencing race talk 131-3, 199
  social construct 10-11
  United Kingdom 113, 123, 138-9
  United States 115, 131-3, 139, 141, 199-200
  universities and 146-7, 151, 169
    differential awards 162-7
  West and 11-13
  white ignorance 128-9
  white-norming 131
  white supremacy 131, 134, 135-40, 198, 199-200
  whiteness studies 129-31, 134, 144, 199
Racine, Josianne and Jean-Luc 191
Radcliffe-Brown, Alfred 65, 191
Raj, Dhooleka Sarhadi 124
Raj, Kapil 67
reading lists 160-1, 190-2
reification 66, 70-1
religion 18-19, 35-7, 175, 177-9

Rhodes, Cecil 101, 140–4, 145, 157
Rhodes-Livingstone Institute (RLI) 66, 68–70
Rhodesia 66, 68–70
Richardson, Eugene 218n9
Risley, Herbert 67
Rivera Cusicanqui, Silvia 28, 43, 57, 117, 206
Rizvi, Uzma 77, 78
Roberts, Nathaniel 110–12, 137, 167
rogue colonialism 33
romantic colonialism 34
Rosa, Jonathan 136
Roth, G.K. 70
Rouse, Carolyn 11, 26, 115, 117–18, 144

Said, Edward 12, 108, 196
Sanchez, Andrew 178
Sanghera, Satnam 107–9
Scheper-Hughes, Nancy 64
schools, silencing race talk 131–3, 199
Schreiner, Olive 142–3
Schucan Bird, K. 161
semiological knowledge 189
settler colonialism 31, 37–40, 58, 72, 136, 171
Shankar, Shalini 193–4
Shoemaker, Nancy 30, 34, 101
Sikhs 124
silencing race talk 131–3, 199
Silverman, Sydel 73
Simpson, Audra 187, 198
Singh, Hardeep 124
slavery 31, 58, 194–6
Smith, Goldwin 143
social justice 39, 42–3, 61, 153–4, 159
Somalia 80–1
Somerville, Alice Te Punga 89–90

soul decolonization 35–7
Sousa Santos, Boaventura de 147
South Africa
  colonial anthropology 72
  decolonization theory 200
  Rhodes Must Fall movement 140
  universities 25, 169, 200
    curricula 155, 158–60
    non-white students 151–2
Spivak, Gayatri Chakravorty 154
Srinivas, Tulasi 178–9
statues wars 140–4, 145
Stevenson, Robert Louis 34
Stommel, Jesse 168
Stoolman, Jessie 87, 97, 115, 116, 117, 118–19, 122, 131
Strathern, Marilyn 119–20, 121, 207
student collaboration 22–4

Táíwò, Olúfémi 49, 51, 52–4, 61, 206
Táíwò, Olúfémi O. 61, 203, 211
TallBear, Kim 201
Tobin, Jeffrey 88–90
Todd, Zoe 62
trade colonialism 31–2
transport colonialism 32
Trask, Haunani-Kay 88–90
Trembath, Sarah 42
Trouillot, Michel-Rolph 125
Tuamotus Islands 33
Tuck, Eve 37–40, 214
Tuhiwai Smith, Linda 75
Turkey 187–8, 212
Twain, Mark 45, 52
Tyler, Katharine 130, 131
Tylor, Edward Burnett 67, 191

UKIP 124–5
ungrading 168
United Kingdom
  anthropology 116–17
  anthropology teaching
    191–2
  anti-colonial history 106
  Brexit 92–3
  Chinese Opium War 32
  colonial anthropology 65–73
  colonial migration 59
  colonial wealth extraction
    101–4
  imperial amnesia 107–9
  imperial power colonialism
    32
  postcolonial colonialism 34
  race 113, 123, 138–9
  Rhodes Must Fall movement
    140–4
  rogue colonialism 33
  Sikhs 124
  universities 116–17, 150–1,
    162–7
  World War I 124
United States
  anthropology 25, 73, 77, 81,
    97, 116–17, 118, 140
  anthropology teaching 191,
    192
  Christian fundamentalism 92
  Evangelical Christianity 185,
    189–90
  Indigenous Americans
    104–5
  legal colonialism 33
  not-in-my backyard
    colonialism 32–3
  race 115, 131–3, 135–7, 139,
    141, 151, 169, 199–200
  rogue colonialism 33
  settler colonialism 37–40,
    58, 171
  slavery 58, 194–6

transport colonialism 32
universities 116–17, 151,
    153, 160, 169, 218n9
white supremacy 135–7
universalism 55, 149–50, 206
universities
  accidental effects 170–2
  Anglosphere 116–17
  anthropology and 146–74
  changes 149–54
  colonialism and 146–7
  concerns 15
  continuities 152
  curricula. *See* anthropology
    teaching
  decolonizing 25–6
  differential awards 162–7
  evaluating radical ideas
    167–70
  focus on 4–5, 8–9
  gender and 151
  globalization 147–8
  isomorphism 149–50
  non-white students 151–2
  place and 149–50
  promotion of justice 100–4
  Rhodes Must Fall movement
    140–4, 145
  role 210
  social justice and 153–4
  teaching. *See* anthropology
    teaching
  universalism 149–50
  whiteness sites 145, 146–7
Universities UK 163–4

Veracini, Lorenzo 71
Viramma 191
Visweswaran, Kamala 78
Viveiros de Castro, Eduardo
    127, 134

Wade, Peter 10, 44
Waitangi Treaty (1840) 33

Wakefield, Edward 33
Walker, Alice 195
Walker, William 33
Walsh, Katherine 42, 43
Walters, Cyrill 43, 169, 179–80
Wanghia Treaty (1844) 33, 181–2
Wangūi wa Kamoniji 35–6, 181–2
Warlis 16–17
weaving 17–18
Weber, Max 81, 91, 191
Wengrow, David 104–5
Werbner, Richard 69
West
  problem 9–10
  race and 11–13
West Indies 102–3

white supremacy 131, 134, 135–40, 198, 199–200
whiteness studies 129–31, 134, 144, 199
Wilder, Laura Ingalls 219n3
Williams, Eric 102–3
Williamson, Gavin 142
Wilson, Godfrey 68–9
Wiredu, Kwasi 36
witchcraft 192–3
women
  period taboos 186–7
  university students 151
World War I 124

Yang, Wayne 37–40, 214
Yonucu, Deniz 187–8

Zionism 171